Power Grids

How Successful Lawyers
Build Powerful Networks that [
Reputations, Relationships, Referrals, ar   ......

Eric Dewey
49 College Park
Davis, California 95616
ericgdewey@gmail.com

Ordering instructions: Special discounts on quantity sales are available to Bar Associations, Law schools, law firms, and others. For information on bulk discounts, please contact the author at the above address.

Printed in the United States of America.

DEDICATED TO ROBIN, MORGAN, KRISTEN, AND SAMANTHA.

YOU ARE MY POWER GRID.

YOU FUEL MY LIFE.

I LOVE YOU.

MY DEEPEST APPRECIATION TO EVERY LAWYER I HAVE EVER HAD THE PLEASURE TO COACH, TRAIN, OR ADVISE.

YOU HAVE BEEN MY TEACHERS WHETHER YOU REALIZED IT OR NOT. THANK YOU.

TABLE OF CONTENTS

3

Introduction

"Human beings have an innate inner drive to be autonomous, self-determined, and connected to one another. And when that drive is liberated, people achieve more and live richer lives."

-Daniel Pink, Author of Drive. The Surprising Truth About What Motivates Us.

A professional's network of connections is their most significant business asset. 'Who you know' and 'who knows you' is the source of most opportunities for new work. In addition to new engagements, your connections can provide new information, unique insights, introductions to new people, novel ideas, and powerful resources.

However, most lawyers are not intentional about developing and managing their network of contacts. They don't take a strategic approach to building or evolving their network of connections. Fewer still understand the value hidden in their networks or make the effort to consistently share that value with others.

When I start a new coaching assignment, I ask the lawyer to tell me where they get most of their work. I want specifics. I ask them to think back on the last ten matters and give me the names of the people or the specific situations that gave rise to each matter. I always make my point. 85% or more of all the work that comes to you comes through someone you know.

For many lawyers, these opportunities for work are hidden. Don't get me wrong, these opportunities are happening all the time. They just aren't happening for the lawyers who neglect their network of connections. Those opportunities aren't revealed because they aren't connected to the energy of their network, that is, they aren't speaking to the right people regularly. When the energy of your network is released through regular contact, it is a powerful force that can propel your career and the careers of others. I call that force, your power grid.

Everyone has a power grid. Everyone has a network of connections that can fuel their success. It may be small. It may be old or barely used. It may be misconnected or wired wrong. But everyone has one. And anyone can look at their connections and make a plan to make it a more powerful network of connections. Anyone can build a more powerful and more reliable power grid.

To tap the opportunities hidden in your network, you need to know who is in your network. You need to know everyone you know, everyone you have known, and everyone you should know. And you need to decide who the best people are that you will get to know and who will get to know you. Then you need to set off to build a trusted relationship with each of them.

This book will help you do that. It will help you to know the value you can offer others and what others can offer you and the other people in your power network. Most importantly, this book will show you how to reach out to them. How to communicate with them regularly and consistently. It seems simple, even obvious. And yet, so few lawyers follow this simple advice.

This book offers a structured and systematic way to manage and cultivate the value of your network. Its lessons will help you find new opportunities for engagements, learn about market and competitive intelligence, and become more effective in your client development initiatives. Regular outreach fuels business development, collaboration, and better intelligence gathering. But you have to do it every day.

Following the advice in this book will help you build your power grid – the network of connections you develop that act as a source of energy to fuel your professional success. That isn't just theory. I've observed, interviewed, and coached hundreds of business lawyers over more than two decades in the legal industry. I've also observed this process among commercial bankers, financial advisors, management consultants, and commercial real estate brokers, all industries in which I have spent a significant portion of my career. The principles are universal. But the book was written specifically for lawyers. Why?

The simple answer is that lawyers are unique. Law firms are unique. The relationship between lawyers and their clients is unique. The rules that lawyers must follow are unique. Many lawyers have common personality traits that make them exceptional lawyers, but not exceptional marketers. That's unique. It's hard to make lawyers into sales people because much of what sales people are taught conflicts with how lawyers were trained. That's also unique to the profession. Lawyers need their own process. They need to follow what makes sense for them.

The process I describe in this book will make sense to you. It will feel familiar. That familiarity is a sign that the path is correct. Follow this path. It's the path that the most successful lawyers take.

I was inspired to write this book by three events. The first was the response I got to an article I wrote several years ago outlining the difference between 'Networking' and 'Connecting.' I hit a nerve. The idea of 'networking' felt transactional to a lot more people than I realized. They knew deep down, as I do, that what we really want is to connect. The networking advice they were getting wasn't giving them the guidance to do much more than collect business cards and blurt out elevator pitches. They wanted more. The contrast between networking and connecting resonated with them.

I've reprinted the article here to begin a discussion about the importance of connecting with others. And to dispel some of the folklore and poor guidance associated with the legal industry's focus on networking.

The second event was a series of coaching sessions that I conducted with lawyers across the country. I begin my coaching sessions with a series of questions to understand the lawyer's practice, their past efforts to build it, and to help me identify where they can improve their efforts. I look at the specialty areas of law in their practice, the marketing and business development efforts they have done in the past, the content and thought leadership they have shared, and their public profile and exposure. Then I ask about their clients, their list of connections, and how they manage their outreach.

I can count on one hand the number of lawyers I have encountered that take a strategic approach to building their network of connections. For the most part, people's contact lists appear to have developed by accident. And there is minimal effort to maintain these connections over time, let alone improve the quality of their connections methodically and strategically. It is a common and pervasive problem among lawyers.

That was also my experience when I was the chief marketing officer of several large law firms. Most lawyers had not managed, let alone thoughtfully organized, their connections. They hadn't made an effort to ensure they knew the most important people they needed to know and had contact information for them. They didn't keep a list of prospects, didn't keep notes of their conversations, and didn't know much about the personal lives and interests of the people in their network.

Outreach calls were made when they were slow and were often driven by the panic of not knowing where their next project would come from. Many of them relied solely on speaking and publishing for leads, leads which inevitably came in too few numbers. Too many lawyers simply rely on the business development skills of too few other lawyers.

To each of them, the concept of a disciplined, structured outreach program seemed obvious, even necessary. And yet, I only saw a few lawyers who had a process in place. And fewer still that worked that process on a daily basis.

The third reason to write this book struck me during a group coaching program I was doing for a midsize law firm. We kicked off the group coaching process by asking each lawyer to go through the steps outlined in chapter five of this book. We assigned a marketing professional to work individually with each group of lawyers to help them collect and prioritize their contacts. I provided training in what to look for and how to think about each connection which helped the marketing folks guide and educate the lawyers as they developed their lists. They became very knowledgeable about each lawyers' network.

When the marketing folks and I talked about what the lawyers were identifying as value in their connections, we realized that the combined networks of every lawyer participating in the group coaching program represented a hidden asset to the firm. We recognized that the Client Relationship Management system (CRM) used by the firm, while valuable for maintaining contact information and showing who knows whom in the firm (among other important functions), it couldn't reveal the value hidden among those contacts. To understand the value, you had to talk to each lawyer. Only the lawyers understood the resources and people in their networks.

The value in the individual and in the combined networks couldn't be easily harnessed in a contact database. It had to be talked about, examined, researched, and revealed. The group sessions enabled this energy to be released. For the first time, the marketing professionals saw that talking about the connections in each lawyer's network revealed a hidden but very potent asset of the firm, an asset that would be coordinated, exposed, and put to work for the firm through our group coaching program. Our systems in law firms encourage lawyers to be lone wolf hunters. Yet, hunting in groups is wildly more effective.

When I look at the networks of connections of the most successful attorneys that I have observed, I see power grids of energy and an interconnectedness that can fuel the success of everyone on the grid. Lawyers who don't feel they have that highly developed power grid simply need to plug in to it. And by plugging in to it consistently, it grows in potency.

Everyone has a network of connections that can drive their reputations, relationships, referrals, and revenues. Everyone has a network that can help them succeed. I hope to show you how it works based on my observations of numerous successful attorneys over the years. And, you'll be happy to hear that when I've guided other lawyers through this process, they see new engagement opportunities develop within three to four months, sometimes faster.

It's not foolproof, of course. It depends on the commitment and enthusiasm one has for working the process and achieving success. But I've seen even a halfhearted effort in executing this process produce results. It's really just up to you.

How to Use This Book

This book is a guide. It shows the steps and activities to take to build a powerful network of connections, what I call your 'power grid' – a source of energy that fuels growth throughout your career. But, in addition to a 'how to' book, I hope you use it as a reference book. It is full of tips and checklists that you can refer to throughout your career.

I've written this book primarily with a younger, less experienced attorney in mind. If some of what you read seems obvious or elementary, that's why. But the book is also relevant for lawyers who want to take their practice to the next level. In truth, the principles will work for anyone at any level of their career and no one is too experienced to ignore reviewing the fundamentals again on occasion.

I've used these principles and this process with partners in the largest firms, small boutique insurance or immigration firms, and single shingle lawyers in rural communities. It's proven successful with attorneys returning to practice from firm leadership positions, to laterals expediting the switch to a new firm, and to first year associates hoping to get a jump on the partner track. If you follow the process, you will find new opportunities, grow your reputation, meet more influential people, and feel more confident about your future.

While I've recommended specific steps to build a power grid, you may have a different way to accomplish this goal. The most important thing is to create a system that works for you. Create what feels comfortable to you and is easy for you to do every day. It must fit within the demands of client work, the needs of your partners, and the balance between your work life and your personal life. Find that comfort zone. Tweak and adjust your system until you find a rhythm that produces regular daily outreach and provides the balance that enables you to do everything you must do.

Outreach should be your number one priority each day, sharing that top spot only with your commitment to your clients. Several clients I have believe their business development efforts are even more critical than their client work because no one can do business development for them, but they can delegate client work to other lawyers. I agree with that.

Make the maintenance and growth of your power grid a habit. Once you build your network, maintain it and constantly grow it. Make it better. Make it more reliable. Reach higher into organizations and expand who you know in them. Tend to your connections every day. Keep them strong and powerful. Your connections are the most valuable asset of your practice.

Highly successful business lawyers end up at the center of business activity with their clients because they have mastered both legal expertise and business acumen. Their advice protects while enabling the company to move forward. That is the balance you must strike. Any lawyer can advise a company on how to protect assets, lower risk, or avoid problems. But highly successful lawyers solve problems and give their advice within the context of the business, their operational norms, and their customer or brand experience. The solutions proposed by successful lawyers are accretive to the business. They add value.

To get to that point, you must be curious – curious about your clients and curious about their business and their industry. Ask questions about the operations, the people, the markets, their suppliers and their customers. Visit and experience the business.

Listen to the phone activity and watch the pace of people moving around the factory floor or office. These impressions are important to understanding your clients.

The combination of deep legal knowledge, business acumen, industry know how, and a dynamic network of connections that can help you solve the most challenging problems for your clients is the ultimate differentiator. It simply can not be duplicated. Tend to your relationships. Know your clients and their businesses. Bring your legal and marketplace expertise to every challenge. Those things will be the engine of your success.

The most important of which, and the first order of business, is to build your network of connections. But don't think of this as networking. Focus on connecting.

Connecting is Better Than Networking

Your connections matter. Connecting with people and lending a hand is what matters in business. Connecting the pieces of information from your conversations is what leads to unique insights. And it is connecting yourself to a community of people who care about your success that builds your reputation. Connecting is the essence of what it means to be successful in business.

I'm not a big fan of networking - that rite of passage for anyone with aspirations of career changes or new clients. It has its place, of course. But it's not the business development panacea many would make it out to be. In fact, I think networking can sometimes do more harm than good. When the true purpose of networking is misunderstood or the techniques misapplied, it can cause damage. When the quantity of contacts becomes more important than the quality of those relationships, "networking" earns a bad name. The connections we *have* with people is what drives our success.

To make my point, here are seven ways connecting is better than networking.

1. Networking is about knowing more people.
Connecting is about knowing people more.

LinkedIn is one place to go to network with other professionals. In fact, my LinkedIn profile says that I am connected with 5,190 people. That's not right. I am not "connected" to that many people, not in any meaningful way. I can't be. How could I really know that many people? Studies, history, and common sense indicate that the human mind can know only about 150 people well. Playing the volume game may serve your ego, but it will do little for your happiness, let alone your success.

Technically, you could say I am "networked" with them. But in reality, these people are my community of connections. Communities are potent and dynamic things. They are comprised of people who care about one another's success, who trust and respect each, and who exchange favors and assistance. Connecting is about finding the people most qualified for you to help and who can help you in return. And then building strong bonds with those people. It is about creating a self-supporting ecosystem in which all boats rise together.

2. The objective of networking is to exchange information.
The objective of connecting is, well, to connect.

At networking camp, they teach us to get a business card, find out about the company, and probe for information that can be used later when we follow up. You've probably even been asked to role-play how you'll do this. As such, networking is about how to get what you need from another person. Networking is internal or self-focused. The assertive networker has a list of questions to ask. Their interaction with you is focused on getting what they need. If you've ever been on the receiving end of this type of interrogation, you know the feeling it creates. And you've probably made a mental note to avoid this person in the future.

On the other hand, connecting is about how to get someone else what they need. Connection requires you to give something, advice, thoughts, introductions, or maybe only your genuine participation in the conversation and a sympathetic ear. In building relationships, your focus is on finding ways to help the other person, however trivial that help may seem. As such, connecting is outward or other-focused. Instead of figuring out how to distribute yourself across an ever-larger mass of people, think about how to surround yourself with the most influential and important people.

Create a community of individuals who will contribute to your success and to whose success you will also contribute. Networking feels much better when you approach the process with the mindset, 'how can I make this person feel grateful that they crossed my path?' You'll create a positive impression that is more likely to lead to future work.

3. Networking puts you in uncomfortable situations. Connecting makes situations more comfortable.

The executives that I coach often hate to network. For them, it conjures up images of being stuck at a benefit dinner talking to someone they don't particularly like. I happen to agree with them. They're told to circulate and work the room and chat people up. If you are not a gregarious extrovert, you will probably dread the idea.

Connecting is about finding a person or people whom you like and who like you and exploring your mutual interests. Connecting is about being comfortable in a new environment because you are being yourself- not forced to do uncomfortable things. Sure, when you see someone standing by themselves, you should introduce yourself. But not because they may be your next big client but because you would appreciate someone doing the same for you. Connecting is about being humble and authentic and enjoying the trust, respect, and compatibility that grows between two people as a result.

4. Networking requires an elevator pitch. Connecting requires a dialogue.

Let me ask you a question. Why do you need to memorize a tweet-long response to the question 'what do you do for work'? Is what you usually say so inadequate? You don't need to talk to people in polished elevator pitch bytes? You're not speed dating. Tell people what you do and how your clients benefit from working with you. Keep it short and authentic. Don't worry about whether or not someone will remember what you do for a living. Worry about how they feel after having talked to you. Don't worry about how polished you come across. Worry about how authentic people think you are. Don't worry about putting yourself in the best light. Put the spotlight on the person you are talking to.

5. Networking is focused on the future.
Connecting is focused on the present.

Watch networker-type people in a networking event. Or, better yet, watch their eyes. People under the influence of networking will have shifty, distracted eyes. They'll constantly look around the room for the next person to meet. In conversations, they'll look away rudely to see if there is someone better to meet. Their nervous energy has them thinking ahead, looking toward their next business card fix.

Now, look at the connectors. They are engaged and focused. They are present in the conversation, listening and speaking as if the other person is the only one in the room. It's an enjoyable dialogue, and you can tell the two have made a connection. And those connections will generate new opportunities much more quickly than the flighty pollinating of the networker bee.

6. Networking is imperfect.
Connecting is perfect.

At conferences, organizers often have to bribe people to meet each other with games and drawings. Networking is admittedly an imperfect way to grow your business. But it is also the most feared way for so many. That's why event organizers force it on you through organized networking activities. You need that nudge to network. But you never need a nudge to connect.

Connecting comes naturally to almost everyone in business. There's nothing you can do to make it better. You can't force a connection. You can't give it away as a prize. And you can't file away a connection anywhere but in your heart. Making a connection IS the prize, and everybody wins.

7. Failing at networking is more painful than failing to connect.

When networking doesn't work, people worry they are doing something wrong. Or worse, that they look foolish. They doubt themselves, curse the process, and renew their commitment never to do it again. Networking is unfamiliar territory for most people. Forcing an introvert to be an extrovert feels awkward and is a difficult behavior to master in front of a live audience. Failing to network makes you question yourself.

When people fail to find people they connect with, they don't view that failure as their fault. In fact, it is pretty trivial. That may be because people have been connecting with other people since their first breath of air. No matter how introverted you are, and no matter how secluded your existence has been, you know how to connect when you meet someone you like. Making a connection produces a sense of euphoria. And it energizes us to connect more.

Networking creates contacts. Connecting creates relationships. With the ubiquity of the internet and social media, we don't really need more contacts. But we do need more connection. Focus on connecting with others and your business will thrive. As will you.

1

The Power of a Robust Network

"A friendship founded on business is better than a business founded on friendship."

-John D. Rockefeller

Power Grids Fuel Success

Your connections are the most valuable asset you have. Not only are they your primary source of referrals, but they also validate your reputation and give you the influence and leverage you need to get things done. When lawyers actively seek to develop, nurture, and manage a wide network of strategic relationships, they will build the kind of relational capital that leads to high levels of success.

Powerful networks of connections require you to cross many personal, professional, and geographical boundaries. Through your relationships, you can tap deep reserves of experience, knowledge, and skills. What's more, the people in your network have their own networks. As you add people to your network, its value increases geometrically because you'll gain access to other, more diverse connections.

Your connections are unique to you. No one can duplicate the set of relationships you have. Those relationships are valuable for another reason: they're portable. Wherever you go, and throughout your career, you can maintain a strong network by consistently staying in touch with the people you know. In a highly competitive marketplace, the advantage gained by distinguishing yourself based on technology, service, or price is fleeting. These things can be duplicated. Over the long run, what sets you apart, and what no one else can copy, is the quality of your business relationships.

Your network of connections is much more extensive than you might realize. Everyone you know, and everyone you have ever known, is a connection. Your extended network includes not only the people you presently interact with but dozens, if not hundreds, of people whom you once knew. These can include people you knew in law school, previous jobs, and community, religious, and recreational organizations you have belonged to. That's a lot of connections!

You can't know, let alone stay in frequent contact, with everyone you've ever known though. It's impossible. But you can select the most important people you've ever known and create a power grid that works to fuel your success and the success of everyone on the grid. It is a formula for mutually assured construction – the construction of reputations, relationships, referrals, revenues, and, as you'll see, greater life satisfaction.

Four Groups of Connections

In general terms, there are four groupings of connections which I refer to as 1. Critical few connections; 2. Primary connections; 3. Secondary connections; and 4. Extended connections, or put another way, the connections of your connections.

Critical Few Connections

Your critical few connections are the people closest to you, those with whom you communicate daily or weekly. They may be family members, close friends, long time clients, bosses, mentors, advisors, law partners, or peers. These connections are your primary source of personal and professional support and camaraderie. For example, they help you gain perspective on situations, plan various business initiatives, and provide advice on a wide range of issues. Critical few connections typically number between ten to twenty-five people. They are the primary audience for your questions, to brainstorm new ideas, and provide you with support, accountability and advice as you grow your practice.

Acknowledge them. Let them know their important role in your life. These people sustain you and make you who you are. For that reason, you should also consider making these people part of your business development team. Don't do this alone. Tell them your plan for building a power grid. Ask them to help you, even if it is only to remind you every now and then to do it. The critical few are an important part of your life. They should be an important part of your business development efforts as well.

Primary Connections

Like your critical few connections, primary connections are people you know well, though you may not interact with them as often or know them as well as your critical few connections. Primary connections typically include clients, client prospects, industry associates, advisors, other lawyers and referral sources. Primary connections are often a lawyer's most important source of new business. For instance, they may hire you, introduce or recommend you to people who may hire you, and share information that will help you achieve your goals. Because you know your primary connections well, relationships with primary connections are typically based on mutual respect and trust.

Primary connections have become relationships over time because you share specific values and help each other advance your careers and the careers of others in your networks. Communication with primary connections tends to be periodic and situational. You are comfortable reaching out to them when you have a question, want to be introduced, or otherwise want to 'catch up' with them. Depending on your relationship-building skills, career length, and personality, your primary connections may number from 25 to hundreds of people.

Secondary Connections

Primary connections aren't always the top source of new work, new information, or new connections. Surprisingly, a large amount of new work comes from all the other people in your secondary and extended network of connections. These are people with whom you are familiar and who are familiar with you. They are weak connections but connections nonetheless. Unlike critical few connections and primary connections, you do not know as much about your secondary connections and communicate with them only sporadically, if at all.

Secondary connections are still essential because they're often the best connections to expose you to different networks of people, new information, new perspectives, new opportunities, and a greater cross-section of people. They exponentially increase the value of your network because they provide access to potentially large numbers of people you might not otherwise come across. These 'weak' connections can typically number hundreds, even thousands, of people.

Your secondary connections are the audience for your content marketing initiatives—things like law journal articles, blog posts, client alerts, and holiday cards. Because you can't build individual relationships with that many people, including your secondary connections in your content marketing initiatives ensures they remain familiar with you, your work, your accomplishments, and your insights.

Extended Networks

The connections of your connections are the fourth level of your network, and it too has great potential, though often untapped potential. Just like the game, Six Degrees of Kevin Bacon, where you attempt to draw connections to the actor Kevin Bacon in six or fewer degrees of connections, your extended network offers an entry to a broad and almost limitless range of people.

As we'll discuss in more detail, your ability to access the extended network correlates with the value you invest in your primary network and the relationships that you build with them. Through this diligent and continuous commitment, you can reap the rewards buried in your extended network of connections. But you must give to receive. If you attempt to tap the extended network without having invested, over time, in those relationships you can earn a reputation as a taker, someone who is looking only out for yourself. You don't want that reputation.

Creating a Power Grid

As I'll explain in more detail in chapter five, you will select people for your power grid from these tiers of connections. Most of them will come from your primary network of connections. Some will be drawn from your secondary contacts and a few may come from your extended network. I explain what to look for and who should be in your power grid as well. Those that don't make the cut to be in your power grid are still people with whom you want to stay in touch. I'll share the numerous ways that you can do that too. But for now, I want to describe how to recognize a power grid.

Your power grid is made up of the most influential people you know, the best candidates or conduits for new opportunities, and the resources to get tough problems solved. They share your business values and work equally as hard as you do to make a difference and help other people. You want the best people you know in your power grid but you also want to continuously improve the energy and value that your power grid represents. The hundred plus people in your power grid will generate most of your work and should be the primary focus of your marketing and business development efforts. No article. No speaking engagement. No conference you can attend is as important as keeping the fire going in your power grid.

What Does a Power Grid Look Like?

How do you know when you have built a powerful network of connections? Or, maybe you think you have one already. What does one look like, you ask? Powerful networks exhibit four qualities. They are broad, deep, diverse, and responsive.

Broad

A broad network of connections reaches numerous industries, a wide range of companies, big and small, and companies that serve different roles, such as manufacturers and suppliers. They include contacts from service providers like accountants, law firms, and engineering firms; financial institutions such as banks, investment brokers, private equity firms, and insurance companies; and real estate and other brokers of assets.

The network should also be spread broadly among various cities and states. You should have multiple connections in the major cities of commerce and a good selection of the states. If you work in international markets, your contacts should also come from the countries where you do business and service clients.

Deep

Powerful networks are also deep networks. They include contacts above your equivalent position, among people at your level, and people below your level. Your network should reach several departments in specific companies and include relationships with finance people, operations people, HR people, marketing and sales, and other departments where the knowledge and connections could prove helpful.

Diverse

Studies indicate that diverse groups produce more innovative ideas, solve problems faster, and develop better solutions. The variety of perspectives in a diverse group causes everyone to consider new perspectives, look at issues from different angles, and be more open-minded. Your network should also be diverse and inspire you with creative new approaches, new information and more knowledge. It should reflect the diversity of the country

24

in every respect. It's also helpful to include different political viewpoints, religious beliefs, genders, cultural backgrounds, and ethnicities to build a more diverse network.

Responsive

Responsiveness is an important indicator of the strength of relationships. People are responsive to the people they respect and find valuable to have as a connection. They follow through and do what they say. If you are responsive to those in your network, there's a good chance that they will be responsive to you. You should plan to return calls and messages within 24 hours. And hope that those in your network do the same.

In chapter five, you'll compile a master list of your connections. When you do this, think about where you might want to increase your network's breadth, depth, or diversity. And think about their responsiveness to you. If you called them for information or an introduction, would they get back to you within a day or so? To increase the responsiveness of your network, always deliver relevant and meaningful value in your interactions. Gain a reputation for someone who always contributes to others without the expectation of getting something in return. Do this and the responsiveness of your network will grow.

Your Power Grid Is a Force Multiplier

'Force multiplier' is a military term which indicates a factor or a combination of factors that gives personnel or weapons (or other hardware) the ability to accomplish greater feats than without it. The expected size increase required to have the same effectiveness without that advantage is the *multiplication factor*. Because the connections in your power grid share your values, commitment, and goals, your power grid is a force multiplier. It multiplies your strengths, reach and utility by all those in your power grid. When you've built a deep, broad, diverse, and responsive network, your ability to navigate and find solutions increases exponentially. You can access better and higher quality opportunities, better and more specific intelligence, leverage the resources in other people's network, and access information not available to others.

Your business development job requires you to constantly improve and increase the value inherent in your network to use it as an ever more powerful multiplier. Just as you would work to increase the value of a company by building its financial, intellectual, talent, and operational value, you must also work to increase the value of your network of connections.

Your network won't maintain itself. You must manage and cultivate it. Networks can fall into disrepair. Your connections can grow weak and unfamiliar. It takes a diligent and constant effort to ensure your network of connections produces value and that that value constantly increases. As I outline in this book, done well, your network of relationships will propel your personal and professional success.

With today's interconnected world, we're drowning in available connections. Facebook, LinkedIn, Instagram, and others not only present us with a constant flow of new and influential people, but they drain our attention away from the valuable connections we already have in our networks. You should focus on those people before launching into the big wild world of social media.

Reaching out to your connections is important for your marketing and business development plan. But so too are other business development strategies such as publishing; client service; understanding the trends and emerging issues your clients face; learning about business and the industries in which you practice; seizing the potential of technology; and learning how to improve the effectiveness and efficiency of your work. Interestingly, each of these strategies can be facilitated through your network. Your network is the source of a tremendous amount of value. It offers so many benefits.

The Value Hidden in Your Power Grid

When we speak of value, most people think of the opportunity for engagements. But networks are a rich source of other forms of value, too. That value is not confined to your primary professional network. It extends to your secondary connections and the connections that are one or two degrees beyond the people you know. The most often tapped value though is information, insights, and resources.

Information

Today, there are numerous ways to access public information. New technologies aggregate business information and give everyone equal access to broadly-held information. It may cost money to get it, but it is available if you have the means. On the other hand, your network represents a trove of closely-held information, only accessible through the strength of your relationships. Your ability to stay in close contact with the people in your network who cultivate this information provides a significant advantage in all kinds of situations.

The types of information available in your network runs the gamut from who knows whom to technical information someone may have about various topics. It can include advance notice of developments that may impact your practice or your clients; job openings; executive moves; information that clarifies financial or strategic moves companies make; or new entrants into the marketplace. The breadth of information in your network includes competitive intelligence, market intelligence, inter-relationship intelligence, and data points that can connect the dots for you in ways that broadly-held information cannot.

As you build your network, think about what types of information each contact might have access to. Note anything significant that might be useful to you or others in your network.

Insights and Perspectives

The people in your network can also help you solve problems, provide new perspectives, or help you think differently about various situations or projects. A robust and diverse network gives you access to new and different viewpoints that can help you to learn new things. We all have mental blind spots and confidence biases. And we don't always recognize when these come into play in our thinking. Seeking the input of others in your power grid can help you guard against limited thinking, develop unique perspectives, solve more challenging problems, and reveal new creative approaches.

The relationships in your power grid, what I call the energizers of your power grid, can also help you build new skills and capabilities. Substantial research indicates that diverse relationships increase your creativity by presenting differing views and opinions. New ideas and approaches can help you re-direct your thinking and spark novel ways of looking at things.

Additional Resources

Everyone in your power grid is a resource. And these resources know other resources. Resources are people with special knowledge, special skills, unique relationships, unique experiences, or original thinking about various subjects. Resources can also be organizations that can help you or that have information you need. They may have access to funding, funding advice, or investments in companies. These resources may be mentors, career advisors, or provide business advice and counseling. All of these resources should be strong relationships that enable you to help yourself and others.

The more you build your network, the more access you get to new resources from networks spread across geographies, disciplines, industries, and social networks. If you have ever moved to a new city and looked back at your connections years later, you'll see how diverse and far-reaching your connections are compared to before your move.

The Personal Benefits of a Power Grid

You benefit personally from the relationships you have with your connections. These are just some of the ways that you can benefit.

Identity

Your connections are a reflection of who you are. Whom you know and associate with gives others a sense of your identity and what they can expect from you. Like it or not, your connections help to establish your social status and your ability to make things happen. Today, those connections are easier to see than at any time in our history. Others can look at your connections on your LinkedIn profile. They can see who your friends are on Facebook and other social media. These mediums may not accurately represent everyone you know, but they create an impression nonetheless.

Status

Your proximity to influential people can bestow status that your title alone cannot. The secretary of a high-ranking executive in the company can have an elevated status due to his proximity and relationship with that executive. Another example comes from my personal experience. The managing partner in a law firm I worked at used one of the graphic designers in my department to do his power point presentations. The designer made a lot of presentations for the managing partner and spent hours building these presentations with him in his office. Over time, they grew close. The graphic designer, who otherwise would be low on the totem pole, gained a higher status in the firm. People often asked him questions of how the managing partner was likely to view various topics before they would approach the managing partner. He had achieved a new status and a new role yet his title never changed.

Access

Your strategic relationships can give you access to the people you should or want to know. The connections of your connections are a wealth of knowledge, influence, and resources. Getting introductions to them is a meaningful way to increase the value of your network.

As an example, a friend of mine explained how this affected him. My friend was a musician who made no secret of his love for playing and performing music. He talked about music to anyone who would listen and loved to go to the open blues jams in town. He met several company executives who were 'closet' or former musicians at those blues jams. He had the idea to try to meet other executives in area companies who also played music and put on a benefit concert.

They organized the benefit, calling it 'Suits that Rock'. At one of the practices, he met the vice president of a company that his firm had been trying to work with for years. Over the course of preparing for and organizing the benefit, his relationship with that person grew closer. They shared a lot in common, even though he was an IT service representative in his company and the VP ran global sales for his company. Over several months that relationship grew to the point where he felt comfortable enough to talk to the VP about his company's interest in working with them. The VP was happy to meet with them. He arranged a meeting with the VP and his company's sale manager, much to the dismay of his boss.

Credibility

The people in your network can give you a degree of credibility in the eyes of others. The quality of the people you know enables you to borrow credibility from them. Connections with influential or knowledgeable people imply an endorsement of your knowledge and capabilities. Testimonials and referrals do this more specifically, but connections also suggest a standard of integrity, knowledge, and accomplishment. Your proximity to influential and powerful people can make others see you differently.

Power

People who are better connected have more power and reap higher rewards. One need only look at the administrative assistant who guards the gate for her powerful boss. Make her mad, and you may have a more challenging time scheduling a meeting with her boss.

The people you know can sometimes give you power that you might not get otherwise.

Imagine you play volleyball at the local YMCA and one of the regular players is the chief financial officer of a large corporation in town. Most nights after volleyball you all grab a drink together. One night your boss is at the restaurant where the group has its post practice happy hours. Your boss sees you laughing it up with the CFO. Suddenly, the boss that has known you for years has a new, elevated impression of you. You could not have achieved that without the apparent friendship of this powerful company leader. That's the power of influential connections.

Who Should Be in Your Power Grid?

Everyone's power network is different. This difference is the DNA of the competitive advantage your unique network provides you. However, several types of people make a power grid particularly powerful. A good mix of these people makes your network more robust, valuable, and effective.

Each type is loosely defined. Think about the general qualities described and which of your contacts fit into these descriptions. People will typically fit more than one role. It's not uncommon for people to be three or four types, depending on their role, position, age, and personality types. You'll be able to tell who is which type when you think about their personality. If you can't assign them a character type or two, it's a sure sign you need to know them better. Review your primary network and see how many of these people you have in your network.

Technicians
Some people are sought for their legal or technical expertise. They are the subject matter experts on specific business problems and have a hard-earned reputation for their expertise. They showcase their knowledge by writing articles and white papers, speaking at conferences, posting on social media, and other activities to

demonstrate and spread awareness of their specialized knowledge. They are the *technicians*. The expert doers. They are the people companies want working on their particular problem.

Navigators

Navigators are the people who can find the problem technicians quickly. They are the ultimate power grid connectors. They know the capabilities and resources in their network and are known as 'first call' individuals. You can recognize them by how people refer to them. You'll hear things like, "Ed will know someone that can help us". Or, "Let's have Ed take a look at this and see what he thinks." They understand business, understand business needs, can recommend the best people, and facilitate the introductions. They are network navigators and their role is to navigate within their network to find the best people to solve problems more quickly.

The best navigators often hang on the outskirts to ensure their recommendation went well and the company is benefiting from the people they introduced them to. And, by the way, navigators don't limit their advice to lawyers. In their networks, you'll find accountants, plumbers, management consultants, supply chain experts, painters, realtors, bankers, reporters, media folks, and most professions that someone may need. They realize that referrals of any kind create goodwill and encourage reciprocity. They look for ways to proactively refer or connect any two people who might benefit from a connection.

Decision-Makers

This group is prominent. For lawyers, these are the people who decide which lawyers are assigned to solve the company's problems, work on issues, or pursue the company's opportunities. They need not always be in the legal department or be the company's chief legal counsel. Sometimes they are CEOs, CFOs, human resource directors, engineers, or others who determine or substantively influence who will be assigned legal work. Keep in mind that numerous people often weigh in on decisions in highly matrixed organizations.

Influencers

Influencers have a stake in or an interest in the outcome of the legal issues, problems, or opportunities and, importantly, often insert themselves into a wide variety of company decisions. They can be chief financial officers, department heads, technology, or project professionals. They tend to be on the periphery of the kinds of problems you solve in organizations.

These people can help you understand the internal decision and prioritization process in their organization. They give insights into the unintended consequences, potential implications, and the impact of various legal solutions. Their input can help you better understand an organization's operational culture. Influencers frequently have the power to say no, but rarely hold the responsibility of saying yes to a proposal.

Non-Legal Resources

Resources are people you can go to for information outside of your expertise or experience. These people have technical knowledge or experience that frequently comes in handy and that lives outside of a legal practice. For instance, they might be business professors, economists, or people knowledgeable about international trade. Resource people depend in large part on the nature of your legal practice. They are people you can count on to get the information and introductions to solve problems but are not directly involved in implementing the solution.

Referral Sources

Referral sources are people who are in positions to hear of or know about opportunities. These can be bankers, private equity professionals, stockbrokers, other lawyers, accountants, or other professionals who are in a position to see opportunities for work for you or others.

Guides, Coaches, and Mentors

Lastly, we have the people who support you in building your network, gaining perspective, and growing as a person and professional. Guides are committed to your success, and they show it in their genuine interest in your development. They give objective advice and hold you accountable as appropriate. These individuals can be critical to your success as both a business person or lawyer and as an individual who supports you in your career.

Qualities to Look for in Your Power Grid Connections

The best power grid connections have your same mindset about the importance of sharing knowledge, contacts, and ideas. In looking at the personal characteristics of effective connectors, several qualities tend to stand out. Each of these qualities will not apply in every case. Instead, this is a list of the qualities to look for when thinking about the best people to include in your power grid.

Authentic
Authenticity is an attractive quality. It is often the foundation of deeply personal relationships. We need people around us who are 'real' and act consistently with their values. We need to be able to depend on people for showing up consistently. Authentic people are genuine, honest, and transparent. They are self-confident and feel comfortable to be around.

Trustworthy
Power grid connectors build relationships based on mutual trust. They have excellent reputations and the results to back it up. They have unquestionable integrity. Their word is their bond. They trust you and show it by sharing their valuable social and professional network.

They Care About You

Good power grid connections should be genuinely interested in you and your success. They take the time to hear your ideas, brainstorm with you and ask about how they can help. They are thoughtful and caring. They show genuine concern for you and others and appear tuned in to the needs and challenges you and others face.

They Are Good Listeners

Good listeners are usually people with natural curiosity and good emotional intelligence. These two attributes make for good power grid connections because they will seek out new information and glean insights. They are eager to learn about the projects others are working on and their challenges and successes making them a good source for new information. When asked, they offer meaningful help and advice.

They Are Positive

The power of positivity is hard to overstate. Your power grid connections should be positive and upbeat people, where possible. They speak the language of possibility and look at life as a sacred opportunity to help others. You feel good around them because their outlook is genuine and sincere. They are happy, optimistic people who see the bright side of situations.

They Are Connected

They actively develop and maintain connections with other people. As a result, they know many people. Look at their connections on LinkedIn. They are broad, deep and diverse. They circulate in their own networks and easily cross into different ecosystems. They often have many side interests (either business or personal) that expose them to new people. Others genuinely care for them and are attracted to them. And it is evident in their reactions to them when they enter the room.

2

The Habits and Qualities of Powerful Connectors

"The deepest principle in human nature is the craving to be appreciated."

– Philosopher William James

The Power of Consistent Outreach

Big goals don't get accomplished overnight. The most significant goals are often a series of steps that need to be done consistently and over a long period. That is precisely the case with building a power grid. It requires not only the initial network building activities but a constant effort to upstream the quality of that network so it becomes even more valuable and productive. You'll likely never stop building your network.

Developing a routine helps you to achieve your goals. Routines can become habits. Think about the routine that would work best for your lifestyle and work style. Focus on building a system that works best for you. The only requirements are that the system is easy for you to use, you can use your process to record who is in your network, and the system can store the information that is helpful to know about each contact.

To give you an example of how simple your system can be, one client of mine begins each month transposing the names and phone numbers of every person he plans to speak with during the month. It is typically one letter-size sheet of paper with names and numbers filling the front and back of a sheet of paper. He adds notes to the margins either before or after his calls.

He gives his list to his administrative support person each month to run through a research protocol. She performs an internet search on each contact and checks their LinkedIn profile looking for professional changes, articles, news, and other relevant information to pass along. She takes a couple of hours each month to prepare the report for him, which he says is critical since she usually finds information to mention in his conversations. This system works for him. He has done it so long that it is now part of his routine. And it produces a tremendous amount of work. At the time, he had a $6 million book of business. It's probably much more today.

What Constitutes 'Outreach'?

Throughout this book, I mainly refer to outreach as phone calls. But in fact, outreach can be any activity in which you engage others in conversation. That can be by email, phone, a social media post, a meal together, a meeting, or a visit to your client's offices. Because the volume of outreach needs to be high and it needs to be done consistently, you should find ways to reach out that are comfortable for you, fit in your schedule, and a process that you can commit to doing consistently.

The purpose of outreach is to connect with people, hopefully with influential and important people. Those people are, by their very nature, busy. By their very nature, they also appreciate connecting with other people - especially people who understand the importance of building their network and providing meaning and value in their interactions. You must strike a balance between 'the easiest, most effective way' to stay in touch and the 'best medium for building meaning, trust, and engagement' in your interactions. For me, that balance falls to phone calls.

Phone calls, in my opinion, strike that happy medium between convenience and effectiveness. Phone calls are inherently personal but can be done relatively quickly. Your voice can still transmit the inflection and tone to communicate your mood and emotions almost as well as a video call. Video calls take more planning but are better in for longer conversations. Emails, social media messages, tweets, and texts are difficult mediums to build personal rapport. Phone calls (or video calls) will work best for the majority of your outreach.

Visits to your clients offices is the best outreach as it gives you the chance to learn more about the company and meet others you might not otherwise. Of course, it takes more planning and time. But you should try to visit the offices of those in power grid at least once.

Some people have preferences as to how and when they want to be contacted, preferring emails or late afternoon phone calls. Don't be afraid to ask the question of whether your contact has a preference for when you should reach out to them. Most won't, but asking shows that you are focused on adapting to their needs. Make a note in your contact record of their preference.

There are many ways to reach out, and all of them can be positive steps in building an outreach habit and deeper relationships. Choose a primary medium (I recommend the phone) to do most of your outreach and use the other mediums to augment your efforts. Over time, you'll learn what combination works best for you and which mediums your connections prefer.

Make the Commitment to ABRO

You've taken the first step in growing your book of business by reading this book. Congratulations. But like any journey to build new habits, you will have good days and bad days. Progress will come in fits and starts. Sometimes the effort to reach out will feel like a burden. You'll have excuses, some of them valid. Client work, family time, work demands, and travel are legitimate excuses. But they are still excuses. You must find the time to reach out every day.

A terrifying feeling for consultants and legal practitioners can be that anxious feeling when they don't know where their next project will come from. When times are good and work is plentiful, it's easy to forget the need to 'always be reaching out' (ABRO). But when projects conclude and there is nothing scheduled, it can be hard to restart the flow of work. For some, it's a terrifying thought not to know where your next project will come from.

Regular outreach aims to smooth out this ebb and flow of work opportunities. If you've stopped all outreach activity, it can take several months to go from zero work to a full plate of work. Through regular and strategic outreach, you can maintain a steady flow of work opportunities.

Over time, it will become much easier, almost second nature to maintain your outreach flow. You will find that reaching out to others becomes the needed break in your day. You'll come to enjoy these discussions, learn fascinating new things, begin to see new opportunities, and embrace the process as fundamental to your practice's success. I promise all of these things will happen. And I promise it will happen sooner than you expect if you do it every day.

The key to ABRO and your success is finding a way to work in the outreach activity even when other demands tell you that it is not a priority. Client demands, administrative work, other competing business development or marketing tasks, or time entries push your outreach back a step in your priorities. Don't let this happen.

I've found the best way is to block time out on your calendar and commit to doing it every day. Block out thirty minutes to make calls, schedule a lunch or breakfast meeting, and arrange to meet someone for drinks. That's potentially six connections made in a single day. That one day of outreach could fulfill your quota for the week.

At the very least, you should plan to reach out to at least one person in your power grid every day. That should be your minimum commitment. I advise my clients to call between one to three people each day. To accelerate results, make three calls per day. Most of my clients see results of new work within three months when they make that level of outreach. Your timeframe may be more or less. But it won't vary by much.

Get Help from Others

Use your critical few and other support people to help you. Your administrative assistant or professionals in your marketing department may be able to help do some of the leg work required of a robust outreach program. For instance, they can research prospective clients, pull financial reports, analyze cross-marketing opportunities, document your conversations, maintain your contact lists, and update contact information. They can also help you hold yourself accountable for daily activity and help you track your progress. Use all of your support options and create 'Team YOU' to work as a group toward your success.

There are many ways in which others can support you in your business development program. Ask for their help, share your plan with them, tell them who you will be calling each week, and keep them updated on how it is going. Encourage them to gently hold you accountable for doing what you say you want to do. The team you build can help you stay on track and make the process easier. They can also support you through difficult times. Most importantly, they can ask you every day whether or not you reached out. Especially in the beginning, holding you accountable to daily outreach is hugely beneficial.

Note: Log on to www.elegaltraining.com and go to the legal forms page. Search for the form entitled, Administrative Support for Business Development. Use 'Power Grids' in the coupon to download your free copy.

Gather Competitive and Market Intelligence

Outreach to your power grid should include an effort to gather competitive and market intelligence. The currency of consultants and advisors is knowledge. Consultants know what's happening in markets, industries, and among their client's competitors. Include learning market and competitive intelligence as part of your call objectives for any call.

Market intelligence refers to gathering and analyzing information relevant to a company's market - these include business trends, emerging issues, competitor information, and customer monitoring. It is a subtype of competitive intelligence, which is data and information gathered by companies that provide continuous insight into market trends such as competitors' and customers' values and preferences.

Essentially, you should have your finger on the pulse of the industry or region. You can do this through an ongoing market monitoring program, reading legal publications and the publications in the industries in which you and your clients operate. You can also read the white papers and posts from the major management consulting groups and accounting firms. These provide a rich source of new and evolving issues and ideas.

Use the significant events or emerging issues to begin the intelligence-gathering portion of the conversation. You can say something like, 'I saw that XYZ is opening two new locations in the southern region. What other information do you hear about expansion in the industry?

Start with a specific piece of information but pivot to a general question about developments in the area. Don't be afraid to probe for more information.

Adopt a Giving Mindset

Since providing value is the spark that ignites the energy of power grids, we will discuss how you can provide value to your network in the next chapter. But let's first talk about the mindset of giving because it should be at the heart of your intentions and efforts to provide value to others.

Most of us believe that hard work, long hours, good grades from a top law school, intelligence, creativity, integrity, and client service are the key qualities that drive the success of a lawyer's practice. But recent studies point to a more powerful force that drives professional success: how you interact with others and the degree to which you give your time, energy, and resources without the expectation of reciprocity. This is the giving mindset.

In his book entitled *Give and Take*, Adam Grant, a professor at the Wharton School of Business, writes about the power of giving, mentoring, and altruism in business. He describes people as falling into one of three categories based on how they interact with others: Takers, Matchers, and Givers. In short, he describes Takers as people who strive to get as much as possible from others; Matchers as people who aim to trade evenly in all of their interactions; and Givers as people who contribute to others without expecting anything in return.

> Lawyers, in particular, worry about giving advice or insights outside of a formal engagement. Certainly, there is some validity to this concern. But I'd caution you not to allow it to inhibit you. You can preface your insights or advice with, 'I don't know the specifics of your situation necessary to give legal advice, but here's what I think….'

The giving mindset can be counterintuitive for many people because of the fear that giving too freely will allow others to take advantage of their generosity. But, in reality, Takers represent a small group, and they are easy to recognize so you can avoid them as much as possible.

Takers frequently ask for favors, talk incessantly about themselves, show little genuine interest in others, always have an excuse for not helping others, and know how to manipulate situations and people to their benefit. You probably know at least one person like this. If you find these people in your power grid, try to remove them from your network. Hopefully, they are not a boss or family member because they will drain value from your power grid.

Matchers make up the majority of people in business. Most people do favors for others, expecting that the beneficiary will reciprocate when they can return the favor. Matchers who keep track of whom they have done favors for or express their expectations for reciprocity before doing the favor can harm their relationships. In general, though, Matchers view helping others as a business transaction. On the other hand, Givers have a sincere interest in helping others and do so without the expectation of reciprocity. Often, they have experienced the benefit of a Giver in their career and understand the lasting impression such acts of selfless concern for others can have.

Hopefully, you are convinced that being a Giver is a good thing and the type of person you want to be (if you are not already). If you need more convincing by chance, consider that giving is also good for your health.

There is substantial scientific evidence that a giving mindset reduces cortisol levels in the brain and increases oxytocin, a hormone that induces feelings of warmth and connection to others. On the other hand, high cortisol levels, a stress hormone, are unhealthy and can even lead to premature death, so you want to do whatever you can to lower your cortisol levels. Giving to others can help do that.

According to The Greater Good Project at the University of California, Berkeley, a psychology think tank, "Giving reduces stress and makes you feel more connected to others. Regardless of whether you're on the giving or receiving end of a gift, that gift can elicit feelings of gratitude. The gift of your time, energy, or resources is both a way of expressing gratitude and a way to instill gratitude in others. Research has found that gratitude is integral to happiness, health, and social bonds."

Giving promotes cooperation and social connection. Several studies have suggested that when you give to others, your generosity is likely to be rewarded by others down the line—sometimes by the person you gave to, sometimes by someone else. These exchanges promote a sense of trust and cooperation that strengthens our ties to others—and research has shown that having positive social interactions is central to good mental and physical health.

Giving encourages collaboration in teams, builds trust, and reduces social anxiety. A giving mindset can help those who fear networking situations. Studies suggest the act of giving minimizes the fear of rejection, thereby improving confidence in social interactions. It increases your happiness and encourages positivity in those around you. A reputation as a giver can even make you more approachable. Most importantly, giving appears to be contagious and inspires others around you to give, creating a fortuitous, value-enhancing cycle.

Giving can help deal with social anxiety. Social anxiety can be crippling, leading to lost opportunities in the office and elsewhere. A new study finds that performing acts of kindness can help people with social anxiety mingle with others more easily. It can be challenging for socially anxious people to get close to others. Naturally, they tend to have fewer friends and can lose out on that vital source of pleasure and support.

Canadian researchers Jennifer Trew and Lynn Alden wanted to see if performing acts of kindness might benefit the socially anxious. People recruited into the study were put into one of three groups for four weeks:

- One group performed acts of kindness, like doing their roommates' dishes.
- Another group were exposed to various social interactions without the acts of kindness.
- A third group who did nothing special acted as a control.

At the end of the study, those who'd performed acts of kindness felt more comfortable in social interactions. The actions of service seemed to help people deal with worries about rejection.

Dr. Jennifer Trew said: "Acts of kindness may help counter negative social expectations by promoting more positive perceptions and expectations of a person's social environment. It helps to reduce their levels of social anxiety and, in turn, makes them less likely to want to avoid social situations."

Professor Lynn Alden said: "An intervention using this technique may work especially well early on while participants anticipate positive reactions from others in response to their kindness."

The study was published in the journal Motivation and Emotion (Trew & Alden, 2015).

Building Trustworthy Relationships

A giving mindset alone won't be all you need to be successful. You'll also need people to trust you. But how can you get people to trust you? If people do not trust you, they will not like you, want to work with you or refer you to others. You can't 'fake it until you make it' with someone's trust. The only way to be trusted is to be trustworthy.

Trust is the glue of social relationships. It is hard to gain and easy to lose. Without someone's trust, you will not be able to persuade them or get them to follow your advice. Trust is one of those things that we know when we experience it but an be difficult to explain or describe the exact behaviors that build trust in other people. Worse, when we need someone to trust us, we often find it hard to build trust swiftly. This is a skill set that you should continuously work on, even when you think you are highly trustworthy. You can never get too good at engendering trust.

Two Types of Trust

So how do we build trust? First, it's important to clarify that there are two types of trust: competence trust and interpersonal trust. Clients and the people you work with must trust that you are a competent lawyer, first and foremost. Competence relates to your legal expertise and experience, and your business acumen. Clients, prospects, referral sources and other lawyers look for evidence of your competence in recommendations from peers, in the cases and matters you've handled, in your attention to detail, the quality of your work product, by the prestigious clients you've worked with, and in the clarity of your writing and thought processes.

Higher levels of competence are shown by your ability to integrate the company's business needs, operational norms, and business strategy into how you achieve results for the client. Technical competence is relatively easy for one lawyer to assess in another lawyer as they routinely scan the technical competencies of other lawyers as a function of their training. It may be more difficult to assess by non-lawyers.

The Three Cs of Interpersonal Trust Building

Interpersonal trust is much harder to quantify or build. Yet it is at the heart of relationship building – it is, in fact, the purpose of relationship building. Interpersonal trust is built through commitment, care and candor.

Commitment is the degree to which you are focused on your client's needs. In developing a working relationship, you will have opportunities to demonstrate your commitment to the client and their business objectives. You will have this same opportunity to demonstrate your commitment to your partners. It is a commitment to both the individual and the business's success, and it comes out in what you do more so than anything you can say. Examples of commitment can be seen by being available to clients after hours or on weekends, re-scheduling activities to meet your client's timeframe, anticipating your client's needs, and delivering ahead of deadline, just to name a few.

Demonstrating a commitment to others comes in numerous subtle but essential actions which are sometimes difficult to describe succinctly. Some would describe commitment as finding ways to make your client's job easier or as making your client look good. Others define a committed working relationship as being responsive or available at any time. Or some might describe commitment as doing whatever it takes to get the matter resolved in the client's favor. Whatever way you describe it, commitment is a deeply-rooted sense of purpose and priority that your clients and co-workers consistently detect in your actions.

Care refers to the service level and concern you have for a person's or their company's success. It is an empathetic approach to your client's circumstances. You can show your care and concern by adopting their perspective, acting proactively, and doing a little extra. There are many ways to demonstrate that you care.

Lastly, candor relates to the integrity and objectivity of your communications with clients and others. While you must be biased in your commitment to the client, your advice should be unbiased. Candor is committed to providing business-focused, practical, and objective input into the client's issues. When offering advice, many lawyers suggest a list of options that the company can pursue. They often don't state which option they would advise the company to pursue. This is a mistake and a missed opportunity to demonstrate all three components of trust: care, commitment, and candor.

Discussions held within an organization often get colored by the internal politics, their institutional knowledge base, and the organization's cultural values. This can lead to oversights or even a miscalculation of the best strategy choice. Clients need advisors who provide a counterbalance to the internally developed views of the organization and are confident enough in their analysis that they can recommend a single option to pursue. It is a discipline that provides extraordinary value and is essential to developing a trusted advisor role with the client.

Trust Building Qualities

You can increase the perception of your trustworthiness when you exhibit certain qualities. These are the most common qualities found among people who are perceived as trustworthy. To be trusted, you should:

Be Predictable

Acting consistently and predictably builds trust. The opposite destroys trust. When you are inconsistent, act unpredictably, and have emotional ups and downs, people will be less trusting of you because they can't predict how you will respond. Great leadership and client relations require a steady, consistent and predictable approach. Those who are even-keeled also tend to be relied on more consistently for their ideas, assistance, and advice.

Be More Familiar

People trust those with whom they are most familiar. They have more time to observe and confirm your behaviors in different situations. The more they know you, the more they understand how you will behave. Spending time with clients and prospects, either by visiting their place of business, working with them, or socializing with them, is a powerful way to build trust and respect.

Many lawyers become friends with their clients. This is typically because they have spent a great deal of time together. Researchers have documented how much time you have to spend with another person in order to form friendships. Research indicates it takes 60 hours together to form "light friendship," 100 hours to get to a full-fledged friend status, and that best friend forever you've always wanted? That will require 200 hours together.

Be Positive and Friendly

Cheerful, friendly people attract others to them. They are easier to be around and influence others to be more positive and accepting. Positivity also suggests the absence of negativity. Negative attitudes, criticism, and pessimism repel other people. Don't speak ill of others. Negativity sticks in your mind like spinach in your teeth. You don't usually know it's there, but boy does it leave an impression.

If you'll talk negatively about someone else, it's reasonable to assume that you will also speak ill of them. Negative comments imply as much about you as they do about others. Often, more about you. It takes tremendous conversational discipline to monitor yourself for negativity, especially if you are naturally a negative person. But reducing those comments goes a long way in building the trust others will have in you.

Be Confident

Confidence engenders trust. Confidence is like an insurance policy that helps people feel more comfortable with their decision to work with you or be their friend. Even if you do not feel confident, act as if you are. Act as if you know what you are doing and are sure it is the right thing to do. Act as if you have the right and authority to do and say what you do. Others trust those who are confident in what they do, especially if they do not know how to do it themselves.

Be Vulnerable

One way to speed up the time to stronger bonds is through self-disclosure or by being more vulnerable. Share a little bit about your personal life, your values, your challenges, or your dreams. Many people find it difficult to be vulnerable or disclose personal aspects of their lives. They live two separate lives: a professional life and their personal life. But as Brene Brown says, you should "lean into the discomfort of vulnerability."

That's right, showing vulnerability, first in low doses, and then in increasing amounts as you get positive feedback (that is, as vulnerability is shared back), increases the speed in which friendship bonds are formed. The demonstration of vulnerability turbo charges relationships.

You don't have to confess to an addiction, your childhood trauma, or your horrible marriage- although I see that increasingly on LinkedIn. Just simply share aspects of your life or personality that gives some insight into who you are, what you like, and the challenges you have faced. It makes you more approachable and authentic.

Acts of self-disclosure and demonstrating vulnerability can be helpful in lots of different areas, too. Besides making bonds happen more quickly, vulnerability makes apologies more convincing. It makes people more attentive to what you are saying. It makes it easier to get good feedback from clients. There are hundreds of ways that showing more vulnerability can grease the slope of relationship bonds. It shows you care enough to trust them that they won't use that against you, or think less of you. It takes confidence and self-awareness which, by the way, are traits strongly correlated to the most successful lawyers.

A friend of mine, Susan Freeman, does a conference for professional women which she calls Empowered Women events that focus on getting real discussions going among attendees. The speakers speak authentically and tell their story of how they have survived and thrived in their work cultures. In short, they each share deeply personal thoughts and feelings they have about their professional lives. They share their vulnerabilities.

I haven't been invited but the reviews are amazing. Women gush about the conference on social media and say things like 'I've never made so many best friends so quickly.' Susan creates an environment where women feel safe and the results are new friendships, strong bonds, and deeper relationships. And those relationships fuel everyone's growth and happiness. That's the power of vulnerability in building trusted relationships.

Apologize Quickly and Sincerely

If you make a mistake admit it quickly and apologize. When you have broken the trust of others, make it right as quickly as you can. Apologizing for mistakes can build trust, besides being the right thing to do. It's also an opportunity to show your vulnerability, another trust-building technique. Demonstrating vulnerability, in which you seem like the other person can hurt you, must be done genuinely and authentically. But suppose you've made a mistake and are willing to admit it. In that case, you'll probably be genuinely vulnerable, and both the apology and the demonstrated vulnerability can build, or in this case rebuild, trust.

Don't mistake building trust with being likable. The two qualities are not interchangeable. Making yourself more likable is also important. You can be likable but not trusted. Building trust requires demonstrating competence and acting consistently with unquestionable integrity, even when that means someone might not like you for it.

The Importance of Likability

Too many believe that being likable comes from natural, unteachable traits that belong only to a lucky few — the good-looking, the fiercely social, and the incredibly quick-witted. It's easy to fall for this misconception. Very likable people seem to have a magical mix of qualities that appear impossible to duplicate. But likability can be developed, just like good habits.

Being likable is under your control. The same way you can change your mindset, you can improve your likability with a little effort. According to Dr. Travis Bradbury, Author of Emotional Intelligence 2.0, the most likable people tend to share the following traits. They are authentic. They smile, use people's names and exhibit positive body language.

Likeable people don't seek attention or pass judgment on other people or their ideas. They are open minded and communicate clearly and concisely. They make good first impressions and, here's the one I would not have guessed: likable people balance their passion with the ability to have fun. According to Dr. Bradbury, "at work, they are serious yet friendly. They get things done because they are socially effective and can capitalize on valuable social moments. They minimize small talk and gossip and instead focus on having meaningful interactions with their coworkers. They remember what you said yesterday or last week, which shows that you're just as important to them as their work."

Likable people are invaluable and unique. They network with ease, promote harmony in the workplace, bring out the best in everyone around them, and generally seem to have the most fun. Add these skills to your repertoire and watch your likability soar!

The Disciplines That Build Network Value

It takes a deep commitment to building a power grid that can drive better reputations, more referrals, deeper relationships, and higher revenues. It requires that you adopt specific disciplines in your life. While these disciplines may seem obvious, the point is to be intentional about incorporating each discipline into your workday and your business development process.

The first discipline is *organization*. When your outreach program involves many primary outreach connections, you need a system to ensure you keep in touch with each person, diligently record the substance of your discussions, and take appropriate actions to deliver value to your connection. If your firm uses a client relationship management system or CRM system, this technology will help you stay organized and keep accurate records. But it may not be enough to record everything and maintain good records about your connections. Develop a system that works for you. If your firm does not have a CRM, develop a process to ensure you stay organized and keep accurate records of your conversations.

The second discipline is *consistency*. Developing a powerful network of connections requires a constant outreach effort. You must make time for this in your daily activities and make it as routine as brushing your teeth each day. I can't stress this enough. Only through regular and consistent outreach can you build the habits and processes that pay off for you. You have to develop the habits daily. But do it daily for two or three months, and you'll find it becomes second nature for you.

The third discipline is *dependability*. It can be a challenge to follow up consistently after each conversation. Even more challenging to do it on a timely basis. A quick email reiterating what you agreed to do or to thank them for the meeting makes a big impression. So does following up with additional information, an insightful article, or sharing a new idea inspired by your talk. The follow-up shows that your conversation created an impact. This little extra follow-up is flattering to the person you were speaking with. And of course, when you deliver on what you said you would do and do it quickly, you create a sense of dependability in that other person, thereby increasing their trust in you.

The fourth disciple is *accessibility*. People in your primary network should feel they have easy access to you. This means giving your connections your cell phone number and other contact information. It also means answering emails and returning phone calls even when you are busy or off work. Access and responsiveness demonstrate respect, caring, and concern for others. It is a powerful way to encourage people to connect with you more deeply.

The fifth disciple is *active listening*. Active listening enables you to build trust and rapport and to identify ways in which you can add value. Active listening allows you to be present in the discussion. But for many, actively listening is a skill that needs to be more developed.

Think about your last few conversations. Did you interrupt the other speaker at any point? Did your mind wander while the other person was speaking? Did you think about what you wanted to say while the other person spoke? These are signs that you are not actively listening. And more than likely, the other person noticed. In general, good listeners speak about thirty percent of the time in a conversation.

Listen Actively for Deeper Understanding

Listening is one of the most important skills you can have. Listening is how your brain retains and processes what you hear. How well you listen has a major impact on your effectiveness in life and on the quality of your relationships with others.

Surprisingly, we're not as good as one would expect given all the listening we do. Research suggests that we only remember between 25 percent and 50 percent of what we hear, as described by Edgar Dale's Cone of Experience. That means that when you talk to your clients, colleagues, friends, or spouse for 10 minutes, they pay attention to less than half of the conversation. Rude, huh?

Turn it around and it reveals that when you are receiving directions or being presented with information, you aren't hearing the whole message either. You hope the important parts are captured in your 25-50 percent, but what if they're not?

Clearly, listening is a skill that we can all benefit by improving. By becoming a better listener, you can improve your productivity, as well as your ability to influence, persuade and negotiate. What's more, you'll avoid more misunderstandings and, potentially, conflicts.

Active listening is where you make a conscious effort to hear not only the words that another person is saying but, more importantly, the complete message being communicated. It is the ability to encourage information sharing and expression without influencing them with your preconceived notions or opinions. It is a communication style that enables a deeper understanding of the person, their problem, or the situation. And it gives you access to the influences, objectives, and perceptions people have about their challenges.

Lawyers are advisors. You help people fix their problems. When a prospect describes a problem they have, it is natural to respond with your suggested solution. After all, you've seen the same problem a hundred times, haven't you? It is in your wheelhouse. You know how to fix the problem.

But the solutions to many of the problems that companies have and the challenges that people face are not always simple or distinct. We often make assumptions about both the listener and what the person is saying. Our experiences in life have taught us to read a person, interpret their words and actions, and form judgments about them quickly, often subconsciously. Research indicates that impressions are formed in as little as seven seconds. We don't listen well and we're quick to judgment. That can't be good.

Active listening skills help us slow this processing in our brains. And it is especially useful when discussing problems with clients. It enables you to explore the core issues and causes of a problem more thoroughly. It can help reveal the emotional costs or damage of a problem. When we give advice too quickly, we miss the opportunity to gather intelligence that will be valuable in crafting the best solution. Active listening and probing for information, as opposed to providing quick advice, builds trust that you understand the company's issues.

Here is how to manage a conversation to actively listen and gather the information you need to provide the best solution or advice.

First of all, be conscientious of your listening and how your listening may be perceived. Think about how well you are listening and stay present in the conversation. Be very aware of body language, yours and the speakers. Face the individual and maintain eye contact with them while they are speaking. Relax your body posture, unfold your arms and create an open, accepting stance. Watch the speaker's body language and note the emotion they appear to be having when speaking.

Keep in mind that studies have shown that seventy to ninety percent of communication is non-verbal. In fact, the words used accounts for only about 7% of understanding. The remainder of understanding comes from vocal tone (38%) and nonverbal cues (55%). Body language, it turns out, is loud.

Focus on what the person is saying and the emotions associated with their words. Avoid the natural inclination to judge what the speaker is saying. Try not to think ahead while they are speaking. Stay in the moment of the conversation and be fully attentive to what the speaker is saying. Check your brain to make sure you are not talking in your head while the speaker is speaking. If you do, refocus on listening to the speaker.

Ask clarifying questions. Use your experience to ask questions. If something is unclear, ask questions that probe the speaker for more information. But when asking clarifying questions, try to avoid asking a question that starts with 'why'. 'Why' questions often imply blame. Instead, use 'what' and 'where' questions. For instance, instead of asking 'Why did you do that?' Ask, 'what was the situation that led to taking that action?' Be non-judgmental. Don't analyze. At least not yet. You need to gather information and requirements for now. Leave the analysis and judgment for later when you need to craft the solution.

Don't interrupt the speaker or finish their sentence. Interrupting can break their thought process and may be perceived as rude. Don't nod excessively. Occasional nods are good, but you can overdo it. Excessive nodding can appear as though you want them to finish so you can speak. Just listen and absorb. If you need to, repeat the information to confirm your understanding of what the speaker is saying.

Use the 'AWE' question to probe deeper. Ask 'and what else' or other questions that probe for more information. Don't be afraid of silence. Silence is uncomfortable but will often lead the speaker to expound on what they have said. A good, strategic pause can spark a thousand more words and new insights.

Maintain eye contact. Eye contact is a powerful way to build trust. The lack of eye contact creates distrust and suspicion. Be careful not to be distracted by your thoughts. As people speak, your mind will want to think about what you should say next or will judge what the other person is saying. Try to avoid doing this. Instead, listen attentively. Let the other person talk. Give subtle feedback by affirming what the speaker has said.

These techniques will build the trust and knowledge needed to find the best solutions for that unique situation or business. When you don't rush to a conclusion and hear the person describe the situations fully, when you probe to understand every corner of the problem, you convey respect and interest. You communicate that they are unique and that you are thorough. And through that process you build more trust and deepen relationships.

Adopt the Right Attitude

Your attitude will make or break your outreach program. In fact, without the right attitude, you may never be able to get traction in your outreach. Attitudes are derived from our beliefs. Whether consciously or subconsciously, we believe certain things to be accurate, and this truth guides our actions and behaviors. But what if your beliefs are wrong? Or worse, what if they are keeping you from achieving success?

Your beliefs drive how you act. Growing up, your parents instilled beliefs that helped guide you in life. The people you are surrounded by can also strongly influence your attitudes and beliefs as a professional. These good and bad beliefs can be deeply ingrained in your thinking, controlling your thoughts and opinions about many things in life. These beliefs can also work subconsciously, influencing your attitudes and ideas in ways that mostly go unrecognized.

The beliefs you hold can limit your ability to learn and grow. To demonstrate how your beliefs can influence your attitude, behavior, and actions, consider the story of a man with his five very rowdy young children on a crowded subway train. The story is taken from Stephen Covey's book, _The Seven Habits of Highly Effective People_.

The children run up and down the aisle, yelling loudly and throwing things at each other. The man sits seemingly oblivious to the chaos created by his children. Passengers are becoming irritated and annoyed by the children.

Why would this man allow his kids to become such a nuisance on the train? Is he a bad parent? Is he on drugs? Does he not care about the people around him?

Some passengers believe what first came to their minds: that the man is a lousy parent and insensitive to the people around him. This belief drives them to admonish the man for not controlling his children.

Now let's turn the clock back and see where the man and his children were before they boarded the train. He and his children just came from the hospital, where his wife died from a sudden heart attack. The children don't yet know that their mother is dead, only that they have spent the last several hours in a hospital waiting room where they had to sit quietly and still for many hours. Getting out of the hospital was liberating, and their pent-up energy exploded when they boarded the train. The man would rather they get that energy out while he thinks about the loss of his wife and how he will go on in life without her. He is lost in his thoughts about how to tell his children.

If you are like most people, this new awareness changes your perspective on the children. You no longer are irritated and annoyed by the children but remorseful and empathetic toward the family. The heavy burden this man carries has changed your belief about the situation. It was not information you could have known. All you saw was your perception of what was going on. But there was more to that story. There is always more to a story.

We adopt these same beliefs about business development and how others will respond to our efforts to reach out to them. Rainmakers understand this fundamental principle. They believe in people's essential goodness, and that connecting with others invigorates relationships.

It may be because of your beliefs if you are an introverted person or someone uncomfortable in social situations. It may be because you don't view yourself as a connector, influencer, or navigator.

Good news. You can change your beliefs, but it requires you to change your perception of yourself first, as James Clear explains in his New York Times bestselling book, _Atomic Habits_. His revolutionary concept hinges on what he calls identity-based habits.

The basic idea of identity-based habits is that the beliefs you have about yourself drive your long-term behavior. Your identity largely forms your habits, that is, how you see yourself. If you don't shift your underlying identity, then it's hard to stick with long-term changes and form new habits.

Clear explains that there are three layers of behavior change: a change in your outcomes, a change in your processes, or a change in your identity. Changes in outcomes are changes that focus on the result of your habits. For instance, you might want to lose 20 pounds or write a best-selling book on business development for lawyers. A change in your processes is the change in how you apply those changes. For example, you may wake up early to get to the gym. You may commit to writing every day to achieve your goal of writing a book. Focusing on the process, as opposed to the result or goal, can go a long way toward developing new habits.

But Clear theorizes that the root of behavioral change and building better habits is rooted in your identity. With an identity-based change, each action you perform is driven by the fundamental belief that the change is possible because you have assumed the new identity of that evolved person. I believe that I am a writer, making it much easier to change the process (writing every day) of developing new habits and achieving the desired result. In other words, if you change your identity (the type of person you believe you are), it's easier to change your actions.

Outcomes result from small changes in habits that lead to changes in your identity. Focus on the process that builds new habits rather than on desired outcomes. Meaningful change does not require radical change. As Clear points out, small habits can make a significant difference by providing evidence of a new identity. And if a change is meaningful, it is a pretty significant change. It's the little changes that achieve big outcomes.

Get to The Woodshed Every Day

One of the best lessons about habit formation I learned in the 'woodshed.' Let me explain.

I started playing drums when I was about seven years old. By the time I was twelve, I was playing with my older brother in local bands. By 15 we had formed one of the best new bands in town. I started to have visions of being the next John Bonham or maybe Stuart Copeland or Butch Trucks, driving the fat-bottomed groove in a mega-popular band like Led Zeppelin, the Police or The Allman Brothers. When my brother went off to The Berklee College of Music, I began to think about studying music. Of course, I was not good enough to get into Berklee. He had better practice habits than me. Plus, I could barely read music. Nonetheless, I was sure a music education would prepare me for a life of stage, lights, hotel rooms, and groupies – just what my younger self thought I wanted.

I was accepted to St. Mary's College in Southern Maryland. Nora Davenport headed the music department there and was a legendary percussionist who played with the Baltimore Symphony and later in the Kennedy Center for the Performing Arts symphony. She was a petite, slight woman barely 90 pounds, but was, by far, the most powerful and skilled multi-instrument drummer I had ever heard.

She knew talent when she saw it and focused her attention on the several percussionists who were truly, insanely talented musicians. I was not one of them. Nora had me play the bass drum in our semi-annual percussion concerts.

She knew I couldn't read music well, but she was committed to me improving under her tutelage. Where the other players got choice music to learn and perform, Nora simply told me to play every day. It didn't matter how much, what I played, or how well I played. She simply wanted me to sit behind the drums or stand at the marimba and play something every day.

Whenever she saw me, she asked if I played that day. If I hadn't played that day, she would cajole me and guilt me to get into a studio to practice. 'I don't care if you only hit the drum once. Get into the studio every day.' 'Play every day,' she said, 'no matter what.'

She was that way with all of us. She hung a huge calendar on the wall in the instrument room and asked us to put our initials on the calendar every day we got into the studio. She told us to 'Never miss a day'. She would tell me, 'Don't worry about how well you drum. Or how long you drum. Only worry about not missing a day.'

I began to see her rationale. Gradually I got into the habit of getting to the woodshed every day (that's what we called the practice studios.) I improved. I started to read better. I began to look forward to my 'shed' time. My skills got better. I began to want to read more and try harder material. I learned that the more consistently you do something, the more it becomes a habit. The more your brain makes the neural connections to make your muscles do things that they could not do weeks earlier. And that habit, and the brain rewiring, changed how I thought of myself. I began to think of myself as worthy of membership in Nora's tight cluster of percussion protegees.

She wanted me to use the techniques that she used to be such a powerful drummer. She taught me how to change how I held the sticks and then had me sit beside a mirror so I could watch the placement of the stick in my hand as I was playing. I realized that she was breaking my skills down to elemental parts and teaching me how to build them back up with proper technique. Each change was small and incremental but over time Nora changed my whole style of playing.

Nora taught me that you need the habit to improve your skills. Forming the habit to improve was the first step. The skills produce results, but repetition is what develops the skills. And those skills form your identity as an accomplished player. Nora had me focus on the process of building a habit rather than the results of that practice. She knew that the results would follow the habit. And the results would form a new identity as a more powerful and skilled player.

Work on What Matters

A second lesson I learned from Nora was that I should focus on what mattered. I would quickly get frustrated if I went to the 'shed' to learn Jon Bonham's drum solo in Moby Dick. More importantly, it would focus my mind on the result of whether I was learning the solo. I was not focusing on the fundamentals that would enable me to build that solo and many others.

She told me to keep it simple. To work on the fundamentals, like trying paradiddles in various combinations on the drums. Do paradiddles because they were the foundation upon which so many drum solos and sticking combinations are built. "There's only one John Bonham Moby Dick drum solo. Once you learned it, then what?" she would ask.

The same is true of business development and reaching out to others. For many, it is a hassle to reach out to three people each day. It can seem like a daunting task considering a busy client work schedule. Indeed, reaching out regularly takes time away from client work, family time, or just the time you need to recharge. But that repetition is critical to your success. The call is what matters the most. The call is the habit. Only by building a habit will you build your network. Because it takes a habit to build the skills that result in deeper connections, expand the people you know, and glean new insights.

Changing Your Mindset

Many of my clients don't reach out to their contacts every day. Intuitively, they know they need to do it. But privately, they see it as time-consuming, disagree with the need to reach out so much, or simply have too many other things to do.

Numerous challenges contribute to the lack of a consistent approach to reaching out. These can include procrastination, a lack of organization, poor time management, failure to delegate enough, a lack of self-awareness, or even self-esteem. These challenges can be improved by changing one's mindset.

Neuroscientific studies suggest a way to deal with the mental obstacles that people create in their minds. The technique is surprisingly simple, having already been proven effective in almost every other case from dealing with loneliness, eating disorders, anxiety, relationships, work performance, and even depression. It does not replace business development training, social skills development, or the need to get out of one's office. Instead, these studies suggest that a simple change in the approach is all that is needed.

As Carol Dweck showed in her seminal book, _Mindsets_, changing a person's mindset is critical to performance improvement. Fortunately, Dweck's techniques can work on anyone quickly. (The article you read at the beginning of this book about networking versus connecting was written to shift readers' mindset about networking.)

A growing body of research suggests that emphasizing the positive outcomes in a situation is enough to form more positive feelings about the situation. Besides finding the good in a situation, Dweck suggests emphasizing the small objectives achieved. Her work shows that focusing the mind on searching for the positive in an interaction or situation further reworks your mindset about that interaction or situation. The simple question, 'What good happened?', releases the benefit.

This focus on finding the positives, however small, is not just good advice for you. It is good advice for law firm leaders. Finding positive outcomes can build more productive cultures, encourage experimentation, and help people bond more deeply. Practice group leaders, peer attorneys, and the firm's leadership all play an essential role in building a pro-business development culture by consciously looking for and soliciting positive achievements.

Guiding and helping to shift the mindset through encouragement and coaching, ideally through professional coaches and internal mentors, can help ensure that a business development culture takes root. Coaching amplifies the effectiveness of business development training by tying business development theory to its practical application. Coaching is most effective when the coaching focuses on more than just the accountability for action but on shaping the perceptions of success. This 'positive framing' encourages people to keep trying and learning from every experience. Positive reinforcement enables people to persist in their efforts. It is that persistence that is needed to learn and apply new skills. Good coaches pluck out the positives and explain why those actions were good. They give context and rationale to the behaviors so they can more easily repeat them.

The mind responds to feelings of empathy and gratitude just as it does to feelings of anxiety and disappointment. The mind's neuroplasticity enables it to choose which emotions it will focus on. Many of us default to negative interpretations of situations where we don't fully know what happened. As a law firm community participant, you can influence how others view and interpret their business and client development initiatives. That, in turn, will also begin to affect you to see things more positively.

Cynicism already runs rampant in most law firms. By their very nature, and maybe due to their training, lawyers are more skeptical than the general population. Skepticism requires a measure of cynicism. While skepticism and cynicism can be good attributes for examining legal issues, they can sap creativity, innovation, and collaboration.

Skepticism douses the flames of opportunity because skepticism focuses the mind on what could go wrong rather than what can go right. How does one turn skepticism into opportunism? Or, more accurately, how do you keep skepticism in its place, only using it when needed? First, recognize the thought pattern as it happens. Ask yourself, am I assuming negative intentions or motivations in the other person? In this activity? Could I have misinterpreted their response? Could I not have a full understanding of the situation? Could other factors beyond my control be at play here?

Similarly, skepticism can blunt innovation and reject new ideas. Skepticism and cynicism have a bias for precedent and proven strategies. But new ideas and innovation offer new paths and ways to do things. Getting caught when considering a new idea in a cycle of examining the problems that could (but probably won't) happen can prevent you from seeing the opportunity and adopting new ways of doing things.

Pioneers in technology and business also think about what could go wrong but don't dwell on it. They determine the likelihood of negative consequences and adopt new ideas when the possibility of a negative result is low. They don't allow themselves to get stuck in the negativity cycle.

Most importantly, skepticism can douse action. Skepticism leads some to examine every corner of an issue. Told to do something new or foreign to them, the minds of some lawyers will litigate the various ways the task won't work. The analysis causes paralysis of action. While I encourage a thoughtful approach to everything you do, an overly thoughtful approach can keep you from doing it. To be sure, action is a better teacher than reflection. Taking action is the fundamental energy that drives business development success.

Earlier I mentioned that you should enroll your critical few in your business development program. An important and valuable way for them to contribute to your efforts is for you to ask them to ask you about the positive experiences, however small, in every effort you make. Ask them to help you to focus on the positive outcomes. Doing that will help you frame your efforts more positively and become more positive about business development. And as I have said from the beginning, a positive attitude is critically important.

3

Business and Their Trusted Advisors

"If you don't understand the details of business, you are going to fail."

-Jeff Bezos, Amazon

Are You a Trusted Advisor?

For many lawyers, a client who describes them as the company's trusted advisor is the greatest compliment they can get. Those two words are the best indicators of client loyalty. But how does one become a trusted advisor? And can any lawyer, in any practice area, assume that mantel?

If you ask ten lawyers what a trusted advisor is, you'll get 15 definitions. It's another one of those I'll-know-it-when-I-see-it-definitions. In my mind, a trusted advisor is the professional in whom companies seek advice and opinions for their most difficult challenges. But I often ask what lawyers think a trusted advisor is.

I remember one definition that I was told when I asked during a program I was giving. One of the participants defined a trusted advisor as "the lawyer who swoops in at the moment of strategic confusion and gives the company the right answer." That's sort of right, in terms of giving the correct answer. But it creates the wrong impression. There's no swooping in and the advice is only right when it fits the company. When I see a trusted advisor, the lawyer has spent the time to get to know their client and their client's business well. They spend time inside the business and the result is advice and solutions that are more relevant and strategic. That advice is tough to give if you only have a cursory understanding of the business.

Being a trusted advisor is really about being part of the business, being there always learning and understanding the business. In that sense, we should refer to trusted advisors as "embedded" advisors to emphasize the need to embed oneself in the business and understand how it ticks.

It's important to visit your clients. Listening to and watching the activity level in the business is essential. Are the phones ringing a lot? Do people move about quickly or slowly? Ask about why things are done the way they are. Look at the business environment. Are there motivational posters on the walls, separate executive spaces, or lots of clutter? Everything you can observe about the business can help you better understand the company, its culture, and how things work there.

When I talk to young lawyers who have just come off of a secondment to a client's business, they are overflowing with knowledge about the business and its people. They have a better understanding of the business than some lawyers who have worked with the company for years. If you can, you should second yourself in your client's business periodically to learn as much as you can. You'll be surprised at how receptive clients are to that and how much you'll learn.

What sets successful lawyers apart is a deeper understanding of not just the legal issues, problems, and opportunities a company may face but also how those challenges can affect that particular business and its operations. They look at not just the first-degree effects but the second and third-degree effects as well. The unintended consequences occur when companies change how they operate. Many lawyers think about legal problems in terms of how other lawyers or the courts will think about them. They think in terms of rigorous logic, legal strategy, and precedent. This is certainly appropriate.

But legal solutions exist within the business context and must synergize with how the company operates. The less disruption to the normal operations of the business, the better. That's not always possible, of course, but reducing disruption to the company should always be a primary concern when crafting a legal solution. Striking that fine line between legal rigor and business practicality is the line that the most successful lawyers walk.

Knowing how vital understanding the business (and having business acumen) is to be a great business lawyer, let's review some basic business concepts and metrics you'll need to understand the business better.

Common Business Concepts

I can't cover everything you need to know about business in this book. But I can share some basic concepts that will help you in your conversations with business leaders. More importantly than learning the concepts and principles of business, I urge you to be curious about your clients' businesses. I know many lawyers who are not considered the top experts in their area of the law but are, nonetheless, trusted advisors to major corporations. Because of this curiosity, their willingness to embed themselves in their client's business, and their acquired business acumen, they can reach that apex relationship with their clients. The following concepts will help you gain a better understanding of your clients' and prospective clients' businesses.

The Concept of Growth Rates

Growth rates are how fast something is growing or contracting. A healthy business is a growing business. Tracking growth helps the company analyze whether or not the business is growing and by how much over a specified timeframe. If the company is growing at a slower rate than its competitors, that's likely a sign that it needs to be doing something differently. You want a positive delta (change) in all areas of the business.

Growth rates are typically expressed as year-over-year (YOY) growth rates, quarterly growth (growth from one quarter to the next or growth in one quarter compared to the same quarter the previous year), or month-to-month (MTM) growth (either against the previous month or the month compared to the same month of the previous year).

Growth should be put in context. It's best to look at the metric that is used to track growth and compare it to industry averages, peer or competitor averages, or regional averages. Growth rates must be comparable to have meaning. In other words, comparing one company's earnings before taxes, interest, depreciation, and amortization (EBITDA) to another company's gross sales revenues will give you an inaccurate comparison.

There are many ways to track growth in a company. The metrics should track what the company is trying to accomplish and where its focus is. If the company is primarily focused on its profitability, it can measure profit in several ways. Gross profit (net sales – cost of goods sold) measures the company's sales less the cost to produce those sales. Operating profits (operating costs, including selling and administrative expenses) adds in the overhead to the cost of goods sold to get a more accurate picture of profits generated from sales. Net profit tracks the total income-generating activities in addition to the total operating profit of the business to arrive at the net profits of the organization (operating profit + any other income) – (additional expenses) – (taxes).

But the company may also track growth rates in other areas, typically where it wants to focus the organization's efforts. For instance, the company may be focused on customer acquisition and retention. In that case, it may evaluate customer acquisition costs, customer lifetime value, customer churn (also known as turnover), cross-selling, upselling, or customer loyalty and retention metrics. A company or organization can use a wide variety of measurements to help it understand how efficiently and effectively it is performing. Ask your clients which metrics they track, why they use those measurements, and what they learn from those results.

The Concept of Returns

Simply put, a return is the value created after deducting the investment made to create that value. This is a fundamental concept that lies at the heart of organizational purpose. Expressed as some form of return on investment, companies, organizations, non-profits, and even governments can't continue to thrive unless the outputs of their efforts are greater than the inputs required to produce those efforts. The difference is expressed as the return on those efforts.

Organizations have many ways to describe and use the concept of return. They often use return on investment. But you may also hear terms like cost-benefit, cash-on-cash return, internal rate of return, and cash multiple, among others. Charitable organizations and non-profits may express the same concept differently. As socially or environmentally conscious and focused organizations, their metrics will also reflect their missions. They will use metrics describing how well they deploy their resources to affect their missions. For instance, they may tout the number of families served during a fundraising campaign.

These terms all communicate the same concept. No matter how you describe it, an organization's return is how they measure what they spent for what they got. It is a way to track whether they are getting more effective and efficient at investing their resources or getting worse at it. The point is to understand what they measure, why they measure it the way they do, and the results they have achieved.

When you are beginning to get to know a company take the time to understand how value is created and understand the leadership's drive to maximize returns. Organizations that are people-focused tend to have more people-oriented measurements. Companies that are production-oriented tend to focus more acutely on production measurements. It's a cliché but true. What gets measured gets done. Ask how they measure returns and how those measurements change depending on their goals and plans. In learning about a company or its business, your objective should be to understand how a company maximizes its returns, so that you can align your thinking and your service delivery to how those inside the company think about their jobs.

The Concept of Constraints

In business, constraints are obstacles to success. A constraint is anything that limits or controls what the organization can do. For instance, a lack of access to water or electricity may constrain real estate development. Limits on the availability of raw materials due to supply chain constraints can constrain production. Increasing costs can constrain a company's ability to invest in research and development. A lack of qualified candidates for an open position can constrain the completion of an important project. Constraints come in many forms and can be found in every aspect of the business.

Ask your contact what their biggest constraints are on their business—probe for root constraints. Money may be the obvious challenge but dig deeper. Even all of the money available to a company may not move some constraints aside. Ask, what constrains their ability to do their job or achieve success in their area of responsibility? What constraints do they see looming on the horizon? Explore the big, macro constraints as well as the little, less critical constraints. Business people think in terms of constraints. To speak their language, think in terms of constraints as well.

The Concept of Business Strategy

A company's business strategy is a clear set of plans, actions, and goals that outlines how a business will compete in a particular market, or markets, with a product or number of products or services. Business strategy uses a combination of pricing and differentiation to design the strategy that works best for the markets or clients it wants to target.

These strategies can be either generic strategies or focused strategies. For instance, a generic pricing strategy example would be Walmart (low-cost leadership). A generic differentiated strategy would be Nordstrom (high service levels). A focused strategy focuses more narrowly on one or both of those. Apple is an example of a focused innovation differentiation strategy. Redbox Video rental is an example of a focused low-cost strategy, they only do red box video stations offered at very low prices.

Understanding the differences that underlie generic strategies is important because different generic strategies offer considerably different value propositions to customers. In other words, a firm focusing on pricing leadership will have a different value-chain configuration than a firm whose strategy focuses on differentiation.

The same is true of focused pricing and focused differentiation strategies. One way to understand a company better is to identify its business strategy and then look at the value chain built to deliver that strategy. If the value chain does not seem to align completely with the business strategy, change the business strategy and look again. Keep reconfiguring these combinations with respect to the value chain, and you will soon understand how that company ticks.

The Concept of Competitive Advantage

Competitive advantage is the mirror image of business strategy. That is, the company's competitive advantage is how the company's business strategy shows up to the customer. Competitive advantage is what makes a customer choose your business over another, and business strategy is how the company puts a competitive advantage in place. By understanding and promoting such an advantage, companies can win a greater market share.

Competitive advantage comes from how the business sources, prices, protects, markets, or distributes its products and services, again, their business strategy. Companies can gain a competitive advantage through a wide combination of these configurations in the value chain. They can achieve a low-cost leadership advantage. They can achieve an advantage through intellectual property rights protections, through brand or reputation management, or through producing a service or product that no one else can.

To understand the strength of a company's competitive advantage in the marketplace, look to its competitors. The strength of a company's competitive advantage can be understood in terms of its competitor's ability to duplicate that advantage. Competitors that can deliver a similar product or service for a similar price with similar differentiating attributes can minimize that company's competitive advantage. If duplicating those attributes are difficult or costly, the barriers to achieving that advantage are considered high and the competitive advantage strong.

The Concept of a Value Chain

We've mentioned the value chain, and you'll sometimes hear the words "value chain" in conversations with business leaders about their business. When business people talk about their value chain, they refer to the range of activities they use to bring a product or service from its conception to its end use or consumption. It is the source of their competitive advantage so the value chain is not often discussed openly or with great specificity.

All of the activities and resources a company must align to deliver its products, services and experiences to its target customers or markets make up its value chain. This includes research, design, production, marketing, distribution, and customer support, among others.

Some think of the value chain as being in two parts, a production value chain (that is, the value produced on the production side of the business) and a customer value chain (the value created in serving customers). This is helpful because each value chain may produce value in different ways and contribute to the company's competitive advantage in different but symbiotic ways.

The Concept of a Business Model

A business model is essentially the plan a business has for making money. It's a graphical explanation of how the company delivers value to its customers at an appropriate cost. Business models are a relatively new concept. It wasn't until the early 2000s, during the explosion of the Internet and the birth of the dot com era, that investors in these new business concepts and the entrepreneurs who created new business ideas saw the need to talk about them more clearly. The growth of new business models and new distribution channels caused the value chain and business strategy to merge. It became necessary for business strategy and how companies create a value chain to be better defined. And investors needed a way to compare one new business idea to another business conception to evaluate their investments and understand better how the company planned to disrupt markets or compete more aggressively.

As Joan Magretta writes in her 2002 book, "*Why Business Models Matter*," a business model answers the fundamental questions every manager must ask: How do we make money in this business? What underlying economic logic explains how we can deliver value to customers at an appropriate cost?" This loosely defined understanding got more specific in 2005 when Alex Osterwalder, along with dozens of the world's marketing experts as contributors, defined what a business model is more specifically in his seminal book, *Business Model Canvas*. They identified nine "building blocks" of the business model design template that came to be called the Business Model Canvas. These building blocks offer an exceptional way to think about and evaluate a company's business. The nine building blocks cover four main activities of the company and describe its infrastructure, offering, customers, and finances.

Specifically, the nine building blocks are:

The Infrastructure building blocks:

1. *Key activities*: The most important activities in executing a company's value proposition. An example for Lenova, the computer manufacturer, would be to describe how it creates an efficient supply chain to drive down costs.

2. *Key resources*: The resources that are necessary to create value for the customer. They are considered assets to a company that are needed to sustain and support the business. These resources could be human, financial, physical, or intellectual capital.

3. *Partner network*: In order to optimize operations and reduce risks of a business model, organizations usually cultivate buyer-supplier relationships so they can focus on their core activity. Complementary business alliances also can be considered through joint ventures or strategic alliances with either competitors or non-competitors.

The Offering building block:

1. *Value propositions*: The collection of products and services a business offers to meet the needs of its customers. According to Osterwalder, a company's value proposition is what distinguishes it from its competitors. The value proposition provides value through various elements such as newness, performance, customization, "getting the job done", design, brand/status, price, cost reduction, risk reduction, accessibility, and convenience/usability. Amazon's value proposition is convenience and useability.

The Customers building blocks:

1. *Customer segments*: To build an effective business model, a company must identify which customers it tries to serve. Various sets of customers can be segmented based on their different needs and attributes to ensure appropriate implementation of corporate strategy to meet the characteristics of selected groups of customers.

2. *Channels*: A company can deliver its value proposition to its targeted customers through different channels. Effective channels will distribute a company's value proposition in ways that are fast, efficient, and cost-effective. An organization can reach its clients through its own channels (store front), partner channels (major distributors), through the Internet, or a combination.

3. *Customer relationships*: To ensure the survival and success of any business, companies must identify the type of relationship they want to create with their customer segments. Their customer strategy should address three critical steps in a customer's relationship: How the business will get new customers, how the business will keep customers purchasing or using its services, and how the business will grow its revenue from its current customers.

The Finances building blocks:

1. *Cost structure*: This describes the most important monetary consequences while operating under different business models. Costs can be in terms of spending or investment as well as in terms of perceived costs or losses such as lost opportunity costs.

2. *Revenue streams*: The way a company makes income from each customer segment.

If you are interested in learning more, plenty of information is available to study. But for now, understanding these key concepts will help you better understand the language of business and how businesses work.

Questions to Understand a Company and Its Businesses

To know the company in more detail, use this checklist to get a more comprehensive understanding of the business. Try to answer as many questions as you can through your own research. Develop any additional questions you have that came up from the research or that you were unable to answer through your research. Prepare your questions for a discussion with your prospect or client.

Goals, Critical Issues, and Challenges

1. What is the company's stated strategy, and what long-term goals does it have?

2. What has been the company's financial performance over the past few years? (Consider revenues, profit margin, amount of debt, cash reserves, Return on Equity, Price Earnings Ratio, etc.) Is the company growing or shrinking, meeting its financial goals, and what consequences or opportunities has the company experienced due to its financial performance?

3. Which divisions or products and services of the company have grown the most, shrank the most, and why?

4. What is the *business model* of the organization? What makes it unique? How is it differentiated in the marketplace? What is its value proposition and how does the business align its suppliers, processes, resources, and talent to deliver unique products and services to customers?

5. What legislative issues, pending legislation, regulatory issues, and changes or other governmental actions affect the company, its business, its suppliers, or its customers?

The Organization

1. Who is on the Board of Directors, past and current? Which other company boards do directors sit on? What unique disciplines and skills do they each have? What does that imply about the strategic direction of the company or the resources the company needs? Are board members investors in the company? How significant is that investment?

2. Who are the key executives in the company? (Consider the CEO, finance, operations, marketing, legal, HR, regional presidents, etc.) What are their backgrounds, previous company experiences, and expertise?

3. What are their responsibilities? What decision-making authority do they have? Are operations compartmentalized (for instance, Regional Presidents have the power to select attorneys), or are the decisions centralized? Which direction is the company moving toward in terms of consolidating or dispersing decision authority?

The Company's Corporate Tree and Related Companies

1. What other companies or divisions are part of the corporate tree?

2. What is the business structure and performance of these related companies? (Description of the products or services, operational structure, geographic reach, financial performance, etc.)

3. Is the company adding or subtracting from its corporate tree over time, and what conclusions can you draw from these changes?

Key Financial Indicators

With public companies, this data will be easily accessible. Private companies will require a meeting with company leaders to get this information. Where possible, compare this information to the company's competitors and industry peer group to get a sense of the company's comparative performance.

1. In the company's annual report (or 10K) pay special attention to accounting and management comments. Review the company's balance sheet (assets, liabilities, and shareholder equity). If possible, monitor the trends in those areas. You can also compare the financial results to the company's competitors to get a better sense of the company's performance.

2. Review the company's liquidity. Liquidity is a key factor in assessing a company's basic financial health. Liquidity is the amount of cash and easily-convertible-to-cash assets a company owns to manage its short-term debt obligations. The two most common metrics used to measure liquidity are the *current* and *quick ratios*.

3. Review the company's solvency. Closely related to liquidity is the concept of solvency, a company's ability to meet its debt obligations on an ongoing basis, not just over the short term. Solvency ratios calculate a company's long-term debt in relation to its assets or equity. The *Debt-to-Equity Ratio* is a good indicator of solvency for most businesses.

4. Review the company's operating efficiency. A company's operating efficiency is key to its financial success. Its *operating margin* is the best indicator of its operating efficiency. This metric indicates a company's operating profit margin after deducting the variable costs of

producing and marketing the company's products or services. It shows how well the company's management controls costs.

5. Review the company's profitability. While liquidity, the company's solvency, and its operating efficiency are all essential factors to consider in evaluating its financial condition, the bottom line remains a company's bottom line: its net profitability. Companies can indeed survive for years without being profitable, operating on the goodwill of creditors and investors. But to survive in the long run, a company must eventually attain and maintain profitability. The best metric for evaluating profitability is *net margin*, the ratio of profits to total revenues. Generally, higher margins produce more profits.

Key Operational Initiatives

1. What are the company's revenue and profit growth, stock price, market share, and competitive rankings?

2. Which of the company's business lines or divisions generate the largest amount of the company's revenues? Are those revenues increasing or decreasing? Which business lines or divisions account for its most significant losses or gains?

3. What initiatives or major projects are planned for the next three, and five years? What is the status of each? Consider new products, cost-cutting measures, process improvements, new technology or personnel investments.

Major Competitors

1. Who are the primary direct competitors of the company?

2. Describe the competitive experience of the company in terms of the number of competitors, types of competitors,

and pricing pressure. Which players have the largest share of the market?

3. What are the alternative substitutes to the company's services or products? How big or small is the cost advantage between the company and its alternatives? What benefits or sacrifices would a customer experience if the company or alternative is chosen?

Market Trends and Emerging Issues

1. What are the four to five most important trends or market forces affecting this company's business? Consider changes in demographics, technology, sourcing, distribution, economic pressures, international trade, regulations, and legislation.

2. If different, what market trends affect the company's industry, individual locations, or other segments of the company's operations.

The Customer Base

1. Who are the key or largest customers of the company? How much revenue is concentrated among the best customers of the company? How vulnerable is the company to the loss of one or more key customers?

2. What is the typical buyer's profile for the company's products or services? How does the company describe its ideal customer?

3. How long do customers tend to remain with the company? Are they relational buyers or transactional buyers? Do they buy multiple products or services or tend to be one off buyers? How long is the sales cycle to gain a new customer?

4. In what ways does the company build client loyalty or integrate with business clients?

The Suppliers

1. Who are the major suppliers in the company's value chain?

2. What product, service, or role do the suppliers play and where do they come into play in the product or service delivery chain?

3. How critical are the suppliers to the company's ability to deliver to its customers? Are there numerous alternative suppliers or are the suppliers specialized and scarce? Does the company have easy access to suppliers in the U.S. or does it use foreign suppliers? What are the regulatory issues that affect the company's suppliers?

Partnerships, Alliances, Associations, and Regulatory Ties

1. What companies act in concert or partner with the company to deliver its services or products?

2. What associations or alliances act in cooperation to influence the market for the company's products or services? How critical is their role, and how large or influential is the group? How significant is the role of the company in the group?

3. What regulatory authorities work to facilitate or monitor the delivery, quality, impact, research, or other company outputs?

Company Culture

1. What are the core values of the company? How would you describe the company's culture? How do people inside the company describe the company's culture?

2. What is the company's mission? What are its stated values or service commitments?

3. What societal challenges does the company care about?

4. Is the company involved with or a member of a specific community or professional organization? In which of those organizations is the company most active?

5. What evidence can you cite that demonstrates the company's commitment to perpetuating the company's culture and societal or community obligations? Consider hiring practices, community involvement and charitable initiatives, investments, statements by the top executives, decision-making process, vendor selection criteria, etc.

Legal Issues Management

1. Does the company have lawyers on staff? How many?

2. Do any of the board of directors or C-suite positions hold law degrees?

3. What practice areas do these individuals and those of the in-house lawyers practice in?

4. How is the legal department organized?

5. What vendors and software do they use for knowledge management, e-discovery, case and document management, e-billing? What others do they use?

Litigation History

1. What types of litigation has the company faced in recent history? Is there a pattern in the types of cases or matters or the type that are taken to trial?

2. Does the company have any open or pending litigation cases?

3. Are there any areas of litigation that the company expects to have to deal with soon? Why? (Consider litigation sparked by product development, research practices, consumer access to services or products, litigation related to their facilities, product performance, regulatory changes, and any pending or proposed legislation, etc.)

Mergers and Acquisitions

1. What are the companies that have been acquired or have merged with the company in recent history? What types of companies were they? What size were they and what has been the history of their financial performance? What new capabilities did these acquisitions bring the company?

2. What was the strategic objective for each of these acquisitions? Consider financial performance, cost of acquisition factors, securing resources, securing suppliers, securing distribution, acquisition of new products or product line extensions, new geographic or demographic segment access, international expansion, and acquisition of talent or human capital.

Intellectual Property

1. What are the intellectual property filings that have been submitted recently? Consider patents, trademarks, and copyrights.

2. What patents does the company have and which patents are owned by its key executives? Are they patented products or business processes?

3. What are the trademarked products or services of the company?

Decision Processes and Controllers

1. Who are the key decision-makers and how do they determine when to hire outside counsel? Is there a regular review process? How are ad hoc legal services hiring decisions made?

2. What impact can you have on the company's operations? What implications are likely to occur in the company as a result of the work that you do? How might the company need to change its operating model or particular aspects of its operations? What are the inherent risks and rewards of addressing the issues for the company?

3. Who are the stakeholders who influence the matters that you handle? What role do they play in the decision process? Where might objections to the changes in operations emanate from within the company?

4. How are budgets determined for legal matters? How are priorities set among competing projects?

It's important to monitor the activities and news about the companies that you provide legal services to and the companies with whom you'd like to provide services. The following is a list of activities that you can monitor to better understand your client's business. These activities can sometimes reveal legal issues, problems, or opportunities to pitch legal solutions.

Monitoring Unusual Business Activities

Wayne Gretsky understood the need to anticipate. He famously attributed his successful career in hockey to being able to skate to where the puck is going to be. Smart investment and commercial bankers do the same thing. They have perfected the art and science of anticipating where a business may experience problems, and they use that information to hedge their bets, seize opportunities, and protect their investments. The same techniques can help lawyers identify reasons to reach out and sometimes anticipate potential legal problems.

A Canary in the Coal Mine

More often than not, companies that run into legal issues had warning signs that provided clues to these developing problems. Warning signs are, almost by definition, easy to see in hindsight. The challenge is to accurately forecast which unusual business activities over time are reliable predictors of future problems for the business.

Fortunately, several industries have cut a path that law firms can follow to help them develop these opportunity forecasting skills. They have shown that the time and effort to monitor and analyze the key companies in their portfolios is well worth it. If you pay close attention to these clues and stay informed of developments in their industries, you will gain a competitive business development advantage. What's more, you will learn a company's business more deeply and can use that understanding to engage company insiders.

What types of legal needs can these clues reveal?

- Companies that may be a target for acquisition by another company or investment firm.
- Companies that may have an appetite for an acquisition.
- Companies that may need to raise capital.
- Companies that may experience regulatory investigations or are dealing with compliance issues.
- Companies that may face various types of litigation.

- Companies that are potentially facing bankruptcy.
- Companies that may be thinking about selling key assets.

I call these techniques 'Forensic Business Development Research (FBDR)' to suggest the importance of thinking like a detective to get behind the numbers and trends to uncover the less obvious, emerging trends. In truth, this is simply a heightened level of business analysis performed consistently over time by people who understand the powerful locus where legal services meet company strategy. Whether this process uncovers an opportunity for you or not, it will help you understand business better and will often provide a good reason to call your connection. It will help you anticipate problems and solutions, making you a much better business lawyer, and make you a more valuable contributor to your power grid.

"What Keeps You Up at Night?"

With today's ubiquity of data and information, it is no longer enough to ask a busy client 'what keeps you up at night'. Clients have neither the time nor interest to educate their outside counsel on information readily available on the internet, in investor call transcripts, or in the footnotes of 10Qs. Clients respond best to lawyers who know the client's business and offer a different and more thoughtful perspective about it. Providing extraordinary value means telling the client something about their business, industry, marketplace, or competitors that they didn't know. To be successful today, lawyers must shift the conversation from 'What keeps you up at night?' to 'Here are some solutions that will help you sleep better.'

The benefits of this more intentional and thorough business analysis are numerous. This early warning monitoring process enables you to target your communications in an environment with little to no competitive pressure. It provides education about the client's business, competitive environment, and industry structure.

Fortunately, or unfortunately, few other lawyers spend the time to understand and analyze a client's business. This heightened analysis and the monitoring over time will allow you to discuss potential legal issues, often before they have occurred. The process also helps you prepare for discussions with prospective clients by providing specific, well-informed questions based on the strategic intelligence you've gathered on the company and its competitors. Most importantly, in house counsel value the opportunity to brainstorm with thoughtful legal practitioners about the dynamics of their unique business challenges. In fact, there is no wider moat to keep competitors at bay than a deep understanding of your clients' businesses.

This business development research methodology requires you to monitor numerous events and activities, including financial indicators, organizational developments, operational changes, competitive moves, supplier changes, and market conditions. It often requires monitoring these indicators over a long period in order to detect trends or slowly developing issues.

The process is not foolproof, of course. But, even if the process does not reveal early-stage problems or potential issues, monitoring and analyzing the breadth of these indicators will provide greater business intelligence and insights into the businesses of the clients and prospects you choose to monitor, a distinct advantage in today's hypercompetitive legal market.

Monitoring Business Activity

One of the most important indicators to monitor is the financial performance indicators, such as changes in cash flows, debt ratios, and contingent liabilities. Each of these indicators may require different calculations and ratios to help reveal trends. A basic understanding of how to calculate each is essential. It is also important to put the information in context to understand any variance. The ratios should be compared to a competitive set of companies, against the company's historical performance, and in light of what the relationship attorney knows about the company.

Too often, lawyers are not paying close enough attention to changes in the company's management practices. These changes can include the creation of new positions or changes in the duties of key executives. They can include departures and arrivals of key executives or board members and the reasons behind these moves. Significant insights can be gleaned from changes in accounting firms or negative accounting firm statements, from investor comments and analysis, from statements made by company leadership or insiders.

A company's operations can also provide clues to developing issues and opportunities. For instance, the loss of a key supplier, alliance, or partner in the business can indicate additional changes and adjustments for the business that will need to be made. A change in business strategy or marketing strategy or significant changes in product quality and service levels may also indicate developing problems.

And, of course, the market itself can change and cause significant stress on the business. New competitors entering the marketplace or other alternatives can quickly upend a market as we have seen with Uber and Lyft and their impact on the taxi industry as well as many other examples.

Any single indicator will rarely lead to the revelation of significant legal problems. More often, the indicators build clarity over time with new evidence emerging and confirming suspicions as the issues become more pronounced. Developing the analytical abilities to assess indicators enables you to get in on the discussion early with clients and prospects and gives you the best shot at helping them with these issues. Even if the indicators do not reveal legal services opportunities, the exercise will significantly educate you on the company's business. Any early warning of a company's developing issues in an intensely competitive marketplace represents a substantial advantage for your business development efforts.

Financial Performance Indicators

The indicators presented here are for illustrative purposes. The information is intended to help you learn about your client's business, identify specific topics for discussion, and, where appropriate, identify potential problem areas. If you do not have the financial analysis training required to interpret changes in financial conditions, you should not rely upon nor act on any of these indicators without first consulting someone who does have that knowledge.

Multiple Periods of Negative Cash Flow

When cash outflows (expenses) exceed cash inflows (revenues), the company has 'negative cash flow.' While it's not unusual to have a month or two of negative cash flow, a prolonged period, or an increasing gap, could indicate that cash in the bank is running low for a company. Without new capital from sales, equity investors, or lenders, a company in this situation can quickly find itself in serious financial trouble.

High Debt to Equity Ratio Compared to Peers

The debt-to-equity ratio is a handy metric for gauging a company's debt default risk. It compares a company's combined long- and short-term debt to shareholders' equity or the 'book value' of the company. High-debt companies have higher debt-to-equity ratios than companies with lower amounts of debt. Comparing the debt profile of multiple companies within an industry helps put the level of debt in context. Some industries operate with a high level of debt, so it's important to take the time to understand the industry norms with respect to debt loads. Either way, the debt-to-equity analysis should be a part of your ongoing monitoring process.

Interest Payments on Debt

A company's income statement will show what it pays to service its debt. The company should be able to pay its expenses and interest obligations from the revenues it is reporting. It probably goes without saying that here should be a comfortable margin above this level to pay profits to the company's owners. In companies that are failing or headed toward default, this gap narrows and may become negative, indicating the company may be on its way to financial distress or failure.

Use the interest coverage ratio to determine the company's ability to pay its debt obligations. The lower the ratio, the harder it is for the company to pay its debts.

Drop in Reserves for Doubtful Accounts

Companies dedicate a reserve amount of money to cover the cost of potentially uncollected receivables. A significant increase in the reserve amount may indicate management's anticipation of collection problems. If the company has only a few large clients, this could present significant challenges. A substantial drop without a reasonable explanation could indicate manipulation of revenues since the reserve goes directly to the bottom line. Either situation is worthy of further investigation and a possible conversation.

Changes in Inventory Volume

Significant changes in the value of the company's inventory can indicate a manipulation of the cost of goods sold, which affects the company's net income. When sales levels remain constant but the value of the company's inventory increases, it may indicate an understatement of the cost of goods sold. As a result, it could indicate an artificially higher net income (assuming actual inventory and sales levels remain constant). If inventory values ramp up faster than sales volume without a reasonable explanation, such as new product releases or increased marketing, that could be a reason for concern. In that case, you may want to do further research or even ask about it.

Changes in Contingent Liabilities

Significant or sudden changes in contingent liabilities without a reasonable explanation can be an indicator of financial trouble. Contingent liabilities are liabilities the company may face that it must set money aside to pay should it be necessary. These can include significant litigation or regulatory fees and other penalties that a company typically experiences. It can also include guarantees made on behalf of associated companies or guarantees made on product or service claims. Regardless, it is worth asking questions when there is a significant or sudden change in the value of contingent liabilities. Ask, what is the company anticipating that caused the liability reserve to increase?

Low Price Earnings Ratio but High Book Value

Plotting the price earnings ratio against a company's book value can help you determine the potential acquirers and acquirees in an industry or geographic market area. Companies with a high price-to-earnings ratio and small book value are companies that are smaller but fast growing. Typically, this growth is the result of a competitive advantage or alternative solution for customers. Larger, slower growing companies (the low-price earnings ratio and larger book value companies) often look for smaller, fast growing companies with competitive advantages or new alternatives to goose their growth or earnings.

Large companies which are growing slowly often look to acquisitions of other companies or their assets to improve their earnings. Plotting the earnings ratio and book value on a 'two over two' graph of the companies in an industry will enable you to isolate the two types of companies and determine which might be potential targets and which potential acquirers. Keep in mind that this is an overly simplified analysis and numerous other factors come into play when considering acquisitions. But as a topic for discussion with clients, a company will likely provide tremendous insights into their growth strategy and competitive advantages when presented with a list of potential suitors or targets.

Management Practice Indicators

Review the risk factors and management's discussion of these risks in their 10Qs or 10Ks. Every 10K and some annual reports include information about the most significant risks that apply to the company or its securities. Companies generally list the risk factors in order of their importance. Some risks may be true for the entire economy, some may apply only to the company's industry sector or geographic region, and some may be unique to the company.

Company leaders also must discuss their perceptions of the risks that the company faces. Pay attention to the points made in this discussion and determine whether company executives have a firm grasp on the scope and intensity of these risks.

Changes in Accounting Firms

In and of itself, a change in the accounting firm is not an indication of problems. However, the advantages over time of using the same accounting firm are powerful enough that a change in firms can be considered an unusual event. If the accounting firm has also refused to provide a clean bill of health in the analysis of the company's financial records (something the accounting firm is required to report), the change in accounting firms is a definite red flag.

The explanation for the change should be sensible and pass the sniff test. In other words, if making the change presents significant benefit to the company, the change may make sense. But if the capabilities of the old and new accounting firm are equal, or there is disagreement between the accounting firm and the company's management, it deserves further investigation.

Lack of a Clean Bill of Health

Accounting firms are required to state their opinion as to the quality of the financial data submitted for review. In some cases, where the accounting firm cannot validate the source or reliability of the information, the firm will make a statement to that affect in the company's filing. In some cases, the accounting firm will state that it does not give the company a clean bill of health. In such cases this is the result of known or perceived improprieties found by the accounting firm. These situations, though rare, universally require further investigation and very often point to a range of emerging legal issues.

New Positions Created

Companies often create new positions to deal with key challenges faced by the company, changes in its business model or changes in its operating strategy. A first-time position dealing with issues such as risk, compliance, or other areas can indicate that it has challenges or plans growth in that area. Ask company representatives about the new positions and how the company plans to address the issues that that new position will have to deal with.

New Skills and Capabilities in New Hires

Similar to when a company creates a new position, a significant change in the description of the skills and capabilities they desire in the candidate can reveal issues that the company is attempting to address in their talent recruitment efforts. This can include new educational or professional certification requirements, experience in particular areas or issues, and other skills and capabilities. Judgment is required to assess whether the change is a response to new market or competitive pressures or whether it is resulting from operational challenges.

Departures of Key Executives

Companies hire and fire executives for a variety of reasons, but some of these reasons can be indications of internal problems. Executive also leave on their own volition for a variety of reasons. In today's market, exiting executives is increasingly common. An exit does not always mean there are legal problems percolating just beneath the surface. But explanations should be reasonable and rational from both sides. It is a rare occurrence for a key executive to leave a company for reasons that might lead to significant legal problems, legal issues beyond employment disputes. But the situation does occur. Taken in combination with other factors experienced by the company, this could be an indicator of developing problems at the company.

Departure of Key Board Members

A change in one or more members of the Board of Directors is a development that requires more research. Research is especially warranted when the exiting board member has a strong reputation and there is a weak explanation of their departure. First, make sure the departure is not a planned term sunset agreement.

Big Insider or Institutional Sales

Key executives in the company and institutional investors have greater knowledge of what's going on inside the company. Executives that begin selling large blocks of stock either in a measured disposal over a short period of time or in one large block can indicate that future problems for the company may be on the horizon.

Dividend Cuts

Companies rarely cut the amount of the dividends that they pay to investors each quarter. Doing so sends a signal to investors that the company needs cash. Reducing the amount of dividends payments to investors is one of the last places a company will look for savings. When this happens, look for more signs of developing problems at the company.

Selling Flagship Products, Equipment or Property

Companies don't sell their prime products, brands, or assets unless they are forced to let them go. In some cases, the sale can be calculated to raise capital for new investments but more often than not, it is an indication of financial difficulties in the company.

Significant Reductions in People or Benefits

If you are going through tough financial times, one of the first things you will likely do is look for ways to cut your expenses. Companies do the same thing. And they will start with the largest expenses first. One of the first large expenses that organizations look to cut are staff positions and employee benefits expenses. Cuts in staffing, especially those made suddenly as opposed to through attrition, are red flags for problems.

The second area often cut is a bit harder to spot. Having reaped the benefits of job cuts, companies often look next to make deep cuts in their health benefits, pension plans, or other employee benefits. Deep and sudden cuts, particularly when they take place in conjunction with other financial indicators, are a sign that trouble may lie ahead.

Operational Indicators

'Operations' generally includes the systems, equipment, people, and processes a company needs to make the organization function properly.

Significant Changes in the Cost or Availability of Raw Materials

Companies which are dependent upon raw materials for the production of their goods and services are particularly vulnerable to changes in the cost of those materials. Monitoring when legislation, market changes, or new regulations affect the cost or availability of materials is one way to anticipate potential legal needs. For example, horizontal drilling technologies tipped the economics of fracking and led to huge increases in the availability of natural gas reserves in the U.S. The companies whose futures contracts were tied to oil and gas prices didn't enjoy the price drops this new supply created. So, those companies began to re-negotiate their contracts and untie their pricing contract from the increasing oil prices. This led to litigation between the contract holder and the supplier, a development you could have anticipated by watching the development of, and cost decreases, in horizontal drilling technologies.

Changes or Loss in Key Suppliers

One doesn't fire a good client unless that client presents little or no future for the business. If the client has not paid its supplier, the first order of business is to stop doing business with the client. Whether the result of the company's inability to pay its bills or due to disagreements in other terms in the agreement, there's a good chance that changes in a key supplier can result in litigation. These situations warrant further investigation.

Significant Price Reductions

Sudden and significant price reductions are often an indication that the business needs more cash to service its debt or pay suppliers. While sometimes a price reduction can indicate investment in a new product or service line, these changes warrant further questions. And again, the answer to why the reduction was made should make sense.

Change in Marketing or Business Strategy

A significant change in marketing or business strategy can indicate a troubled company or, at least, a disconcerting outlook for the company. Companies rarely make an about face on their marketing or business strategy and do so only when conditions or times leave them no other choice. A company that abruptly changes its strategy or business model often are panicking and acting somewhat irrationally.

A change in strategy typically requires a significant investment in marketing and operations in order to affect that change. It brings numerous risks and 'unknowns' for the company and many times forfeits loyal customers for the promise of future, more profitable customers. Therefore, significant changes in strategy should be accompanied by a logical and realistic business case. Where the business case is suspect, look further for other developments that can confirm or deny the potential for developing legal issues.

Loss of a Business Alliance or Partnership

The loss of a strategic business alliance can indicate problems in the relationship between the two companies. In some cases, the benefits to both businesses may simply have run its course. But more likely, a split is an indication of a strong disagreement between the two companies either because they are in competition for the rights to certain assets or technologies or because suspect business practices have wedged the two apart.

Deterioration of Product or Service Quality

Companies that are struggling to pay their bills often look to cut expenses in production and service. This results in the deterioration of product and service quality. With the ubiquity of user review websites and tools such as Yelp, Angie's List and other rating systems, it's becoming easier to monitor an uptick in negative experiences. Many big box retailer sites and shopping sites such as Amazon include user reviews for the major manufacturers and brands featured on the site. This enables a relatively easy way to compare product and service quality across industry players.

Market Condition Indicators

Market forces can substantially alter how a company must operate. They can threaten the viability of a business and force changes, disruptions and closures of businesses. But market forces can also do good. Some companies benefit from market forces and changes to the underlying structure of markets. Every change presents both a threat and an opportunity depending on the strength of the company and the creativity of its business managers.

New Competitors
Strong, new competitors entering a geographic area or industry can upset the balance of that market and, if not managed well, lead a company into financial distress. Walmart is famous for putting smaller retailers out of business in the markets it enters but even lesser-known brands can cause an intensification of the competitive environment that leads some companies toward financial distress. Ask how the company plans to blunt the impact of new competitive entrants.

Alternative Providers
The sudden appearance of a new, well-funded, or game changing alternative provider can fundamentally change a company's business strategy and sometimes lead to financial distress in the affected companies. A prime recent example of this was the introduction of Uber and Lyft, applications which fundamentally changed the taxi cab business over the short course of a few months. (In fact, these applications are now threatening to change the fundamental business models of the local delivery service industry). Once these services gained traction in a couple of big cities, litigation, lobbying efforts, and even taxi cab company bankruptcies quickly followed.

Once again, it's rare that a single market indicator will reveal significant legal problems or business challenges. More often, the indicators build clarity over time with new evidence emerging and confirming your suspicions. More importantly, knowledge of business and the indicators of business stress can help you flag information that you hear in your conversations with your power grid connections.

Developing the analytical abilities to assess indicators early enables you to get the earliest shot at helping the company with these issues. It will help you to have more substantive discussions and can provide access to more useful information about the company. Even if the indicators don't reveal legal services opportunities, the exercise will significantly educate you on the company's business. In an intensely competitive marketplace, knowledge of the business and any early warning of a company's developing issues represents a substantial advantage for your business development efforts.

4

Know Your Practice

"There are things we know, things we don't know, and things we don't know we don't know."

- Donald Rumsfeld, Former U.S. Secretary of Defense.

It might seem odd that I suggest you don't know your practice. Or that knowing your practice better will help you develop a power grid. Obviously, you know what you do. You know who your best clients are. You know where your work typically comes from, and you know the issues and challenges your clients face daily.

I want to ensure you know how to look at your practice objectively. I want to help you remove the confidence bias and familiarity to see your practice as your client sees it. The models I will show you in this chapter will help you evaluate your practice with a clear-eyed and sober assessment. That assessment will enable you to confidently adapt or change your practice and service delivery and be more certain that those changes are the right changes to make. In my experience, having a deeper understanding of your practice will help you market it more effectively, generate referrals more efficiently, and adjust your practice more quickly to your clients' needs. That's what I intend to give you in this chapter.

In the next few pages, we will dive deeper into a more comprehensive understanding of your practice. I'll share with you several tools you can use to understand the market position you hold in your client's mind and how you can use this tool throughout your career to adjust your practice's marketing as needed. We'll look at the price sensitivity of your practice, that is, how much resistance you get to your regular hourly rates. And, we'll examine the factors contributing to that resistance so you can manage them to increase your rates more quickly. Finally, we'll look at the factors that influence you getting hired and how to communicate those qualities more effectively to your power grid.

After reading this chapter, I hope you'll gain new insights and perspectives into your practice, your clients, and your competitors. You'll have a better feel for your place in the market, better understand competitive advantage and how to build it, and be more prepared to market your legal services. But first, let's get some context for the discussion by starting it with a short history of legal marketing strategy.

A Short History of Legal Marketing Strategy

The strategies and techniques of selling professional services have changed over the years. When lawyers were first allowed to formally market or sell their services back in the early seventies, they correctly assumed that what mattered most to clients was the result achieved. The rules of professional conduct limit a lawyer's ability to market themselves in a way that sets certain expectations for the results that could be achieved. But lawyers were allowed to provide information that documented their experience and expertise.

Business lawyers used past performance and other factors to infer their ability to achieve results without the promise of delivering those results. They could ethically cite the quality of the clients they served, provide sample case studies and matter descriptions, and show their articles and thought leadership as evidence of the results they could achieve. This evidentiary model assumed that companies would be transactional in selecting outside counsel, meaning that companies were driven solely by cost and inferred results in choosing outside counsel.

Over time, lawyers recognized that experience and expertise alone did not always win the work. Clients also had to like and respect you. The prevailing view on client development moved to a relationship-building model. This model recognized that clients had the choice of many good lawyers and that the difference in whether you were selected had more to do with whether you had personal chemistry and shared values with the client. Your relationship with the decision-maker was the key to winning work from a company.

This ushered in a period in which attorneys worked hard at building affinity with company representatives. To gain new clients, attorneys had to wine and dine them, take them golfing, sponsor their community programs, and do extracurricular activities that allowed the lawyer and their prospects to get to know one another and build a mutually respected relationship.

Relationship-based selling remains the most common professional service sales philosophy today. Client entertainment continues to be a primary client development strategy for many lawyers. But this client development philosophy doesn't always work. Lawyers are often frustrated by the problem of being good lawyers with relevant experience and great relationships with company managers, only to be passed over by the company in favor of a competitor.

After the recession of 2009, the key to winning engagement and client loyalty became clearer. Companies wanted more value from their lawyers and the law firms that served them. Frustrated by a lack of focus on their business needs and billing practices that rewarded inefficiency, companies began to encourage their outside counsel to find ways to lower costs and improve the delivery of legal services. To some lawyers, the answer was to discount their hourly billing rates. To the business-savvy lawyer, the answer was to deliver more value. They do this by becoming more client-focused and aligned with the company's needs and objectives and using that knowledge to create a greater impact on the business. This is where we are today.

Now that we've discussed the habits and qualities of powerful connectors, learned some business concepts, and gotten a quick history of marketing in the legal profession, let's move on to your practice area. There is a lot to discuss there. Let's start with a broad description of what it takes to succeed in private practice.

Pi-Shaped Professionals

While this book is about building a powerful network of connections (your power grid), it is worthwhile to put your network of connections in the context of the total marketing program for your practice. The legal marketing world is so broad that it is hard to imagine a single book that could do justice to every aspect of legal marketing. I've chosen to focus on building a power grid and reaching out to that network because it is the most productive thing you can do for the success of your practice.

However, it is not the only thing you need to do. It would be best if you also marketed a specialty area of expertise to attract those with the problems you can fix. And you should develop a consistently outstanding service to your clients so they return to you repeatedly.

I tell my clients that business development success depends on how well you manage three aspects of your practice's marketing: 'what you know,' 'who you know,' and 'how much you care.' These three factors make up what I refer to as the Pi-Shaped Professionals formula for business development success.

The symbol 'Pi,' denoted by the Greek letter π - is one of mathematics' most common constants. It is the circumference of any circle, divided by its diameter. Nobody knows its exact numeric value, though. Because, no matter how many digits you calculate it to, the number never ends.

The two pillars and crossbeam of Pi represent the deep knowledge pillars of your relationships and your subject matter expertise held in place by a crossbeam representing the personal qualities that demonstrate how much you care. The symbol should help you remember what it takes to be successful: 'who you know,' 'what you know,' and 'how much you care.' And, of course, it should also remind you to pursue business development continuously like the never-ending constant that is Pi.

What You Know

In the late 80s, IBM introduced a concept called "T-Shaped Professionals," which the company used to describe its ideal engineering professional. T-shaped professionals were characterized by their deep disciplinary knowledge in at least one subject matter, their use of the best systems and processes, their ability to function as "adaptive innovators," and their ability to cross the boundaries between disciplines. This symbolism caught on, and IBM became known as a company dedicated to the power of specialized knowledge.

Lawyers, too, share these same benefits when they distinguish themselves as subject matter experts, users of the best systems and processes, are viewed as adaptive innovators, and can easily move across disciplinary boundaries because they understand the practice areas of their partners. They should aspire to these qualities in their practice: specialized expertise, systems expertise, innovation, industry expertise, and collaboration.

Unfortunately, legal subject matter expertise is increasingly becoming less potent as a differentiator in the highly competitive legal services industry. There are many experts. Today, legal expertise must be accompanied by business and industry expertise. The highest level subject matter experts tend to be industry thought leaders, the recognized legal authorities in an industry on strategically important business issues. These rare lawyers are the ones whose depth of legal knowledge and experience in an area is matched only by their business and industry knowledge and acumen. That is, they are not simply experienced and well-versed in a particular area of the law, they are equally experienced and well-versed in the dynamics and complexities of business and the unique challenges of an industry sector. The depth of their knowledge in both business (their clients' businesses as well as in business principles generally), the industry structure and dynamics, and the law enable them to be nearly prescient about the direction of emerging issues and provide their clients with unparalleled value and advice. What you know about the law is critical. But it should include both the law, industry, and business.

Who You Know

Deep knowledge also applies to your relationships. The people you are connected to are the largest source of your work. That's true for most professional service providers. We all travel through life, meeting new people through various professional, social, spiritual, and educational endeavors. We collect the names from each interaction and add them to our mental database of connections. Some of those connections are weak and temporary- that is, we did not have much of a relationship, and they will move on from our lives. Others are weak, but recurring-that is, we do not have much of a connection, but we share an ecosystem or exist in networks of people and, as a result, connect with them periodically. With others, we form deep connections, and they become part of our social and professional networks. However, all of these connections have value, either to us or others.

Few of us take the time to explore how these various relationships (weak, strong, fleeting, or lasting) can add value to our professional lives. We rarely inventory the knowledge, experience, station, or whom we think they may know of our contacts. Some of us make introductions and try to connect with others. Few, though, set up a regular system for communicating with them and build the tools and resources necessary to contribute to increasing the value inherent in a shared ecosystem of relationships. But rainmakers do. Top-performing lawyers understand that who you know and how you add value to your network are critical to their success.

How Much You Care

The cross beam of the Pi-Shaped Professional model is the characteristics that make up your personality, and that help you succeed as a professional. Some qualities contribute more to your success than others and include behaviors and qualities that build trust, respect, and that generate interest in you. The most common characteristics I observe in successful lawyers include empathy and compassion; a commitment to giving more than receiving; an unrelenting positive outlook; a discipline in executing the fundamentals of business development; and a willingness to invest their time, resources, knowledge and their connections to ensure others benefit from knowing them.

I have observed these qualities in hundreds of successful lawyers. Look carefully, and you will see it as well. While their marketing strategies vary, their personal characteristics vary little. Some lawyers will be more focused on thought leadership and content marketing. Others spend most of their time on their relationships. Others focus on client service to attract prospects. Some exhibit all three equally. A few succeed purely on the grit of their persistent efforts. But these marketing strategies are shared in some degree by every successful lawyer I have ever observed. But, to be clear, the most successful focus relentlessly on their relationships.

Make no mistake. There is no silver business development bullet. These are not easy competencies and disciplines to incorporate into your daily routine. Making these changes takes effort and focus. They require a deep personal commitment, continuous self-awareness, and a relentless focus on improvement. For those willing to take the journey, the payoff is in greater performance, greater happiness, deeper career fulfillment, heightened peer respect, and more interesting relationships, all of which are the benefits reported by the top rainmakers that I have had the intense pleasure to observe and coach.

What Every Lawyer Should Know About Their Practice

It is important to any service business that it is able to step back and get an objective look at itself. That objective look should help you put your practice in context and help you explain the differentiated attributes of your practice to your power grid connections. It should help you understand how competitive forces will affect you and give you better insights into how to price your services and differentiate your practice in the marketplace. Only through regular self-analysis can you gain the perspective to correct course and continue on the path to increasingly profitable and higher growth. The Practice Positioning model is a tool you can use for this process.

The Practice Position Model

Why do you need a model to understand your practice? That is a good question. The answer lies in the nature of legal services and how hard it is for clients to distinguish one lawyer's abilities from another's. The practice position model will help you evaluate your services and capabilities in view of what clients expect from you. And it will help you consistently re-align your skills and abilities to correspond to your practice's position in the legal services marketplace. This understanding will enable you to differentiate your practice from the competition better. And that will make selecting your services, as opposed to someone else's, easier for clients.

Selling services is not like selling products. For one, services are intangible—your clients can't try you before they buy you. Also, services are impermanent. Once services are performed, they generally cannot be reused and they cannot be returned if the buyer is not satisfied. And something else, clients' impressions about the quality of your services are highly subjective. A result that one client finds satisfactory may dismally fail to meet another's expectations.

What's more, you can't provide effective services without the client's cooperation. For instance, a client that withholds or forgets to tell you about important information can hinder you from providing your best legal advice. Consequently, the legal services experience is heavily dependent on the relationship between the client and the attorney.

Another complication is that powerful forces constantly change the dynamics of the playing field. These forces include changes in technology, the governing law, the competitive marketplace, and the economy. The practice position model will help you adapt the marketing of your practice to these changes.

Adapting to Marketplace Changes

Building a sustainable practice requires that you continually adjust your practice and how you deliver your services to adapt to the forces of change and meet clients' expectations of you - expectations that are constantly rising. There are numerous adjustments you may need to make to your practice including learning to handle matters more efficiently, modulating the price of your services to the evolving marketplace, understanding your clients' businesses, and improving your ability to deliver added value, among others. The practice position model can help you understand what adjustments you need to make at any given point in your career. It helps to provide a context, based on the client's point of view, in which to make these decisions more confidently.

The Client's Perspective

The importance of thinking about your practice from your clients' perspective is hard to overstate. Times have changed dramatically for the legal profession. For many years, deep knowledge of a particular legal discipline was sufficient to win clients' trust and loyalty. Today, however, lawyers must work much harder than before to do this. Today's lawyers must not only be legal experts, but also savvy businesspeople. That is, lawyers must thoroughly understand not only the areas of law in which they practice, but also how a client's legal issues, and how the lawyer resolves those issues, affects the client's business.

Clients constantly apply a cost-benefit analysis to most matters, comparing and contrasting various law firms' relative fees and efficiency. That's nothing new. What is new is the intensity of the focus clients have on understanding their business, its operational practices, the culture, and how lawyers can affect change without causing too much disruption inside the organization. The new normal for delivering legal services requires that the lawyer intimately know their clients, along with their businesses, their operations, their industries, and their goals and preferences. Put differently, how lawyers work is becoming just as important as what lawyers know.

There was a time when traditional law firms were practically clients' only source of legal help. Today, though, when corporate and other clients need legal assistance, they have an increasing number of options. For instance, many corporations have in-house legal departments. Others go overseas for certain types of work or use alternative legal service providers (ALSP), like virtual law firms. But, at least for now, most U.S. companies still turn to U.S. law firms for solutions to their legal problems. In doing so, they try to find the lawyer or law firm that is best qualified to handle their legal issue—for the amount of money they are willing to spend.

Put differently, their goal is to match the lawyer's quality—and price—to the work's complexity and strategic importance to their business. Clients don't want a lawyer who is more qualified, and higher priced, than the work requires. By the same token, they certainly don't want an attorney who is underqualified for the specific matter at hand just so they can save money in the short term.

To that end, business clients tend to rely on two criteria to help them decide which lawyers to hire: the specific issue's strategic importance to their business or other interests and the availability of qualified attorneys to do the work that's needed to resolve the issue.

The practice position model uses a two-over-two quadrant format to illustrate these two important criteria. The vertical axis is divided into ten equal segments starting at one in the lower left-hand corner. The horizontal axis also is divided into ten equal parts, with one starting in the left-most position.

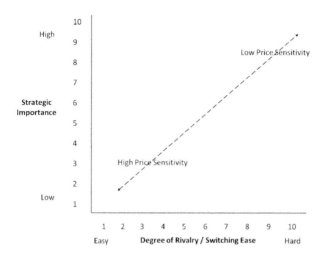

The Vertical Axis: Strategic Importance

The first criterion, strategic importance, is neither universal nor constant. Indeed, strategic importance varies depending on the client, its business model, and its goals. Naturally, what is critical to one client won't be critical to another. Indeed, even a specific client will find that some legal issues, and the work needed to solve them, are more strategically important than others. Even within matters themselves, some tasks are more important to get right than others. To complicate things further, businesses are dynamic and evolving, so work that is crucial today may be less important tomorrow.

Here's how the strategic-importance criterion affects hiring decisions: critically important issues will generally prompt a client to hire attorneys with demonstrated experience and reputations - attorneys that provide the best possible insurance against the critical issue reaching critical mass or that are critically harming the client's interests.

The Horizontal Axis: Competitive Rivalry

This brings us to the second criterion: attorney availability, which refers to the ease of substitution or degree of competitive rivalry for the particular type of work. Put differently, this describes the relative ease with which a client can find and employ a similarly qualified and experienced lawyer at a similar price to do the work. The first criterion drives the second. As a general rule, the more strategically important the work is to a client, the fewer qualified and experienced lawyers there are to do the work—and the less replaceable each qualified lawyer becomes.

This is because vital work often requires much greater expertise, experience, and knowledge of the client's business and industry, than does less important work. Conversely, when the issue's resolution has little impact on the company, getting it wrong poses a relatively low risk. As such, companies can tolerate less qualified, less expensive, and more replaceable attorneys.

A potential client's perception of how qualified you are for the work, and how replaceable you are, will largely determine whether the client hires you or someone else. Keep in mind: it doesn't really matter what *you* think about your qualifications and who *you* think might be able to replace you. All that matters is the client's view of these things.

Risk and Predictability

There are two more factors that influence clients' hiring decisions: the role of risk and the predictability (or unpredictability) of legal matters.

Managers of companies are responsible for minimizing, as much as possible, any risk to their employers' businesses. They generally reduce risk by carefully supervising the business's processes, policies, investments, and people. Risk, as such, is an esoteric concept that's sometimes hard to identify or define. However, in the business realm, when managers say *risk*, they really mean *uncertainty*. Therefore, the way to reduce risk is to reduce uncertainty or increase predictability. Put differently, the more consistent a legal work process is, and the more predictable an outcome is, the less risk is inherent in it.

The concept of risk, or uncertainty, is central to how managers evaluate legal services. In legal services, as in any other industry, you can gauge risk by assessing how predictable certain matters' outcomes are, as well as how consistently the processes that are required to complete certain legal tasks are understood and applied. If the procedure for accomplishing a particular legal task is well understood, or if the outcome of a particular dispute is practically certain, the risk associated with the matter is low. On the other hand, if the legal issue is new and not well understood, or if the dispute's outcome is unpredictable, then that uncertainty presents greater risk.

Risk affects both competitive rivalry and strategic importance. Here's how it affects competitive rivalry: business managers can reduce the risk posed by novel issues and unpredictable disputes if they select lawyers who are especially well-qualified to handle risky matters. After all, the more experience and expertise the lawyers have about the matter, the greater their ability to predict the matter's outcome and reduce the associated risk.

These so-called specialists are comparatively rare, so they face less price resistance than their less-qualified counterparts. Put differently, these attorneys can generally charge higher rates than others, because they are risk minimizers: their superior knowledge and experience lets them handle high-risk matters more expediently, and predict outcomes more confidently, than others could. Conversely, lawyers who take on matters about which they have little practical experience or legal knowledge must generally charge lesser fees than their more qualified counterparts. In doing so, they're essentially paying for the opportunity to gain this experience.

Consider also the barrier to competitors that knowledge of the unique operating practices of the business has on competitive rivalry. Lawyers who have worked closely with a business over months, or even years, gain knowledge about how the company operates that is difficult to know when you don't work directly with the company. That institutional knowledge affords those lawyers the ability to craft solutions that are more aligned with the business' operational practices and norms. It means less disruption in the business because those disruptions can be better anticipated. That thorough knowledge and the customized approach they deliver enables those lawyers to become more entrenched in that client's business. And it gives them greater pricing power because clients recognize and protect their access to that knowledge and efficiency.

Risk, or uncertainty, also drives strategic importance. This is especially true when a brand-new legal issue breaks onto the scene. Generally, the law reflects society, so new legal issues most often emerge due to societal and economic changes, for instance, technological innovation, new legislation, economic fluctuation, and so on. When these issues first emerge, the impact on clients' businesses is largely unknown.

Consequently, in the beginning, not only are there relatively few lawyers who have the needed experience and knowledge to handle the issue due to its novelty, but the issue's very uncertainty makes it more strategically important. That is, managers who seek always to minimize risk must lend as much certainty to the issue as they can, as quickly as they can. Accordingly, addressing the issue becomes more urgent.

Even so, nothing lasts forever. As the issue becomes more prevalent and affects more businesses, the growing volume of work attracts ever more lawyers to address the issue and become more knowledgeable about it. This, in turn, increases competitive rivalry. Further, as lawyers and judges figure out the issue's legal contours over time, the related uncertainty declines—which, in turn, lessens the issue's urgency and, hence, strategic importance.

A recent example of this phenomenon involved the sudden adoption of flying drones for various commercial and personal uses. The prevailing laws were inadequate to address the dangers associated with this emergent technology, so legislators began to write new legislation to do so. At the time, very few lawyers had experience in so-called drone law, because it was so new. However, and quite predictably, hordes of enterprising lawyers rushed to learn the risks and challenges that drones presented and educate themselves as much as they could about the developing field of drone law. As drones became more popular, more lawyers gained expertise and experience handling cases involving drones. This naturally increased drone law's competitive rivalry. Also, as courts and lawyers applied the developing law and struggled through the issues, case-by-case outcomes became more certain. As this happened, the strategic importance of drone-law issues fell.

More recently, the pandemic presented companies with numerous issues which needed to be evaluated and solved quickly. Quarantine, vaccines, work from home policies, and other issues, issues which had not previously been addressed, urgently needed legal interpretation. It was new territory for everyone. Speed was of the essence despite circumstances that were constantly changing. In this environment, research alone didn't make lawyers stand out as irreplaceable. There simply wasn't precedent to rely on. The issues were so novel that companies sought reasoned opinions more so than research. The attorneys who were sharing and updating their thoughts, with intimate knowledge of the business, provided the greatest value to companies.

Price Sensitivity

Price (or in your case, billing rate) sensitivity, also called the *price elasticity of demand*, is the degree to which the supply-to-demand ratio for a service affects the rates that clients are willing to pay for it. As you undoubtedly learned in your college economics course, higher demand for a service, relative to the available supply of service providers, means that customers will generally be less price-sensitive about the service, enabling service providers to charge more. Conversely, lower demand relative to supply makes customers more price-sensitive, so providers can't charge as much.

This is just as true in legal services as it is in any other industry. An oversupply of lawyers in a specific practice area tends to lower the price, or fees, that all qualified attorneys in that practice area can generally charge. Conversely, if demand for work in a particular practice area outstrips the number of lawyers that can provide the needed services, clients will be less price sensitive, which means that qualified practitioners can charge more.

Keep in mind that the company's perceived value of the legal services has many components and vary by client. Obviously, knowledge and experience in the area of law is important. But equally important is the lawyer's knowledge of how business works, the issues and trends within the industry, and maybe more important than knowledge and experience, is the lawyer's knowledge and understanding of the client's business, its operational practices, internal politics, culture, people, and customers.

Today, however, the presence of alternative legal service providers significantly affects the legal service industry's supply-and-demand equation. The simple reality is that certain matters, or tasks within matters, may be more efficiently handled through outsourcing or some technological or virtual solution. This represents an alternative, cost-effective means to produce what is generally an equally positive result to what the client might obtain by hiring a traditional law firm. This, in turn, decreases the demand for traditional legal services and makes clients more price sensitive.

While supply and demand affect the *price* of legal services, the *quality* of the legal services affects how clients perceive those services' intrinsic value. This, in turn, impacts the clients' price sensitivity. Namely, the more valuable that clients believe a particular attorney's services are to them, the less price-sensitive they'll tend to be about those services. This, in turn, permits the attorney to charge higher rates than the attorney could if clients thought his or her services were less valuable. Consequently, understanding, managing, and communicating the value of the services you offer your clients is one way to influence your clients to pay you more - a welcome result, to be sure!

Uses of The Practice Position Model

The practice position model is versatile. It can be used to evaluate Client Perceptions at a legal task level through to multiple law firms in a marketplace. You can use it to evaluate demand and likely price sensitivity for particular work, an individual attorney, a law firm, a practice area, or even a whole industry, depending on the nature of the analysis. You can even use it in your interviews of clients to determine which competitor law firms the client uses and may be vulnerable to a cross-selling pitch from you.

The model was designed as a strategic client assessment tool to help attorneys evaluate and think about practice development more objectively. It can also help you better align your understanding of your practice with the clients. To do this, I use the model in two phases in my coaching. The first phase asks attorneys to predict where their clients would position them on the graph. Then I ask the attorney to meet with their clients and ask their clients to rate them on the two questions. The gap between an attorney's perception and a client's reality is often significant and instructive. Exploring that gap can lead to more practical and client-centered development of their services delivery strategies.

Evaluating the Market Position of Your Practice

Let's apply the Practice Position Model to assess your position in the marketplace. This exercise involves three phases. The purpose of the first two phases is to help you compare and contrast how you think your clients perceive your practice with how your clients actually perceive your practice. The third phase aims to help you reflect generally upon the state of your practice and how you might improve it.

Step 1: Identify the areas of law in which you practice. For each area, use the table below to estimate the average number of billable hours, or the average revenue generated in each practice area, for the past year.

Practice Area	Hours / YR	Revenues
Ex. Employment Counseling	185	$97,125

Set up a graph to enter your information. Repeat the following exercise for each respective sub practice area: on the vertical axis, using a scale of one to ten, plot how strategically important *you believe* the practice area is, from what you believe to be your clients' perspective, to accomplishing the clients' business and other objectives.

Next, on the horizontal axis, using a scale of one to ten, plot the ease with which you think your clients believe they could replace you. This is your *ease of substitution,* which you'll determine by considering the number of attorneys with similar knowledge and experience to yours in the practice area, who could do the work about as effectively and efficiently as you, at a similar rate to what you would charge.

Place a mark at the point on the graph where the vertical and horizontal values intersect for each criterion and each practice subspecialty area. Inflate each mark by the amount of the revenues you produce in each sub practice specialty area either for that one company or for your practice in general. The size of each practice area's bubble will depend on how lucrative the specific practice area is for you; in terms of the average billable hours or revenue it generates. The more lucrative a practice area is, the bigger its bubble; the less lucrative it is, the smaller its bubble. Similarly the bubble size can relate to the number of hours spent in each type of work for that one client or for all of your clients. This will enable you to evaluate each of your most and least lucrative practice areas at a glance, to give you a more holistic view of where your practice stands.

The next step is to get your client's perceptions of the strategic importance of the work you do to the company and your client's ability to substitute another attorney to handle the matters you handle for them. This step can be eye opening. Typically, lawyers have a higher perceived value of the importance of their work than their clients have. Regardless, the conversation provides numerous ways to explore your working relationship with the client and develop strategies to align more tightly with their needs.

This next step will help you identify ways to build barriers to competitors and embed yourself more deeply into your client's business processes. It can also reveal strategies for you to protect your margin and increase your billing rate.

Evaluating The Price Sensitivity of Your Practice

Previously, we reviewed the two main factors that affect clients' price sensitivity, or resistance to your billing rate. These include (1) the strategic importance of the work and (2) the degree of competitive rivalry for the work. Numerous elements drive these two factors. Examining these elements, and applying them to your specific practice, can help you determine the price sensitivity or resistance you'll face from clients. This assessment can also identify areas in which your practice is unique or, alternatively, areas where you should improve your competitiveness.

Below, I've listed and described, in no particular order, the elements that drive price sensitivity. The objective here is for you to evaluate your practice area against these elements, to help you gauge your clients' price sensitivity to your work in that area. If you have several key practice areas, do this exercise for each of them. To complete this evaluation, do the following:

1. From among the various areas of law in which you practice, pick the area you believe most crucial to your career—the area that accounts for most of your prestige, billable hours, or revenue.

2. Read the description of each element affecting price sensitivity below.

3. For each element:

   a. Indicate whether you think that element has a strong, moderate, or weak effect on your clients' price sensitivity to the work.

   b. Then write down:

      i. Why you thought the element had a strong, moderate, or weak effect on price sensitivity.

      ii. At least one feasible thing you could do to mitigate any price sensitivity stemming from that element.

Factors Affecting Price Sensivity

Each of these factors can affect the price sensitivity inherent in your practice. It is not a conclusive list. There may be other factors which influence how much a client is willing to pay for the legal services. For instance, the provider may have done an extraordinary favor for the company and the company is willing to overlook the higher rates out of respect for that history. But these are unique and often arbitrary pressures on prices. The factors below apply to most practice areas and have substantive influence on the price level acceptable to most clients.

Unique Value

To what extent does your work, in the practice area you are examining, provide your clients unique value? Clients tend to be less price resistant towards work that imparts unique value, value that others cannot provide. Unique value can come in many forms such as: deep experience in a particular subject; access to influential, skilled, or knowledgeable colleagues or experts who can sway the matter's outcome or expedite the resolution; or especially streamlined and efficient internal processes.

As you determine unique value's effect on your clients' price sensitivity, think about your process, your workflow, and the resources you bring to the table, together with your particular knowledge and experience. If you conclude that unique value has a strong effect on price sensitivity, this is a good thing! It tends to show that your clients recognize the unique value that you provide.

Describe the unique value you deliver to clients. Write it down. Include both a description of the value and the benefits that clients enjoy as a result of the value you deliver.

The value that I deliver and its associated benefits to the client is:

_____

_____

_____

This element's effect on my clients' price sensitivity is:

➤ *Strong*

➤ *Moderate*

> *Weak*

Explain why the value you deliver affects (or should affect) the client's price sensitivity.

The unique value I deliver has an effect on price sensitivity because:

_____
_____
_____
_____
_____
_____

List the things you can do to improve the client's perception of value and thereby lower the price sensitivity of your practice.

Things I can do to change this element's effect on price sensitivity include:

_____
_____
_____
_____
_____

Ease of Substitution

Ease of substitution is another term for competitive rivalry. The question here is this: to what extent does the client have access to other lawyers who can complete the work with comparable skill and quality to yours? These include in-house lawyers who can do the work, as well as colleagues in other firms with expertise, experience, and qualifications similar to your own.

The greater the number of other available lawyers to do the work, the greater clients' price sensitivity will tend to be. Accordingly, if you determine that ease of substitution has a strong effect, then this would indicate that your clients find you very replaceable, which may make it hard for you to charge higher fees—or even to find work.

This element's effect on my clients' price sensitivity is:

- ➢ *Strong*

- ➢ *Moderate*

- ➢ *Weak*

The reason for this element's effect on price sensitivity is:

_____
_____
_____
_____
_____

Things I can do to reduce this element's effect on price sensitivity:

_____
_____
_____
_____
_____

Total Expenditure Relative to Budget

Total expenditure relative to budget implicates how much your clients spend, compared to their overall legal budgets, for the type of work you chose. Clients tend to be less price resistant towards work whose cost comprises only a small part of their overall legal expenditures. Accordingly, if you determine that total expenditure has a strong effect, then this would indicate that hiring you to do this work costs the client comparatively little in the grand scheme of things, which in turn lets you charge comparatively higher fees.

This element's effect on my clients' price sensitivity is:

> ➤ *Strong*

> ➤ *Moderate*

> ➤ *Weak*

The reason for this element's effect on price sensitivity is:

_____

_____

_____

_____

_____

Things I can do to reduce this element's effect on price sensitivity:

_____

_____

_____

_____

_____

Imputed Benefits

The term *imputed benefits* refers to the ways in which your work helps your clients other than merely by solving their legal problems. For example, your work may save the client time, money, or other resources; help the client mitigate risk or uncertainty; or enable the client to take advantage of a future opportunities. To the extent your work brings imputed benefits, clients will tend to be less price resistant towards it.

If you determine that the notion of imputed benefits has a strong effect on your clients' price sensitivity, then this is a good thing. It shows that your clients understand the various ways in which your work helps them—which makes them more willing to pay you more when they recognize these imputed benefits.

This element's effect on my clients' price sensitivity is:

> *Strong*

> *Moderate*

> *Weak*

The reason for this element's effect on price sensitivity is:

_____
_____
_____
_____
_____

Things I can do to change the client's perception of the imputed benefits I deliver:

_____
_____
_____

_____

_____

Shared Costs and Processes

Clients tend to be less price sensitive towards work whose costs they share with others or work which is part of a shared process. For instance, a company going through an initial public offering may share the cost of legal representation with the underwriter and the placement agency. In cases like this, the group sharing the cost probably won't collectively mind a higher fee, because the members are splitting the cost among themselves.

There is a barrier effect to work that is part of a shared process. Legal processes which are shared between the company and its firm are more difficult to change, and thus less susceptible to price sensitivity. A strong shared cost effect would indicate that your work's cost is often split among multiple payers. A strong shared process effect would indicate that your work is integrated into the client's systems, procedures, or work flow.

This element's effect on my clients' price sensitivity is:

➢ *Strong*

➢ *Moderate*

➢ *Weak*

The reason for this element's effect on price sensitivity is:

_____
_____
_____
_____
_____

Things I can do to change this element's effect on price sensitivity:

_____

_____

_____

_____

_____

Institutional Experience

Institutional experience refers to an established lawyer-client relationship. A lawyer who has a longstanding working relationship with a particular client often suffers less price sensitivity from that client. This is because the lawyer and the client know each other and the lawyer has learned how the client likes to have things done. There is less of a learning curve on new matters, less need to alter the lawyer's processes to suit the client's work flow, and less need to integrate technologies. These things save time and money, which lowers price sensitivity. A strong effect would indicate that your clients recognize the savings you bring due to your deep institutional experience with them.

This element's effect on my clients' price sensitivity is:

- ➢ *Strong*

- ➢ *Moderate*

- ➢ *Weak*

The reason for this element's effect on price sensitivity is:

_____

_____

_____

_____
_____

Things I can do to change this element's effect on price sensitivity:

_____
_____
_____
_____
_____

Reputation

If you have a strong reputation for achieving past results, then this provides the client with a form of insurance that you can achieve the desired future results. That insurance represents real value to the client, which in turn reduces price sensitivity towards the work.

For instance, a litigator with a winning record in a particular court may be able to charge higher fees for work in that court, because clients believe that the lawyer's record of past victories will translate to a greater likelihood of success in present and future matters. A strong effect would indicate that your clients highly regard your reputation, and they appreciate the resulting certainty that you will achieve the best possible outcomes for them.

This element's effect on my clients' price sensitivity is:

> ➤ *Strong*

> ➤ *Moderate*

> ➤ *Weak*

The reason for this element's effect on price sensitivity is:

_____

_____

_____

_____

_____

Things I can do to change this element's effect on price sensitivity:

_____

_____

_____

_____

Urgency

Clients with an immediate and pressing need for your services are almost infallibly less price sensitive towards them. That is because certain matters, if not dealt with quickly and decisively, can severely and negatively impact the client's operations, reputation, or revenue. For that reason, the greater the urgency, the lesser the price sensitivity. A strong effect, then, indicates that your work tends to involve urgent matters requiring immediate action.

This element's effect on my clients' price sensitivity is:

- ➤ *Strong*

- ➤ *Moderate*

- ➤ *Weak*

The reason for this element's effect on price sensitivity is:

_____

_____

_____

_____

_____

Things I can do to change this element's effect on price sensitivity:

_____

_____

_____

_____

_____

Once you've completed this exercise, come up with a plan to make your practice less price sensitive. Review each of these factors and determine the steps you can take to increase the value, create more barriers to competitors, and learn your client's business more intimately. You may want to meet with your clients to get their input on these factors. Often clients are not aware of the variables that factor into their sense of fair pricing. These conversations can benefit you in the future in areas where you have a clear advantage, compared to your likely competitors, and where your clients perceive substantial, maybe even irreplaceable, value.

Practice Differentiation Strategies

You can also use the practice position model to evaluate the differentiation of your practice and service offering. Differentiation refers to the process of distinguishing a service from similar services to make it more attractive to a particular target market. It means setting yourself apart from the competition as well as a way to refer to the uniqueness of your practice. Powerful differentiation enables you to credibly communicate the value *you* can provide but your competitors can't so clients will hire you over the competition. It's a promise of the superior performance that they can expect from you.

Why is differentiation a big deal? In short, it's because clients have vastly greater bargaining power, relative to lawyers, than they once did. Buyers of legal services have much more information and hard data about lawyers and how they handle matters than at any time before. To be sure, legal buyers today are much more sophisticated about buying legal services than lawyers are about selling legal services.

To make matters worse, companies have many more options available to them to solve their legal problems. Companies have pushed to make legal services cheaper and more efficient by pursuing new technologies, creating bidding marketplaces, using alternative legal service providers (ALSP), and focusing on internal process improvements. The result is that clients now care less about a lawyer's impressive credentials than whether a lawyer provides significant and unique value through smart, efficient lawyering and top-notch client service.

The upshot: in today's crowded and demanding legal-services marketplace, you need a differentiation strategy to help you stand out and get noticed. A differentiation strategy is the process through which you do two things: first, credibly communicate the unique value you provide and second assure clients that you can consistently deliver that value. In other words, it's your method to align your knowledge and capabilities with your clients' needs and wants. This creates both value for your clients and a competitive advantage for you.

Differentiation and You

There are three reasons why differentiation is such a powerful marketing strategy. First, it makes marketing more effective and efficient by letting clients clearly see how your services' value differs from your competitors'. This, in turn, helps clients make more informed hiring decisions than they could otherwise.

Second, by clearly and credibly promising unique value to clients, a lawyer helps clients to perceive how the lawyer's work will tangibly benefit them, which, in turn, encourages clients to hire that lawyer over someone else.

Third, and relatedly, lawyers whose clients view their services as providing superior value suffer less price sensitivity. That is, those lawyers can generally charge higher fees than others who have not effectively communicated their own unique value.

Patrick Fuller, Vice President and General Manager of ALM Intelligence, sums it up well: "differentiation creates demand. It steers demand toward you versus your competitors. And in some cases, powerful differentiation strategies can even create new demand."

Establishing a differentiated position in the marketplace is difficult for four main reasons. First, the legal services marketplace is ever-changing. What appeals to clients today may not appeal as much tomorrow.

Second, clients glean information about lawyers from many different sources: for example, peer referrals, websites, seminars, publications, directories, and so on. Conveying a concise and compelling message consistently across these different channels is tough, even for the savviest communicators.

Third, your competitors are constantly looking for ways to improve their own services and gain market share for themselves. Naturally, then, they will continually challenge your value proposition and market their services against yours.

Fourth, how clients perceive your value is built over time, as your reputation grows and evolves. Consequently, creating a successful differentiation strategy requires a clear, consistent, and unwavering focus on your practice development and marketing initiatives. More importantly, it also requires a thorough understanding of clients' needs and wants.

Achieving that depth of understanding is not easy, but there are ways to learn what clients need and want from their lawyers. The key is to be open to learning as much as you can about why clients hire some lawyers, and not others.

The most effective way to get this information is through client interviews. You'll be astounded at what your clients will tell you, if you simply ask them. Indeed, well-developed questions can reveal those attributes, qualities, and behaviors that clients find most appealing and valuable in their lawyers.

Another way to identify potential differentiation strategies is to interview clients (or prospective clients) about the other providers they use, either for legal advice or accounting, management consulting, etc. I call these 'reverse client interviews' because you aren't asking about your service delivery but the delivery the company experiences from its other providers. Very often, you'll learn a great deal about what the company values through these types of interviews.

Short of interviews, you can look to any recent requests for proposals, or RFPs, that your firm, or other firms, might have received. Put simply, an RFP (which stands for Request for Proposal) is where a potential client with a legal issue asks one or more law firms to *propose* how they would resolve that issue to help the client decide which among multiple competitors to hire. Studying RFPs will show you what questions clients tend to ask and the things they tend to emphasize, giving you valuable insight into their lawyer-selection criteria.

Also, we all know that in-house attorneys are generally key decision-makers regarding which outside firms their employers hire. Accordingly, you should check out the Association of Corporate Counsel's website under the Value Challenge tab. This website has lots of information collected from in-house counsel on their preferences and needs in working with outside counsel. Finally, don't forget to ask your fellow attorneys what their experience has taught them about identifying and meeting clients' needs.

Test Your Differentiation Strategy

Once you generally understand clients' needs and wants, you can build your differentiation strategy. The strategy must make a *credible* claim about the unique value that you alone can provide your clients, make charging higher fees easier for you, and make choosing your competitors harder for your clients. To that end, you should ask yourself three questions about each claim you make, to determine both whether it's credible and whether it truly conveys your unique value.

First, is your claim both *true* and *provable*? Put differently, your claims about your services must be both factually accurate and supported by evidence. For instance, if you claim to be an expert on some topic, make sure you can cite articles you've published, presentations you've given, or some other objective proof that you really do know something about that topic. Otherwise, people will tend to disbelieve you.

This also means that exaggerated and embellished claims, or "puffery," can actually do more harm than good. You want to present a compelling description of what you do, but not so outlandish that it's not believable. For this reason, stick to what you know is true and provable.

Second, is your claim *relevant* to your target audience? Does it address something that the client both needs and cares about? For example, every client needs a lawyer without conflicts of interest, so a lawyer who truthfully claims not to be conflicted makes a true, provable claim that addresses a client's need. However, the client may, subjectively, find the conflicts issue unimportant, so making claims about it is a waste of time, because it won't really factor in the client's hiring decision.

Third, is your claim *valuable*? Will it help the client make or save more money than you're charging? After all, businesses exist to generate value for their stakeholders, so your claim will not set you apart if it doesn't show clients how you'll provide them real value (or avoid loss) in financial terms. For example, if you claim that your process includes exhaustive research of an issue, but you can't

134

demonstrate how that thorough research will help the client's bottom line, your claim may not resonate.

Differentiating your practice is difficult. It requires ongoing effort because even once you implement a good differentiation strategy, you must always adapt it to market changes. While the effort is great, so are the benefits. A differentiation strategy will help you grow your practice and attract better, and better paying, clients.

The Three Core Differentiation Strategies

Let's examine the three primary practice differentiation strategies, their challenges, and how each can build a competitive advantage for you.

Earlier, I described how differentiation could help you stand out in the client's mind and get noticed. I also suggested that you need a differentiation *strategy* to help you do this. A differentiation strategy is a way to manage the client's perception of your value. It helps you build and manage your personal brand. While there are innumerable ways to differentiate your legal practice, most fall under one of three general methods or strategies for creating value in the business relationship between you and your client. And as you'll see, these differentiation strategies also tend to track with a company's needs as the predictability of legal outcomes grows more pronounced.

The chart below lists and explains the three basic practice differentiation strategies: practice or service innovation, client intimacy, and operational improvement. The chart describes each strategy and lays out the associated growth drivers. It also articulates the common challenges associated with each and the competitive advantage or value proposition that each creates.

Differentiation Strategies	Innovation	Intimacy	Improvement
Strategy	Early command of emerging issues, first to market with specialized expertise enables premium rates.	Fast customization of solutions to client business model enables client integration and expansion.	Process management and improvement leads to higher predictability, lower risk and better protection of margins.
Growth Driver	*Speed to understanding of issues and implications is key*	*Managing scope and operational integration is key*	*Managing scale and process improvement is key*
Key Activities & Challenges	Industry and Business knowledge; Research & Analysis; Identify risks; potential Implications.	Knowledge of business model & operations; Service delivery skills; communication skills.	Project management; process improvement; competitive positioning; value capturing.
Competitive Advantage / Value Proposition	Specialists & Experts	Client Focused	Best Value Option

Innovation

The first is innovation. Innovation means identifying new or emerging issues, and finding solutions to those issues quicker than your competitors can. In other words, it embraces revolutionizing how you deliver services to clients, along with creating new practice specialty areas that provide solutions for new or uncharted areas of the law.

Innovation requires two things: legal prescience and strong business acumen. Legal prescience means employing robust legal research and analysis skills to help you detect emerging legal issues and forecast which ones will impact clients' interests.

Strong business acumen means understanding how these emerging issues might affect various clients, and how your singular skill set can help solve those issues effectively and efficiently. In other words, be entrepreneurial. Find a need and fill it. Quickness is key here. The speed with which you can identify new issues and develop solutions is the very thing that creates value and competitive advantage in the innovation strategy.

Intimacy

The second strategy is client intimacy, or customization. It means becoming *intimately* familiar with your clients' businesses, so much so that you can customize your service delivery and craft solutions to your clients' specific needs. Client intimacy takes effort. It requires strong understanding of not only the client's business model, but also the client's competitors and industry peers.

Most importantly, it requires a deep understanding of how your legal solutions affect various areas of the business and its operations. With a client intimacy strategy, you must gain a strong sense of the company's operations, culture, philosophies, values and norms. Solutions are often evaluated by business managers in terms of the amount of disruption to current operations that they cause or avoid. To design solutions that minimize operational disruption, you have to know the business exceedingly well.

This effort is worthwhile, though, because customization creates value for clients. It provides effective solutions that fit within their existing business model. This saves them the time and resources they would otherwise have to expend to adapt your services to their own internal processes. This builds loyalty and keeps them coming back to you.

Improvement

The third strategy is an improvement strategy in which you pursue differentiation through operational effectiveness, typically achieved through project management and process improvement. Project management and process improvement helps you create value for clients by streamlining your own workflow, so that you can handle an increasing scale and volume of work. That is, it helps you do the same work using less time and fewer resources, so that you can do more with what you have. This strategy requires strong process improvement and project management skills, as well as ongoing commitment to efficiency. It also requires fluid communication with clients so that you understand the unique aspects of the company's operations and so that they understand the value they derive from your continuous improvements.

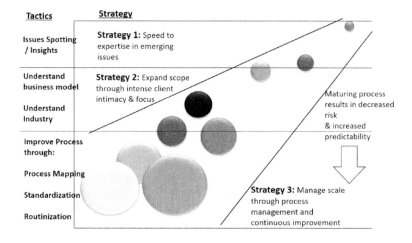

This graph shows the three differentiation strategies as they sit in their respective positions on the practice position model. You'll recall that the upper right-hand corner of the model is the area that has the greatest risk and where matters are unpredictable. Conversely, the lower left-hand corner is where routine, predictable matters sit. Looking at the three main practice differentiation strategies, you can see how each strategy works to accomplish different objectives for you and serves different client needs. The bubbles represent the sub practice areas and their respective volumes and relative position on the chart. The bubbles were taken from an analysis I did on a practice area. Your bubbles may differ.

Of course, no one strategy is exclusive to the others. You can implement multiple strategies at once. Because, for instance, you innovate well and gain quick command of emerging legal issues, it does not mean you will not also be effective at working more efficiently if you put your mind to it. Rather, it simply means that innovation is the strategy you emphasize in your marketing efforts when the issues are new.

The basic practice differentiation strategies are meant as a guide to help you explore specific ways to distinguish your practice. There are numerous ways to combine or segment these basic strategies to create more narrowly defined approaches tailored to your particular practice development needs.

For instance, you may focus your process improvement strategy on your effectiveness at handling matters with large volumes of data to sift through. Or, you may focus on more efficient project management or on the detail of the reports you provide for certain types of work. It all depends upon how well you understand your clients' needs and can develop a value proposition that addresses those needs.

As a practical example, one lawyer I worked with had a paralegal who became very familiar with a client company's trademarked display standards. The paralegal traveled a great deal and routinely visited the stores that carried her client's products whenever she was in a new city. She took pictures, reported when displays were executed wrong, and even looked for counterfeit products. This gave the client an added resource to help maintain display standards and protect its intellectual property assets. And it provided an example of how the attorney and her team routinely went above and beyond what other attorneys would likely do.

It also exemplifies a client-intimacy differentiation strategy focused on a specific practice area (trademarks), which addressed a recurring challenge the company faced: maintaining display standards and watching out for counterfeit products. This benefit to the client produced a deeper sense of loyalty to the lawyer and her paralegal, which encouraged the company to use more of the lawyer's services.

Practice differentiation is all about projecting and validating the value you create. Projecting that value for prospective clients helps those clients envision working with you. Validating that value helps to ensure those clients remain with you. In a few more pages, you will see how to create a unique value proposition to position your practice competitively in the minds of your best client prospects. It is not hard to imagine the value you can deliver to clients. It is intensely difficult, however, to execute that value proposition over time consistently and with numerous different clients.

Evaluating and Differentiating Your Practice

This is an exercise that I encourage you to do. In each set of instructions, or in the questions to follow, a reference to "you" is also a reference to your firm, unless the context clearly indicates otherwise.

This exercise asks you to do two basic things. Part one has you analyze your practice as it is now, to determine how well-differentiated it is. That is, how well you've implemented the three main differentiation strategies of innovation, intimacy, and improvement. Part two encourages you to brainstorm ways that you can better differentiate your practice, using the three differentiation strategies.

Part 1: Evaluating Your Practice Area

For each main differentiation strategy, I'll explain the meaning of it and then ask you a series of questions to help you evaluate how much you have differentiated your practice in that area.

Innovation

You'll recall that innovation means identifying new or emerging issues, and finding solutions to those issues quicker than your competitors can. It can also mean innovating how you deliver legal solutions. In other words, innovation means revolutionizing how you deliver services to clients, along with creating new practice specialty areas that provide solutions for new or uncharted areas of the law.

Innovation requires two things: legal prescience and strong business acumen. Legal prescience means detecting emerging legal issues and forecasting which ones will impact clients' interests. Strong business acumen means understanding how these emerging issues might affect various clients, and how your singular skill set can help solve those issues effectively and efficiently for each business. Quickness is key here, because the quicker you can identify emerging issues and find solutions, the greater competitive advantage you'll reap from innovation.

Instructions

List each of your practice areas on a separate piece of paper. Once you've done this, answer the following questions with respect to each practice area.

1. How relevant, or strategically important, is your practice area to your clients? Describe (1) the uncertainties your clients face when they encounter unresolved issues in this area and (2) the ways in which they benefit or the risks they manage when these issues are resolved.

2. What novel or emergent issues do you see arising in each practice area? List them. To evaluate novelty, you can study several key criteria, including: the volume of scholarly writing about the subject, emphasizing how much has been written and how recently; the number of recent judicial or administrative decisions about the subject; and the extent to which your key competitors have recently taken an interest in the subject.

3. For each issue you identified in the previous question, identify its longevity. That is, how long do you think the issue will continue to provide opportunities to develop new and relevant solutions before judges and lawyers mostly figure out its contours, and further innovation becomes difficult or impossible? Think about, among other things, what needs to happen for the issue to arise less often, and whether events surrounding the issue are trending in that direction.

4. For each issue you identified in #2 above, identify the ways in which you have been an innovator. That is, how have you identified and implemented new and forward-

thinking solutions to resolve these issues favorably to your clients?

Intimacy

Remember that client intimacy, or customization, means becoming *intimately* familiar with your clients' businesses and their industries, so that you can deliver solutions tailored to your clients' specific needs and circumstances. Intimacy requires strong understanding of the client's, its peers', and its competitors' business models.

Instructions

For each of your practice areas, answer the following questions:

1. How have you adapted, or customized, your practice to suit your particular clients' peculiar needs and circumstances? How have you avoided disruption to the company's business operations? As you craft your answer, consider (among other things) each client's business model, the overall industry, and each competitor's business model.

2. Think of this question as a subset of the previous question: how have you customized the way you deliver legal services to adapt to each client's processes, schedules, or policies? As you answer this question, think about things like your clients' billing requirements, the technology your clients use, any reporting schedules they follow, how you have adapted solutions to the company's unique processes or operational norms, and so on. Put another way, think about how you have adapted your legal advice to the ways your clients do things, rather than forcing your clients to adapt to your preset prescriptions.

Improvements

Operational effectiveness, or *process improvement*, helps you create value for clients by streamlining your own workflow, so that you can handle an increasing scale and volume of work. That is, it helps you do the same work using less time and fewer resources, so that you can do more with what you have. This strategy may also save your client time and money and use fewer resources. This strategy requires strong project management skills and ongoing commitment to efficiency. It also requires fluid communication with clients, so they understand the value they derive from your continuous improvements.

Instructions

Take a moment to think about your practice at large: how you run it, your internal processes and procedures, and how you manage your own workflow. With this in mind, answer these questions on separate paper:

1. What changes have you made, over time, to work more efficiently? Think about ways you have streamlined your own processes, eliminated steps (or made steps faster to complete), adopted new technologies, and so on.

2. Over time, what changes have you or your firm made to reduce the cost of serving your clients? For example, you might have down-streamed work to the least qualified and least expensive attorney who could do the work. Or, you might have acquired new software or implemented other changes to reduce time spent performing discrete tasks.

3. How well have you communicated, to your clients, the efficiencies you identified in the prior questions? For instance, think about ways you have collaborated with clients to improve your workflow or to save costs or time.

Think about the degree to which you have reported to clients what you've done.

Part 2: Differentiating Your Practice

Now, let's brainstorm ways for you to improve in each differentiation strategy, to offer more value in each aspect of your practice. The following exercises should help:

1. For each novel or emergent issue you identified in Part 1 under Innovation Question 2, write down at least one way you can resolve the issue to your clients' benefit. Try to think of resolutions that are difficult or impossible for your competitors to achieve.

2. List at least five ways to learn more about your clients' businesses, and to customize your own service delivery to their needs, policies, and procedures.

3. List at least five ways to streamline your own practice and workflow, so that you can do more with less money, time, effort, and resources.

Now that you've evaluated the differentiation in your practice and you've identified ways to improve your competitive advantage by increasing the degree of differentiation, take some time to make a plan for how you will implement each tactic that you identified in the exercise. Remember to write it down and figure out the steps you'll need to take to accomplish the plan. Share it with others. You may even want to do this exercise with a group of your peers. You will get more and better ideas working as a small group to brainstorm differentiation tactics. Plus, you'll have people to help you accomplish your new differentiation goals.

Know Your Unique Value Proposition

Now that you've identified the ways in which you can differentiate your legal services, let's work through how you can talk about this to your clients and prospective clients. The tool for crafting these talking points is the Unique Value Proposition statement.

A unique value proposition (UVP) helps prospective clients understand what differentiates you from other lawyers. It is a marketing tool that helps to set expectations of what prospects can expect when they hire you. Most UVPs focus generally on service delivery, experience and expertise, or process management and improvement. Your UVP should be authentic (capture something that is true about you), valuable to your clients, provable (if possible), and unique.

But a UVP offers more than a soundbite describing how you work with clients. The process of articulating your UVP can help you determine how well differentiated you are and help you build more refined qualities into your practice. As you develop your UVP, think about ways that you can make those differentiating points more easily observable and more consistently delivered. Think about how you might be able to track whether you are delivering on your UVP so that you can continuously improve your clients' experience with you.

The process described in the short worksheet in the addendum section will help you clarify how you currently deliver services (or how you would like to deliver services). The process of developing your UVP will enable you to benchmark your best qualities so that you can stay focused on the delivery standards you promise.

Creating Your UVP

A strong UVP has four main components. They do not need to be in any particular order:

1. The practice description, which describes what you do.

2. The target client profile, which communicates what sorts of clients you work with (or want to work with).

3. A description of the benefits that clients reap by engaging you.

4. A description of how your services are unique or how your practice differs from the competition.

Here's an example:

"I help real estate developers and municipalities resolve land-use issues and business disputes by focusing on common-sense solutions from initial negotiation through the administrative process, trial, and appeal. My clients benefit from my years of success as general counsel of a large real estate developer, where I creatively worked around some of the country's most complex and archaic zoning codes."

1. Practice Description
Let's begin by concisely describing what you do. To start, you might try filling in the blanks below.

I am a(n) _____.

Or,

My practice involves _____.

2. Target Client Profile
Now, let's describe the kinds of clients you work with or want to work with. Remember to portray your ideal client in terms of the relevant industry, legal problem, business type, company size, stage of business maturity, or another feature. To start, you might try filling in the blanks below.

I work with _____ who seek solutions to _____.

Or,

My clients are _____ who _____.

3. Client Benefits
Now, let's describe the primary, or top-ranked, benefits those clients derive from working with you. Here, your task is to articulate how you make your clients better off than they would be without you as succinctly and forcefully as possible. Think about all the various ways you benefit your clients, and from among these, pick the one or two you think most important. To start, you might try filling in the blanks below.

My clients experience _____.

Or,

My clients benefit from _____.

4. Practice Differentiation
Now, let's describe the primary, or top-ranked, ways in which your practice is unique, or different from the competition. Think about all those attributes and qualities that make your work stand out. From among these, pick the one or two that you think are most important to the types of companies you typically work with. Be as succinct and forceful as possible as you write. To start, you might try filling in the blanks below.

My practice is unique, in that _____.

Or,

I've set my practice apart by _____.

How Will You Measure Your UVP?
To internalize these qualities, identify the metrics or activities you can use to measure whether or not you are delivering on your UVP. For instance, if you distinguish your service by being very responsive to your clients, you might track whether you return calls within the same business day. The point here is to identify

metrics, activities, or behaviors that you can easily track to demonstrate that you deliver your promise.

Putting It All Together

Now that you have the components of a good UVP, let's try putting them together to create a final UVP that gets you noticed. Here, you'll combine the separate statements you just crafted into one comprehensive and concise proposition. The separate components don't need to be in any specific order, so experiment with different sequences. Feel free to retool your previous statements as needed to integrate them seamlessly. As you write, try to make your style and tone as conversational as possible while maintaining an appropriate degree of professionalism. You want your UVP to be easy both for you to communicate and for your prospective clients to understand.

Once you're happy with your final UVP, practice speaking it aloud, as if you are presenting it to a prospective client. If you can, record yourself and play it back, critiquing yourself as you listen. Do you sound authentic and natural? Are you convincing, clear, and intelligible? The more you practice your statement, the more natural and convincing it will become.

Finding and Delivering Client Value

"Firms that do their homework, and think not just about themselves, but about you, as a prospective client — those firms are going to be much more successful. Firms should come in and say, "We see certain things about your business model that create certain legal risks," or "There are certain things we've noticed about your intellectual property."

Firms should be able to say, "We studied you. We know what your characteristics are as a company. We've learned a little bit about how you've handled things in the past, and we think we can help you handle them better, and differently, more efficiently, in the future."

-David Leitch,
Group Vice President and General Counsel, Ford Motor Company

Client development has entered a period in which value delivery is the critical differentiator. Creating value for a client is an effective means of gaining a new client and expanding your relationship with existing clients. Getting good results and building close relationships are still important. But to become a trusted advisor to your client, you must create the type of value that the company cannot easily get elsewhere or create without you. Faced with an overabundance of competent lawyers to choose from, value generation can generate the business impact that gets an invitation to work more with the client.

The value creation model of client development requires a thorough understanding of the client's business, methods, and practices, and an ability to think structurally and systematically about the client's problems. To do this you must become a student of the company, its operations, and activities by conducting thorough research on the company to identify potential issues or ways in which you can impact the company and add value. I call this ability your 'speed to business acumen' ability.

You can build your knowledge of a company by studying the company's financial reports; by reading their website content; by reading investor commentary on the company; by reading the company's press releases; by reviewing case and matter history and results; by reading interviews of company executives and media mentions; by interviewing company representatives; and by studying the company's competitors.

But you also must spend time at the business, in their offices, at their factories, or warehouses. Nothing beats the ability to understand a business as taking the opportunity to experience the business. Notice the activity level of the business. Are the phones ringing constantly or only occasionally? Do people walk quickly through the halls or are they more relaxed and slower paced? Are people light hearted or serious? Casually dressed or in business suits? Are there motivational signs or expensive artwork on the walls? All of these observations will help you better understand the business and its culture.

If this sounds like a lot of work, it is. But the time spent understanding a company's business and thinking about ways to add unique value is a surer path to an engagement. The best way to get and keep a client is to make them look good inside their company and make their jobs easier. Your credentials won't do that. Your experience won't do that. Your relationships alone won't do that. Only through understanding their business and from that understanding provide extraordinary value will you be able to make your client look good and their job easier. In doing that, you will build their loyalty to you.

Client Development Through Business Embedding

At the beginning of this chapter, we discussed the practice position model and how to use it to identify where your practice sits in the marketplace of legal services. We also discussed the three core practice differentiation strategies and how you can differentiate your practice based on subject matter expertise, client focus, or process efficiency. Next, I want to use the practice position model to show you how to better understand client needs and priorities and how to align the delivery of legal services with what the client values most. I call this model and the process, the Value Creation Strategy Model.

This model will help you think about how you can focus on the client's business and align with the business' needs. In explaining this philosophy, we'll talk about the imperative to create business value to achieve a legal result. This value creation strategy model suggests why it is a more effective process for winning new clients and deepening your involvement with clients, than simply strong personal relationships and expert lawyering.

To understand this concept, let's first talk about what value means to a company and why simply achieving a result is no longer enough. In business, value is created when processes are improved, risks are reduced, resources secured, and customers are served better. Companies want you to deliver added value and even extraordinary value when you can. The concept of 'added value' or 'extraordinary value' can be obscure. Your idea of value may differ from my description of value if we don't clarify what value means. For me, extraordinary value falls into one of four types of value that companies experience from their service providers.

Companies experience extraordinary value when a lawyer:

1. Identifies a problem the company did not realize it had,
2. finds a solution the company did not know was available to them,
3. finds an opportunity that the company did not know about, or
4. provides access to resources the company could not have accessed otherwise.

Delivering extraordinary value requires strong communication with the client and a thorough knowledge of their business. But it creates an impact on the business that could not have been made without this research, communication, and focus. Opportunities to provide value are hidden in the company's value chain. Michael Porter first described and popularized the value chain concept in his 1985 best-seller, *Competitive Advantage: Creating and Sustaining Superior Performance.*

According to Wikipedia, "The idea of the value chain is based on the process view of organizations, the idea of seeing a manufacturing (or service) organization as a system, made up of subsystems each with inputs, transformation processes and outputs. Inputs, transformation processes, and outputs involve acquiring and consuming resources - money, labor, materials, equipment, buildings, land, administration, and management. How value chain activities are carried out determines costs and affects profits."

A company's value chain is unique to that company. It's like their secret sauce that they use to execute their business strategy. Even lawyers who have worked a long time with a company may not fully understand the company's value chain. That is why lawyers must develop business acumen by educating themselves in the basic concepts of business, economics, finance, and the client's business. It makes it easier to build an understanding of the company's business.

The relationship-building model described earlier lacks the value orientation and business focus required to compete in a highly competitive marketplace. This is why process improvement, project management, knowledge management, and other business process trends are becoming increasingly prevalent today. These are methods for improving the value delivered to companies over simply providing legal advice.

So how does this process work exactly? How do you collaborate with a company? I'll walk you through a concept I use to explain this general process to my clients. I call it the client embedding process and it starts from generating the initial interest in you to engaging your services to collaborating with you as a trusted advisor to the company. It relies heavily on the concept of value alignment which, once you understand the principles, will help you deliver greater value through each stage of the lifecycle of your work with any type of company. It traces the practice position model and identifies the differentiation strategies that you can use at each stage of the maturing process of legal issues and solutions.

The Value Creation Strategy Model

As the General Counsel of Ford Motor company implied, conversations should start with a statement similar to this: "I've been looking at your business, your competitors, and the issues similar clients of ours face. I'd like to share with you some of the things I think you should be focused on and get your thoughts on those ideas."

The value creation strategy model is built on the practice position model. I use it to identify the legal services delivery strategy that will provide clients with the relevant value they seek. In this model, you should start the relationship focused on research and planning by learning as much as you can about your client, their business issue, and the key performance indicators (KPIs) that determine the success of the results. This activity begins in the upper right-hand quadrant of the graph. As this knowledge builds and a solution strategy is identified, you can work more collaboratively with the client to align the legal solutions to the company's business processes, goals, and needs.

Once you are familiar with the company's unique business needs, you can focus on execution by constantly looking for ways to improve the workflow and the efficiency of the tasks involved in the work. Your objective should be to reduce the time and resources required to solve the client's problem while trying to achieve the best possible result. In a value creation strategy, you will want to capture these reductions and improvements for use in future matters. In this process, you will gain valuable knowledge about the company's business, which will help you become more integrated and aligned with the company.

The client embedding process follows the three stages in the value creation strategy model depicted below. Those stages are the solutions innovation stage, client intimacy stage, and the operational effectiveness stage. As a side note, each of these stages occur at all levels in the legal services delivery process. They simply tend to take on more importance at certain points in the maturing process, either the maturing of the client relationship or the maturing of the legal issue or both. It is a tool that can be applied to ensure value alignment at the individual task level, the matter level, or at a client-attorney relationship level.

Lawyers create value for their clients through the speed at which they find strategic solutions to client problems, the depth of the alignment of those solutions to the client's business, and the degree of efficiency they have in handling matters. As matters and relationships mature, companies continuously demand more value. This requires you to continuously adjust your service delivery to re-align your methods and processes to continuously improve the value you deliver.

The chart below shows this process. The value creation strategy follows the natural commoditization path of legal matters. In other words, as matters become more familiar to lawyers and businesses, their outcomes become more predictable, the risks lessen, and they become candidates for process improvement to eliminate the waste in their work processes. Following this path is also how you essentially embed your services into the client's business.

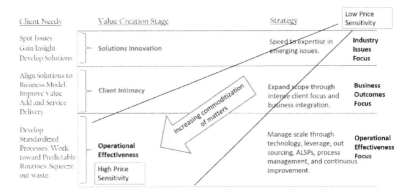

By deeply understanding the client's business and developing strategies to impact the business's success, you can deliver extraordinary value to your clients. That value will earn your entry to additional areas of the client's business and even more proprietary information about the business. It is a virtuous cycle and is the essential method for earning a trusted advisor relationship with the company.

Putting the Value Creation Strategy into Practice

Looking again at the first-time client relationship, a general counsel considering hiring you is doing so primarily on faith. That is, without actually experiencing working alongside you and understanding firsthand the degree to which you instinctively look out for the company's needs and interests, the hire decision is a gamble. And the company will be cautious until a degree of trust is built.

That trust can begin to be built through recommendations from your peers (power grid connections) and through the evidence you provide through your writing, case studies, and client testimonials. Conventional marketing suggests that prospective clients must first become aware of you and your services. Once aware of you, they must be interested in your services, either because they have identified a need for your services or because you have educated them about the need for them.

One way to begin this trust-building process is to attract interest from prospective clients through your thought leadership. Thought leadership educates companies about legal issues and can demonstrate to potential clients how you think about problems and how your thinking aligns with how a company operates. As such, most professional service businesses use thought leadership to gain the attention and interest of prospective clients.

Novel and insightful perspectives provide the best chance to gain the interest of company managers and their legal advisors. Thought leadership that is written in the style of writing familiar to business managers is more universally consumed than is writing written exclusively for consumption by legal professionals. It's easier to read by a wider audience and implicates an understanding of business that legalese struggles to convey.

Let's talk a little about how thought leadership works and how you can use your writing and thoughtfulness to create value for companies with whom you do not currently work.

Generating Interest Through Thought Leadership

Once you understand the company and its needs, business practices, and how you can provide value, it's time to formulate a strategy for attracting interest in your ideas and knowledge. As I said, a common way to generate awareness and interest is through thought leadership and content marketing. Thought leadership is what you share (your thoughts, ideas, and opinions), while content marketing is how you share it (through client alerts, articles, webinars, podcasts, etc.).

According to Wikipedia, a thought leader is "an individual or firm that is recognized as an authority in a specialized field and whose expertise is sought and often rewarded." Law firms and lawyers routinely share their knowledge through client alerts, white papers, articles, opinion pieces, webinars, podcasts, and other means. In doing so, they are advertising themselves as an expert in an area of law. And in some areas of the law, the field of experts is crowded.

In the value creation process, the effectiveness of a thought leadership strategy correlates to the degree to which the information is both relevant to the company and delivered timely. In other words, you can email your client new case decisions but if it is delivered long past the same case decisions sent by your competitors, it is of little use. Conversely, you can get new information to your client's mailbox quickly, but if it isn't relevant to the issues the client is dealing with, it will likely go unread. You need speed and relevance to be effective in thought leadership and content marketing.

To keep this otherwise complicated topic simple, let's discuss the speed of delivery and the relevance of the information you present to prospective clients and how they will perceive the value of that information considering its timeliness and relevance. Through this, you'll see the importance of tailoring information to the company's needs and delivering that information quickly as a means of starting a dialogue.

Hind Sights, Insights, and Foresights

Information distributed by lawyers can be categorized into one of three categories of information: Hind sights, Insights, and Foresights. Hind sights are the simple reporting of facts such as recent developments, case decisions, legal precedents, or new issues. As reported information, Hind sights don't offer advice or predict outcomes. They are simply a reporting of facts. If you send reported information to a client and are the first to make them aware of that information, they will probably view you as helpful. I call this first in position a notifier.

If you are the fifteenth to send them that information, you'll likely be considered an irritant, cluttering up the client's mailbox. Acting slow with less relevant information can cause you to potentially be an irritant. With Hind sights, value is created through the speed of reporting new, relevant and important information.

'Insights' is information presented in the context of the client's business or industry, including recommendations and advice. Insights don't just report developments but interpret how those developments will or could impact the company's business or their industry. The value of insights is created through the depth of understanding that the lawyer has of the issue, the client's business, and their industry. The ability to put new information in context, that is, apply it to the client's business or industry, is what differentiates the information. Speed is still important as competitors are also trying to deliver insights quickly to clients. But differentiation is most pronounced when insights tightly align with company needs and business practices or are particularly novel or insightful.

Foresights are the most difficult type of information to develop. 'Foresights' is information that predicts the future development of an issue and the potential consequences to the business or industry. Foresights require astute analysis, frequently tying unrelated issues together into a credible description of what the future state of legal affairs will likely be for that company or its industry.

Clients prize foresight above all other types of information because it helps them avoid risk and seize opportunities ahead of their competitors. Lawyers, by training, are biased toward facts, precedent, and evidence. They typically constrain their analysis to known legal issues and trends. But accountants and management consultants are increasingly crossing the boundaries by including legal analysis the way lawyers should include business analysis. And their information is often predictive of future trends. Lawyers should do the same, with qualification of course.

Foresights, and to a lesser degree, Insights, create the kind of value that can attract client interest. Lawyers who meet with prospective clients armed with an understanding of a client's business and a perspective on the business' direction are much more likely to engage them in meaningful dialogue that can lead to a working relationship. This level of preparation for the prospective discussion is critically important and sets a substantially different tone for the conversation.

One you've generated interest in your services and are handling an engagement for your new client, check in with your client to see how your plan for handling the matter will affect the client's operations. Depending upon your practice area and the company's issue, it may not have much of an effect on their operations. Often, though, it will. Sit down with your client to explore the impact and implications of the work you will be doing for them making sure to ask about the people in the company who will be responsible or will have a role in implementing the changes in the company. Ask how your advice could affect how the company currently operates, what unintended consequences could arise, and the aspects of the company that you should know in formulating a solution to their problem. These questions will not only provide you with additional information that you need to craft the best solution, but will give you valuable insights into how the company operates.

As you get into working with the company, keep your eye on ways to do the work more efficiently, squeeze waste out of the process, and improve the effectiveness and value of the solution. Collaborate with your client as much as you can and make your client a partner in the solution. Remember, you know the law better than they do. But they know how the solution needs to work inside their company. Focus as much as you can on reducing the amount of disruption they will experience while at the same time maximizing the effectiveness of your advice.

Practice Power Points

Practice power points provide leverage to your business development efforts. They are aspects of your practice or how you deliver services that help differentiate you. Think about them as talking points. You want to have several compelling sound bites that are notable about you or your practice that you can use in conversations and in your marketing materials.

We've talked about your market position, the price sensitivity of your practice, and how your practice is unique and differentiated. The following topics are what you need to know to market your practice effectively using practice power points, some of which you may not have thought about before. Some of these, you may not have thought about for your practice before. But they each relate to how to position and promote your legal services.

As you go through this list, think about how each concept affects you and your practice. Are there ways to better understand each?

Are there things you can do to take more control of each topic? How can you use each of these topics to your advantage? Hopefully, each issue makes you think harder about how to market your practice more effectively.

Opportunity Triggers

An opportunity trigger is a comment, event, or activity that indicates a potential need for your legal services. Depending on the practice area, that need can be 'triggered' by changes in a company's financial status, changes in management or operations, changes in a company's strategy, the sale or acquisition of assets, or changes in the talent pool in an organization, among many other triggers. Triggers can also come in the form of comments made in conversations. These are the triggers or verbal prompts to listen for that may indicate a need for your services. How you respond to those is key.

Think about the activities, events, or information that could indicate a company or individual has a need for your assistance. What might someone say that could indicate that they need your help? Which events or financial disclosures would indicate a company needs your services? Take a few moments and think about the comments, activities, and events related to your area of practice that can indicate a need for your services.

Why is this important to know? Because you want others to look for opportunities for you. To make that easy, the list of comments, events, or activities can help prepare others to be on the lookout for the specific triggers that indicate a need for your help. While obvious to you, they may not be obvious to your partners and referral sources. By providing the triggers to watch or listen for, you help them be more effective in identifying opportunities for you.

Examples of Unique Expertise or Experience

An obvious practice power point is the unique experience or expertise you have acquired. You know your past clients, past matters, most interesting cases, and the specific problems or issues you address for your clients. If someone asks, there is no doubt that you could explain what you do. But your partners and referrers will not invest the time to know your practice as thoroughly as you know it. Your partners and referral sources have a general idea of what you do, but they don't know how to position what you do or create the interest for others to want more information. To help them help you, give them one or two notable achievements that exemplify your work.

An example may help illustrate what I'm suggesting. Let's imagine that you do labor and employment work. You defend national retailers against attempts by their employees to unionize. When asked for referrals to a labor defense lawyer, your partners would likely respond with your name and that you represent national retailers. Of course, this is good. A national retailer wants a lawyer who understands the challenges of defending against unionization efforts in different states. But that description doesn't give them a way for you to stand out from the other referral requests they are making in their other attorney relationships.

A better response states your name, legal expertise, and industry experience but adds a wow factor to help you stand out. That wow factor could be a well-known case, a highly regarded client, a particularly challenging matter, a uniquely creative approach, or a result that was extraordinary. Think about the one or two aspects of either your expertise or your experience that is impressive, unusual, or highly effective about your practice. Then ask partners and referral sources to include that in any discussion of your capabilities.

An example of a good response by a referral source when asked for the name of a good labor defense lawyer would be: 'I'll set up an introduction to Bill Baggadonuts. Bill is really well-regarded in that area of the law and is certified by the state board.'

A better response would be: 'I'll set up an introduction to Bill Baggadonuts. Bill is really well-regarded in that area of the law and is certified by the state board. The CEO of The Limited first introduced us and uses him.'

Write out the two or three most notable aspects of your career and share those with your partners. It will help them refer you more powerfully.

Value-Added Services

Here again, think through how you add value to your client relationships. Identify one or two examples that will impress a prospect and share those with your partners. Give examples of how the client benefited from that extra effort and what the result was.

Tell the story but keep it short and specific. You want your partners to be able to remember the example and easily recite it. Stories facilitate memory and recall. Frame the value-added service as a short story, if you can.

Here's an example: 'Bill noticed his client kept losing in the fifth district, both with his cases and other law firms his client was using. He did some research and found out that cases with two specific evidentiary issues were most often the ones that got overturned. He created a review process so his client would know when those evidentiary issues were present and they should seek a change of venue.'

Client Service Delivery Strategies and Standards

Client service is the glue that binds clients to us. What's your secret sauce for delivering exceptional client service? What standards do you hold yourself to in terms of service delivery? What can you tell new clients to expect from you when they start working with you? Do you return calls quickly? Make yourself available at a moment's notice? Are you flexible and able to adapt quickly? Do you have an uncanny ability to put the right lawyers on the right tasks in a project? Do you foresee problems better, provide deeper insights, and find better solutions because you understand the client's business or industry better than others?

There are many facets of service. Scour your past client relationships and inventory the aspects of your service delivery formula that has been most meaningful to your clients. Then, identify the one or two standards or practices that rise to the top. Share those with your partners and referral sources.

In addition, spend some time articulating what you do to deliver exceptional service. Think about how you could demonstrate or prove that you do those things. Where possible, create standards and memorialize the behaviors and activities that clients appreciate most. Make them your standard operating procedures for your service delivery. Consider taking courses on how to deliver client service excellence. Review your standards to identify ways in which you can track your client service using key performance indicators. Using metrics will enable you to focus on and improve the areas in which you distinguish your service from others.

Creative Approaches and Results

Clients want attorneys who take a creative approach to their problems. In what ways or in which matters have you delivered creative legal work? How might you deliver that level of creativity time and again? Is there something in how you manage matters, understand the client's business, understand their goals and strategy, or learn about the people involved in the issue that lets you find and deliver creative solutions to their problems. What results can you tie back to those creative approaches? Can you document them and make them into case studies or get testimonials from your clients describing what you did? As much as you can, identify your process for bringing creativity to develop better solutions. Be able to articulate this to your partners.

Practice Synergies

Some practices tend to lead to work in other practice areas, while others are rarely found combined. Identify the most common synergies between your practice and the others in your firm. Think about the attorneys you know in those practices and the referrals you get from them. Think about the practice synergies and how they change from industry to industry for your practice area. Be able to explain them to your partners and why there are synergies between those practices.

Look back on your past matters that arose from inside the firm. Are there any other legal practice areas that predated your work on the matter? Try to distinguish whether those matters developed as a result of the synergy between practice areas or the synergy between lawyers with whom you have a good relationship. Identify the practice areas that feed work to you and focus on developing relationships with lawyers in those practice areas.

A Core Group of Partners

I recommend forming a core group of 6 to 8 partners whose practices you can learn, get to know well, and collaborate on presentations and pitches. These should be partners whom you respect, who share your work ethic, and who you would be proud to work alongside with any of your clients. Learn about their practices, clients, and their experience in different industries. Choose lawyers from practices that complement your own, if you can. Regardless, think of these partners as your hunting party. Get to know them, meet and talk frequently, and strategize with them regularly. The more you do this, the easier it will be to form business development partnerships with them and others.

These attorneys can not only become a core pitch team to present to new clients but act as a support group for you in your business development efforts. You might even ask them to read this book so they share an understanding of the process and principles you are following to build your practice.

Operational Efficiencies

Think about how you handle matters or cases. How do you improve the effectiveness of your work? How do you improve the efficiency of how you handle matters and cases? How do you make matters more predictable in their outcomes? Are there technologies you use or systems that help you manage your work better? Do you have checklists? Write down what these are and be able to discuss them with potential clients and referrers. Think about the onboarding process right on through the post matter review and how you make each step increasingly efficient.

The Urgency Experienced by Clients for the Solutions You Provide

The urgency in which clients need your solutions determines the length of the sales cycle and the complexity of the hiring decision.

Some decisions to hire outside counsel can be made quickly, while others take time and consideration. Knowing where your practice falls on this continuum helps you to understand the buyer's motivations and some of the potential obstacles to buying your services.

To get a sense of what I am talking about, let's apply a DIB assessment tool. I created this tool to help my clients understand the urgency in which clients make decisions to solve the problems they have. The urgency drives the sales cycle. Longer sales cycles happen when companies don't have a pressing need to solve their problem. Shorter sales cycles result from problems which are pressing and must be solved quickly.

DIB stands for Discretion, Importance, and Budget. Discretion suggests the degree to which a company can delay the decision or even opt not to solve their legal issue. Importance indicates the strategic importance of the issue to the company. And budget indicates the resources, time, and money set aside, or not set aside, to deal with the issue.

If an issue is critical to the company's operations, they have little discretion as to whether or not to address the issue. Alternatively, a legal issue may be important but not critically important. Some issues are important because they have far-reaching implications for how the company operates. In this case, they may be able to put off the decision until the company understands those implications better. Thirdly, a company may consider the issue important and have little discretion as to whether they address it or not but did not prioritize it by allocating resources to dealing with it. Each of these criteria helps you to evaluate the company's motivation, or lack thereof, to address the issues you bring to their attention.

Let's use two examples to illustrate. We'll use a class-action lawsuit and a proposal to review a company's technology contracts as examples to illustrate how to interpret a client's motivation to solve their legal issues. A class-action case that implicates a substantial payout to class members would be a critically important issue to the company. The pending court schedule would make it an urgent issue to address. And the risk of losing the battle would incentivize the company to pool its resources to fight the action.

Now let's consider a company faced with the suggestion that its technology contracts might be outdated. The issue could be important but may fall well below the importance of other projects. The company could delay the decision and put it into a plan to address later since there is no specific, known risk. And the lower importance and greater discretion mean that the company can prioritize investigating the issue and assign it the resources later.

The DIB assessment is a way to answer the question, 'Is this issue something that the company must address now and has the resources dedicated to addressing it.' Using these two examples, your sales approach on each would be necessarily different.

You can test your practice area by ranking your answers to each of these three questions on a scale of one to five, with one being not important, lots of discretion, and no budget. Conversely, a five would rank the issue extremely important, with no discretion (it must be resolved), and an appropriate budget. Remember to do your analysis from the perspective of the company.

Leveraging Emerging Issues and Disruptive Forces

Whether you primarily focus on specific industries or orient your practice toward specific legal areas, there are issues on the horizon that threaten your clients and prospects. You will know many of these issues, but do research to be sure you capture all of the emerging issues. Write them down.

Maintaining a list of the emerging issues and potential disruptions that companies and industries face will help you formulate marketing and business development strategies as well as content marketing strategies. Thinking about them in advance can also prepare you to respond more quickly when the issues come to light.

Another way to find emerging issues is to think about the issues that have plagued one industry and potentially affect a different industry. Issues often impact more than one industry. And they also impact the supply chains within different industries. Think up and down the supply chain to inventory the issues and disruptions your clients and prospective clients are likely to encounter.

You should also think about the disruptive forces that could affect your clients. Disruptive forces are significant shifts in demographics, technological capabilities, new technologies, biological or chemical developments, weather influences, and other forces which have the potential to disrupt the normal balance of things. Here again, consider how different forces could be combined or whose interplay might bring new threats or changes that make them hard to predict.

Think about the emerging issues and disruptive forces which could be the source of work for your practice in the coming three to five years. Use the worksheet in the addendum to capture and assess the opportunities in each issue or disruptive force.

Identifying Emerging Issues and Disruptive Forces

Instructions:
The following exercise is intended to help you catalog and assess the emerging issues and disruptive forces facing your clients or the industries you target. Use this process to identify potential subspecialty or niche areas for further practice development as well as to identify topics for thought leadership and content marketing.

Some issues and forces are high stakes, while others present little challenge to business. Rating the issues can help determine which topics should be the focus of additional research. Evaluate issues regarding their potential impact on clients and industries and your ability to serve clients' potential future needs. Keep the rating

system consistent from category to category and between each
successive emerging issues or disruptive force analysis.

Consider how issues unique to one industry could potentially
impact another industry sector. Look at the suppliers and ancillary
service providers and how they could be affected. Do the same for
regulations, legislation, judicial decisions, and political, social, or
technical trends. It is not necessary to accurately predict an
emerging issue so much as it is to stimulate your thinking on how
various issues could potentially play out. Some issues may seem
unlikely to develop or have too little potential using this technique,
but others may reveal real issues that companies will have to
address or even forces capable of disrupting businesses and
industries.

Create a worksheet using each of the following factors as a column
heading. Use the last column to enter the rating of each factor on a
scale of 1 – 5. Use one for the least impact and five for the most
impact. List all of the emerging issues and potential disruptions
that will or could affect your clients and prospective clients. Rate
each answer on the one to five scale. This exercise helps you to
identify the issues and disruptive forces with the greatest impact
and greatest opportunity for you.

Emerging Issues

In this first column, list the issues you feel are new or just
emerging in the marketplace, or that you anticipate developing,
and that present challenges for businesses and organizations. The
more specific the description of the emerging issue, the better the
analysis of the issues will be. Emerging issues should present a
formidable risk to a company and be substantive, meaning they are
not rumors or theories. Do this exercise for disruptive forces as a
separate entry on your worksheet.

Knowledge Strength

Rate the strength of your knowledge on a scale of one to five, with
five being extremely knowledgeable about the issue and its
implications for the business. Be as objective as possible. Think
about the full range of issues and the industries that may be
affected and rank your knowledge in all of those aspects. Consider

the number of attorneys inside the firm who know how to solve the issue, the depth and scope of their knowledge, and any gaps in their knowledge or experience. The rating should reflect the total knowledge inside the firm about the issue. A rating of five would be extremely knowledgeable with few competitors with a similar level of knowledge in their firms.

At-Risk Client Population
Determine the number of existing clients likely to be impacted by this emerging issue. Rate the number of clients on a scale of one to five, with five being a substantial number of the firm's clients having a risk associated with the emerging issue.

At-Risk Non-Client Population
How many businesses that are not existing clients would likely be impacted by this issue? Use this to analyze potential new business opportunities, new industries, and other untapped opportunities that this issue would likely present. Rank on a scale of one to five with five indicating a large number of businesses being at risk of the issue.

Growth Potential and Speed of Growth
How much potential for growth does this new source of risk or emerging issue present? Is the change occurring quickly or slowly? Rate the growth potential on a scale of one to five, with five being high growth potential which is developing quickly.

Strategic Importance of Issue to Business
Consider the degree of risk the issue has to the company's business. Rank the issue on a scale of one to five with five being bet-the-company level strategic importance.

Competitive Availability
How many other lawyers or law firms have knowledge of the issues that can provide solutions to companies in this emerging issue. Rank the competitive environment on a scale of one to five, with five being very few competitors, if any, have the knowledge and experience to provide solutions in this area.

Now that you've completed an assessment of the emerging issues, which of the issues present the greatest opportunity for your practice? Use this analysis to meet with your marketing professionals and other lawyers in your practice to brainstorm how you can take advantage of these trends and attract more clients.

Having read this chapter, you should have a much deeper understanding of your practice and its marketing opportunities. Now let's look at the people you know and take a deep dive on your connections.

5

Knowing Who You Know

"There is immense power when a group of people with similar interests gets together to work toward the same goals."

— Idowu Koyenikan

Creating a Master List of Connections

A strong network of connections is essential to building a successful legal practice. No matter what career stage you are in, you most likely already have an extensive network. But can you access the right person at a moment's notice? Do you know who the most important 150 people, influencers and referrals sources are among your contacts? Can you efficiently communicate with your entire network or segments of your network when need to? Probably not.

Like most professionals today, you may have hundreds of contacts scattered across work and personal cell phones, tablets, and computers. Your contacts may be in physical address books or in stacks of business cards. You may have people you know on Facebook and connections on LinkedIn. Some of us have multiple email accounts and have separate contact records in the firm's Client Relationship Management (CRM) system. And, of course, there may be other connections for whom you never physically collected contact information. There are numerous places where you have contacts or can reference the people you know.

Maintaining those contacts across multiple sources is not the most effective way to manage your network, especially as your network grows. That's why creating a master list of your connections is so important.

In this chapter, I will help you assemble a master list of connections, figure out who you should talk to regularly, and discuss how to evaluate the quality of your network of relationships and the people in it.

Of course, even after you build your master list, the work continues. Each time you meet a new person that you would like to include in your network, you should add them to your master list as soon as possible. As for existing connections, information will change from time to time. Maintaining this list is important, though time-consuming. The more help you can get in maintaining it, the easier it will be.

Finally, your master list of connections is a storage vault of value. Your connections have information, they are resources, and they can provide support, insights and different perspectives. Your connections are incredibly valuable. But you have to be able to access that information quickly. The more information you can save in your contact records, and the more you learn about your connections, the more valuable your network of connections becomes.

Creating a master list of connections will take some effort. But it will pay off for you in numerous ways. You'll be able to find who you know more quickly, it'll make it easier to do a mass mailing or email blast, and you'll learn more about the people in your life and how each of them can contribute to you and others in your community.

Collect Your Contacts

The first step in building your book of business is to know everyone you know. In this first step of the process, we'll review who is in your contact list, who is not and who may be missing from your contacts that you should know.

Let's start by collecting your contacts from the CRM system, your email accounts, and LinkedIn connections. Then we'll review those contacts to consider who is missing or who you should know that you don't. Then, I'll ask you to categorize your connections and prioritize them based on your goals for building your practice. Your goal should be to identify 150 contacts from among your clients, company prospects, and referral sources. This group will make up the largest portion of your power grid. These are the people that will produce work for you in the shortest amount of time.

Follow these steps to build your key connections list. (Your administrative support professionals, such as your assistant or an assigned business development manager, may be able to help with this process.)

Identify all the places where you keep contact information. These could include:

• Client-relationship management (CRM) system contacts
• Personal email address books. i.e., Outlook, Gmail, Hotmail, etc.
• LinkedIn connections, first-degree contacts
• Facebook friends
• Twitter followers
• Miscellaneous address books or paper Rolodexes
• School alumni directories
• Professional organization membership directories

Your bias for who should be included on your list at this point should be towards inclusion. That is, when in doubt, include their name on the list.

Consolidate Your Contacts

Download or input all your contact information into a single Excel spreadsheet, keeping each discrete bit of contact information in a separate field. For instance, put your contact's first name in one field, last name in a second, street number and address in a third, city in a fourth, state in a fifth, zip code in a sixth, phone number(s) in a seventh, email address(es) in an eighth, and so on.

If you have multiple spreadsheets with contact information, cut and paste the columns to be in the same order. Doing this will make the data easier to export into an email marketing program or to use the list in a mail merge.

Now, go back through the list and fill in any missing information about each incomplete contact record. At a minimum, you will want the first and last name, title, company name, and email or phone number. This may take some time. Focus on getting completed information for those contacts that you will likely include on a professional newsletter. Remember, this is an iterative and ongoing process. The hardest part of this process is getting a complete and updated master list of contacts. But the payoff is huge so don't cut corners or leave this step incomplete.

Plan to periodically update this list. Your administrative assistant may be able to help research contact information and organize and maintain the list.

Note: LinkedIn's help page has directions for how to download a list of your first-degree connections. Go to LinkedIn.com/help and search using the phrase 'Export my LinkedIn connections.'

Remove Duplicate Contacts

Run a check to remove or fix any duplicate information. Excel has a function to do this easily. Go to the Data tab and select 'Remove Duplicates.' You'll select the fields to use to compare entries. Select First, Last, Company Name and email address. This will get rid of the vast majority of duplicate entries.

Review the contacts, sorting the list in different ways to double-check for any duplicates you might have missed and decide what to do about them. For instance, if you have two records of one individual, and both have different email addresses (e.g., personal and work, or a new and old address), decide whether to keep both contact records or combine them. Sometimes you may have old information in a contact record. Your administrative assistant, a paralegal or a business development professional in your firm may be able to assist you in updating this information.

Identify Missing Contact Information

Your master list will likely be missing various types of information, including addresses, phone numbers, and email addresses. Of course, the amount of information you may want about your contacts can be extensive. It's up to you how much information you collect and maintain. At a minimum, you should have a work email address, a work phone number, a full name, a position title, and a company name in your contact record. You may also want to have the contact's home phone number, cell phone number, home address, home email address, administrative support contact information, and spouse's name in your record. You won't be able to collect this information for all of your contacts, nor would you want to. But having detailed contact information for the most important connections in your power network is a worthy goal to work toward.

Search Your Memory Bank

Now, let's add people you may not have contact information for but who should be among your key connections. Think about your past jobs, the schools you've attended, past deals or matters, and the religious groups and extracurricular activities you have participated in. Make a list of the people with whom you developed a good relationship. Many people find this step enjoyable and productive because the process helps you renew old friendships and identify new relationship opportunities.

Write down all of the information you have about that person. If all you have is a name, plan to research them to get more information for your contact record. As you are thinking about these people, filter them in terms of the people you think could potentially be a valued part of your network- either because they could refer work or contribute to your network in some meaningful way.

Think about the people you know or knew from these categories of relationships:

• Attorneys and business leaders from past deals, cases, or matters
• Undergraduate and graduate school alumni
• Previous employers and colleagues
• Professional service providers (accountants, bankers, and so on)
• Vendors or suppliers
• Professional associations
• Religious or spiritual institutions
• Gym members or sports activities
• Social or fraternal organizations
• Close friends and neighbors
• Children's or family activities
• Community or volunteer organizations

Add as much information as you have on these contacts. If you don't have the basic contact information, you can search LinkedIn, their company's website, or google the names to find available information. It may require some research to find these people. Concentrate on the ones that will likely be power grid contacts for you. It probably goes without saying but you should review your list on a regular basis. I suggest reviewing your master list at least once a year, twice annually is best though.

Categorize Your Connections

The next step is to categorize your connections based on how you know them and their role in your network. I recommend you categorize connections by whether they are an existing client, a prospective client, a referral source, a peer or partner, or a friend or family member. You may have other categories to add that would be helpful. Consider the ten categories of people you should know as you categorize your contacts. The list is on the next page.

Categorizing enables you to segment your contacts into groups and flag each for easy reference. The categories can also determine how those groups might be used or communicated with. For instance, you might want to mail a newsletter to all your clients and prospects but not to family and friends. Or you could have a special message for those who are in a position to refer work to you.

Conversely, you may want to include family and friends in your holiday card list but maybe not among your resource contacts. Remember that you can 'sort' the list to show everyone within each column heading. Some contacts may end up included in two different headings. Pick the most important classification for those contacts.

Ten Groups of People to Know

The following are suggested categories for your list.

a.   *Referral Resources*: Professionals with the potential to refer work/new clients. These can include accountants, other lawyers, business consultants, investment professionals, insurance professionals, and bankers, among others.

b.   *Industry Connections*: Professionals who have knowledge of trends and emerging issues or are influencers in an industry. These might include industry conference organizers, members of professional associations, lobbyists and industry influencers or business leaders.

c.   *Clients*: Here include both former and current, active clients. In addition to your legal work contact, also include anyone associated with the company such as business line managers, department heads, support personnel, etc.

d.   *Prospects*: Include the names of prospective clients (the companies that you would like to work for) and anyone you are actively pursuing for work.

e.   *Media Contacts*: The media are important people to know and you should know as many as you can. List reporters and media contacts who can help create awareness of your practice, who report on the issues you handle. Include both paper and online distribution channels like blogs, podcast producers and similar contacts. Remember to include reporters, editors, producers, bloggers, etc. Anyone who fits in to the general description of media.

f.   *Business Managers*: Include a category of business leaders and other professionals that are not associated with active or former clients (you should already have a category for them). Include any business leader that you think can provide value to your network of connections or that might have information or perspectives that you would benefit from.

g.   *Educators*: Include university or law school alumni, professors, CLE providers or educators that influence knowledge in the your industry or others.

h.   *Lawyers*: Make a special category for the lawyers you know that are not clients. Think about the competitor or ally lawyers that you have worked with or against in past matters, deals or cases. Include lawyers who are not in your practice area as they could be referral sources. Don't forget to include the partners and associates in your firm.

i.   *Advisors*: You likely know people who you could classify as an advisor to you. Include mentors, coaches, or any advisor to whom you can turn to for assistance or support.

j.   *Others*: If there are others who are not listed in the above categories, include them in a designated category.

k.

Review Your list

Take a look at the people in your list and ask yourself these questions:

- How many people do I have in my list? Is it too many or too few?
- What is the quality of the people in my list considering what I would like to accomplish?
- Are there any roles missing from the list that would make my list more valuable? Are there categories of people that are lightly populated and that I should try to add more connections?
- Do I have enough contacts in the industries in which I would like to work? What types of connections do I have in each? Do my contacts cover a broad range of responsibilities in those industries?
- Do I have people that can refer business to me?
- Are most of my contacts other lawyers, or do I have a good mix of business professionals and attorneys?
- Do the attorneys in my list cover a wide range of practice areas or are they concentrated in one or two practice areas?

Reviewing the list should provide insight into the types of people you have in your list. In those categories in which you have few contacts, consider whether you should make an effort to meet more contacts for that category.

Review the list for the information, resources, and influential people. How would their knowledge, their access to resources, or their influence help others on your list? As you go through the list, keep in mind that the next step involves marking those who will be in your power grid. These are the people you'll reach out to regularly.

Add Information Important to Your Practice or Industry

Think about any other information you want to maintain in this spreadsheet of your contacts. Add columns to capture that information. This could include the names of their administrative assistant, their supervisor, and their spouse or children. You should include notes about the conversations you have had with them. But you can also include notes about how you met and the names and connections to others who work in the organization. Include interests and activities you have in common.

Think about other column headings that are unique to your practice and add those column headings. For instance, you might want to add an industry code; a column to record the number of matters you have done for them; a column to indicate related companies or suppliers; or some other code denoting information related to your practice area. The level of information collection is up to you. Collect what you believe you need that will be helpful to you in the future. The column headings are how you sort and segment your list. So think about the unique information in which you would want to sort your contacts.

Identify Your Power Grid Connections

Now that you know who you know, let's build your power grid. Remember, the people in your power grid are clients, prospects, referral sources, and anyone who could potentially engage you or refer work to you. Your power grid will also include resources, influencers, technicians, and others who provide value to your network of connections. You should try to have a power grid of approximately 150 people.

Designate a column heading for your power grid connections so you can easily sort them into a sub list.

Over time, your job is to continuously improve the quality of the people in your power grid. Add and subtract people from your power grid to evolve your network to where it is increasingly valuable and generates increasing amounts of work for you and the others in your power grid.

I recommend that you reach out to each of these contacts a minimum of one time every three months. To put this in perspective, that volume of communication would require approximately three outreach calls every day over those three months. This is a difficult pace but it is a level of outreach made by the most successful lawyers I have observed.

Suppose your list falls short of 150 names. You can brainstorm ways that you could meet more people or think about people you may not have included when you thought through your past co-workers and people in your social circles. Try to expand your list to at least 100 total key contacts. Ideally, your list should include 150 (but not more than 150) in your power grid.

Go through your master contact list and mark each a *power grid contact* if they meet one of more of the following criteria:

- They are a current or potential prospect for your legal services
- They are a dormant or past client
- They are a lawyer who has or could refer work to you (either from inside or outside of your firm)
- They are a business professional who has or could refer work to you (Banker, Accountant, etc.)
- They are a high-level manager or C-suite business executive in a company with whom you could potentially do work
- They are well-known, reputable and/or an industry influencer likely to hear about work that you could do
- They have unique knowledge, experience, or access to resources that might be helpful to you or others in your network.

If you have more than 150 contacts in this list, consider prioritizing the list further. Use your judgment, but identify those contacts that likely have a current need for your services as a top priority. The second priority should be contacts who are in a position to hear about new opportunities for you.

Remember, your power grid should constantly improve in value. That means that you will need to review this list periodically and add and delete from the group to continuously improve the value and increase its 'power' to drive results for you.

Questions to Ask About Your Power Grid

Once you've identified the primary connections that will make up your power grid, go through the list and ask yourself these questions:

1. Look at the makeup of your power grid. How many of the categories are well-populated when looking only at the power grid connections? Are there categories that need to be better represented in your power grid? Which ones are they and how will you go about identifying and adding them to your power grid? Does your power grid include connections that reach a broad array of industries and geographies? Do your connections reach deep into the companies that you would like to work for? Does your power grid include a diverse cross section of people?

2. Look at the outreach activity level of your power grid. What is the level of outreach activity you have had with the people in your power grid? How often do you reach out to them? How many have you not contacted in a long time or at all?

3. Review the extended networks of the people in your power grid. How much do you know about the networks of the people in your power grid? Can you trace the spheres of influence of the people in this group?

4. Consider how you've cultivated the relationships in your power grid. For which of your connections have you done or given something of value? Which ones have you entertained? Provided information to? Helped them on a project? Provided a referral to or reference for? What is the level of your giving to the people in your power grid?

5. Think about how responsive your power grid would be. If you needed to reach a decision-maker at a large corporation or organization, how long would it take? How many different people would you need to work through? Would the people in your power grid likely respond to a request from you within a day or two?

6. Do your power grid connections exert influence? How effective would your power grid connections be in making things happen in their jobs, their communities, or their industries? In what ways do they have influence? Are there other influential people that you should include in your power grid? How many of them would you consider thought leaders in their areas of expertise?

7. How do you stay connected? Do you have a process for staying connected with your power grid connections? Do you monitor news, announcements, and other developments in their lives? Do you monitor their birthdays, work anniversaries, accomplishments, awards, speaking and publishing to find ways to connect with them?

With this analysis complete, you should know enough now about how your power grid should develop over time. Identify specific objectives for improving the quality of your power grid and the steps you will take to accomplish those objectives. Keep the plan simple and refer to it often. The plan should guide how you consistently improve the quality and productivity of your power grid.

Tracking Prospects and Outreach

You may have as many as 100 to 150 people in your power grid. If you are regularly reaching out to them, you'll need a way to keep track of the information you develop about them and about their company. At a minimum, you will want to record the date of the last contact you had with them and what you discussed. Keep notes on what needs they may have or opportunities you have identified for them. Keep track of the things you've done for them and they have done for you.

To develop a thorough contact record, I recommend five main areas of information to keep track of: conversations, people, interests, facts, and news.

Conversation records are brief notes about your discussions with your connection. These should be detailed enough to cover the main subjects discussed and key information revealed in your discussions but not so detailed as to be difficult to record or process. Anything of substance that you've gleaned during your conversation should be recorded in your notes, though.

You may also want to include notes about your sales efforts with that individual. This could include the proposals you've made to them, their responses to your overtures, objections they have had, and any other decision makers and stakeholders who have been involved in those discussions. Make sure you mark the date of every conversation. You'll be surprised at how helpful having dates on your discussions can be.

Make notes of the significant people in their lives. This could be spouses and children(s) names, their boss' name, and, of course, their administrative assistant's name and contact information. If there are others in the company that you might interact with, keep track of those people as well.

Keep track of their interests, hobbies, birthdays and anniversaries. Include professional associations and industry groups in which they are a member or hold positions in. If they have a favorite sports team or musical group, record that info as well.

Facts include any notable information about them or their company. For instance, they may have a special degree or advanced education. Record their alma mater or schools they have attended. Keep track of the basic facts about the business such as number of employees, number of patents, locations, key suppliers, and other information relevant to either your practice or that will help you achieve your goals for the connection.

You may also want to document significant events or news about the individual or their company. Include links to company news and press releases, financial reports or filings, events they have attended, and mergers or acquisitions. All of this information can help you prepare for your calls, remind you of developments and challenges the company or individual may have, and spark ideas for questions for your next discussion.

The depth of information that you collect and maintain on your contacts is up to you. It will likely evolve as you work through this process. Regardless, get in the habit of keeping track of information about your power grid connections. It will definitely come in handy and on a regular basis.

Selecting Secondary Connections

I previously introduced the idea that your power grid should include some of your secondary, or "weak" connections. In this section, I will discuss the factors that will help you determine which of these connections are right for inclusion in your power grid.

One goal in creating your power grid is to identify connections from diverse circumstances. Your secondary connections can be a place to find those diverse connections. People tend to gravitate toward others that are most like themselves. However, this phenomenon, called homophily, has been shown to reduce opportunities for innovation and creativity. To tap those qualities, select connections that represent diverse backgrounds, experiences, perspectives, interests, and demographics.

You may want to have a variety of industries represented in your power grid. Think about the industries that use your services or benefit from your knowledge and make a list of them. Then identify the people on your secondary list that work in those industries. This will be one factor among several in your analysis of who, from among your secondary connections, should be moved to your power grid.

The next area of diversity is organizational diversity. Power networks should connect people from different organizational functions, such as human resources, research, operations, marketing, finance, and accounting. Include different ranks within an organization, from secretaries to chief executive officers. Remember that people at every level of an organization have perspectives and information that can be valuable to you or someone else in your network. Even the lowest person on the totem pole can often wield influence inside an organization, so avoid making assumptions about connections based simply on title or rank.

You should also strive for geographic diversity among the people in your power grid, even if you concentrate your work in one local area. You never know when a referral to a professional in another area will come in handy. For example, imagine the value you can provide a client moving to another city if you can recommend a real estate agent, lawyer, or other professionals in that city.

Next, think about the generational and gender diversity of your network. Do you know people much older than you and people younger? Do you have many more connections of one gender than the other? People of different generations and genders have unique perspectives and needs, so you will add more value to your network by including people of different ages and genders.

After you've identified potential candidates for your power grid from your secondary connections based on diversity, you should further consider each connection based on personal attributes. For each connection, ask yourself if he or she is someone you would like to get to know better. Based on what you know about them and whatever initial interactions you have had, do you like them, and do they seem to like you? Do you share common interests or hobbies? Strong relationships typically start because two people like each other and have common interests.

Finally, you should select people you believe you can trust for your power grid. Ask yourself, from what you know about them, do they share your values? Do they have integrity? Are they credible? Do they deal honestly with others? Do they have a good reputation? Do they gossip about others or tend to have a negative or pessimistic view of the world? The people you know is a powerful reflection of who you are as a person. As an old Mexican proverb goes, "tell me with whom you walk, and I'll tell you who you are." Select people with whom you would be proud to be associated.

When you have identified secondary connections that represent diverse perspectives, experiences, and interests, that you like and who seem to like you, and that you believe have integrity, add them to your power grid.

Who Else Should You Know?

If you have done a thorough job cataloging all of the people you know, you have a very impressive list of connections. But what if you want to add more people to your network? What do you do next? Of course, your network will grow organically through new referrals and the new people you will meet in the regular course of your professional and personal activities. But if you want to be proactive, consider these key sources for new connections.

First, look at companies that serve the industries you represent in your legal practice. This is a broad category of companies that can include software companies, public relations firms, accounting firms, banks, real estate companies, and a multitude of vendors, just to name a few examples. Salespeople and advisors in companies that service the same community that you do can be a terrific source of information, new connections, and referrals. If you are not already familiar with these organizations, ask your clients which companies support their businesses. And if you don't already have a contact there, consider asking your client to connect you to someone at the company.

If you do a lot of work with clients within a specific industry, get involved with that industry's professional association. Industry association meetings are a great place to meet and connect with others. New business can result from meeting with many association members in the near or long term. Try to meet with some of the more influential members of the organization. They might be willing to share their insights about industry developments and the needs that will arise from these developments.

Get to know government officials, politicians, and lobbyists. Politicians, especially, survive by their ability to connect to a wide range of networks and cross numerous boundaries. They are influencers of trends and collectors of intelligence. Regulatory agents in your industry practice are also tremendous sources of information. They see your competition from a unique position and understand the key issues that players in an industry grapple with. Think about the people who you know or should know that are politicians or governmental employees. With politicians, start with your local politicians. They are easier to meet and, when necessary, can introduce you to state and national figures.

Your network should include people in finance, venture capital, private equity, insurance, accounting, and banking. Especially if you are a transactional attorney, you can benefit greatly from knowing people in these industries. At a minimum, you should know two or three good bankers and two or three investors. Bankers and investment bankers are what I call 'leverage' contacts because they have a stake in connecting people for their own purposes and can help you connect or acquire information.

People in the media also can significantly help you gain visibility for your practice, leading to new opportunities. But reporters that cover specific industries also have a wealth of information about the industry and usually have a wealth of high-level connections. Local, regional, and national reporters and editors are always on the lookout for story ideas and subject matter experts to interview.

If you work for a large firm, your firm's public relations staff may primarily develop these relationships. But you should still try to create these relationships on your own. Journalists are frequently well connected, know the competitors, and understand the issues and challenges in the industries or subjects they cover. Ensure your outreach includes all relevant outlets, in print, broadcast, and digital media.

In many practice areas, academics and industry educators have a significant impact on the direction of the industry. They may study the issues in greater depth than others you regularly consult with and are often on the cutting edge of their field. You can learn a lot from these educators about the developments that may affect your clients in the future.

Finally, consider getting involved with your practice area's community and non-profit organizations. The Board of Directors of non-profit organizations can be useful as they enable you to meet monthly with influential members of the community. Leaders and board members of community organizations, especially those involved in fundraising, have a unique perspective on the business community and other community organizations and are a rich source of information and connections.

I've given you a lot of ideas for getting to know more people who can significantly add value to your network. Focus on those most relevant to your practice and start devoting time to identifying, meeting, and cultivating relationships with these important potential connections each week.

Check for Navigators, Influencers, and Decision-Makers

Now that your network crosses numerous industries and disciplines let's look at the vibrancy of the people in your network of connections. By 'vibrancy,' I'm referring to whether the people in your network are engaged and actively looking to help others. In chapter one, I talked about the different types of people who should be in your power grid. I referred to these people as 'navigators', 'influencers,' 'decision makers', and others. Now is the time to look at whether those types exist in your power grid.

Consider whether you have navigators who can direct you to new resources and connections. Whether you know the influencers and decision-makers in the companies you work with or want to work with. Make a note of the type of person you believe each to be in your power grid. If you need, look back on the section in chapter one entitled Who Should be in Your Power Network to review the types.

You should feel good about where you are in this process right now. Putting together a master list and identifying your power grid is a big achievement. It takes a lot of work. Don't let this work spoil. Review your list at least quarterly and keep it updated. If you maintain it regularly, you'll never have to go through this process again. And you'll have quick access to the people in your power grid who can help you and others.

Now that you have assembled your power grid, it's time to prepare to reach out to them.

6

Preparing to Reach Out

"He who masters the power formed by a group of people working together has within his grasp one of the greatest powers known to man."

— Idowu Koyenikan

In this chapter, I'm going to share with you the steps I think you need to take before you reach out to your power grid connections. But first, let's figure out how many calls you need to make every week in order to achieve your revenue goals.

How Much Should You Reach Out?

You know that you need to devote more time to outreach to expand your business. But how much more time? How many calls should you expect to have to make to generate a new matter? What level of outreach activity should you be doing each week to achieve the revenue and new client acquisition goals that you have for yourself? I'm not suggesting you call 150 people per quarter cause the number seems right. I'm suggesting that volume because research suggests that number is what produces results. But every practice area is different. 150 calls per quarter may be required for one practice type but another may only require 80 calls per quarter. You need a way to estimate what the right volume of outreach is right for your practice. That's what we are going to work through now.

The first step in determining how much outreach to do and how much time to spend on it is to decide how much new revenue you want to generate. Revenues that you generate and that are from clients that are yours — as opposed to business from pre-existing firm clients — are called "originations." For purposes of this discussion, let's assume you want to generate one million dollars in new originations.

Next, you need to determine the average revenue that each new matter generates on average. If you don't know how much revenue a new matter of the type you are pursuing brings in on average, your accounting department may be able to help. You may know intuitively, but try to validate what you think with statistics from your firm's billing data.

When you have that figure, divide the average revenue number into your originations goals to determine how many new matters you need to acquire. In our example, we'll say that an average matter for you brings in $80,000. Considering your goal of $1 million in new originations, you would need to acquire 12.5 new matters (one million divided by eighty thousand).

Next, let's apply a "close rate" to estimate how much outreach may be necessary to generate the target number of new matters. Not everyone you speak to will end up working with you. The 'close rate' is the number of clients and prospective clients with qualifying work that you speak to that produces new engagements. I use an aggressive close rate of 20 percent, meaning that you expect to sign one new engagement for every five clients you talk to over time. If you think that you close new engagements at a higher (or more likely lower) rate in your actual calculations, you should, of course, use that rate. Divide the number of new matters you need by your chosen close rate.

In our example, 12.5 new matters divided by .20 (20 percent) equals 62.5 prospects you would need to reach out to achieve your originations goal. Of course, you can only reach out to this number of prospects if you have at least that many in your power grid. If not, you need to identify additional prospects or reduce the originations goal.

With a target number of prospects for your outreach, you can determine next how many conversations you will likely need to have with each to develop them in to a prospect. Typically, that number is 8 - on average. In other words, you will need to have eight conversations before an engagement opportunity comes up. Of course, this number will vary depending on the lawyer's reputation, the prospect's active legal needs, the strength of the connection, the urgency of the legal need, the degree of competition, and numerous other factors. But in general, 8 is an average number reported by a broad range of similar industries. So I think it is a good number to use in determining how many times you must contact a prospect to achieve your goals.

To estimate the total outreach activity you will need to do, multiply the number of outreaches per prospect (we are using 8) by the number of prospects you previously calculated (62.5). That totals 500 outreaches to generate one million dollars in new business. Divide that number by the number of weeks you will work in the year to get the number of outreach calls and meetings you need to do weekly. If you work 50 weeks a year, you'll need to maintain a pace of outreach each week to ten prospects. Now do you see why I had you collect the contacts for everyone you know? This level of activity requires you to do a lot of talking to a lot of different people.

Lastly, estimate how much time you will need for each typical outreach so that you can plan your schedule accordingly. I usually do this based on only making phone calls. You'll also have meetings you can credit to your outreach program but for now, focus on making the volume of calls you need to make. Remember to factor in time to prepare for the call or meeting, conduct the actual call or meeting, and follow up and record the details of the conversation. Perhaps that's 30 minutes per call. Thus, 500 times one-half hour equals 250 hours, or about five hours a week.

To sum up the steps for calculating your needed outreach:

1. Determine your originations goal.

2. Determine the average revenue amount per new matter. Divide that number into the originations goal to find the number of new matters you need to generate.

3. Divide your target number of new matters by your chosen close rate to determine how many prospects you need to reach out to.

4. Multiply the target number of prospects by 8 (or another appropriate number of outreaches per prospect) to determine the total number of outreach activities you need to perform during the year.

5. Divide the annual target of outreaches by the number of weeks you work to determine how many outreach activities you should conduct each week. Multiply that number by the average amount of time you think you will spend on each call or meeting to calculate how much time per week to set aside for outreach.

There you have it. It may seem daunting at first but at least you know what you need to do. You can plan for it and work at getting better and more efficient at making your calls. Focus on making the required calls every day. Focus on building the habit of calling and it will pay off. Over time, with repetition, it will become easier and you will get more effective. It will become second nature. It'll become just how you work.

Making The Call

For a long time, I thought making calls to people in my network was a simple process. I picked up the phone, made the call, and 'shot the breeze' with them. It was, I thought, an intuitive exercise. No one needed to teach me how to call someone I know. The purpose, I thought, was simply to keep my name fresh in their minds. As long as I made an effort to call, the conversation would develop as it was supposed to. I trusted myself to adapt and go with the flow, and I trusted the person I was calling to do the same. I almost always had good conversations.

It wasn't until later on that I realized that these calls weren't producing the results I wanted. So, I thought more carefully about how I was making my calls. I realized:

- I wasn't clear about what I was trying to achieve on the call.
- I didn't focus on the next incremental step I could take in the relationship.
- I wasn't prepared for the call and often learned things I should have known going into the call.
- I hadn't thought about how to manage the conversation so that it was short *and* productive, and
- I often felt like I got more out of the call than my callee. That didn't seem right.

I needed a call plan to help me prepare for the call, manage the call, and ensure that both people got something out of it. I realized I needed to plan the call better, set an objective for every call, and develop a format to follow that would ensure I included each of the most important elements of the call. Let's start with setting call objectives.

Setting Call Objectives

Now that you know how many people to reach out to, let's talk about what you want to accomplish in your calls. Call objectives define the purpose of your call. Every interaction with your power grid should have purpose. Setting an objective helps you focus on having a purpose for every outreach call. An objective not only helps you to determine why you are making the call but it helps you identify next specific action step to take in the relationship with your connection. Think about the action you would like your caller to take? Be as specific as possible.

Before each call or meeting, take a moment to think about the reason for making the call. There may be numerous purposes for your call. Think about which one or two would create the most benefit to you and/or your caller. Don't set more than one, or at most two, objectives for each call.

Your objective should be clear, simple, and achievable. It should be achievable for you in the sense that you can see how to manage the conversation to get to where you can accomplish the objective. And it should be achievable for your caller because it is something they can do or would want to know about.

Here are some examples to help you think about defining an objective for your calls.

I'm going to ask _____ for permission to send them my latest article.
I'm going to ask _____ to attend our CLE presentation in March.
I'm going to ask the name of the law firm doing their employment work.
I am going to ask _____ about the company's increasing debt to equity ratio.
I am going to ask _____ to introduce me to _____.
I am going to share my insight on the _____ case.
I am going to get _____'s opinion on the company's new chief legal officer.
I am going to ask for _____'s input on our proposal.
I'm going to ask _____ to explain the implications of their competitor's announcement that they are moving out of the _____ business.

While the idea of determining the purpose of your call may seem intuitive, thinking through the various reasons for making the call is worthwhile. It gives you a perspective on the quality of the relationship you have with that person. It enables you to select the best reason to call. That is, one that is most likely to advance the relationship. It helps you think more strategically about the relationship and, as such, how to structure the conversation to achieve your desired outcome. And it ensures that your call is adding value and accomplishing something substantive.

In part, the objective you set will depend on the level of familiarity with the person you are reaching out to. If you are not very familiar with them or their type of issues, your objective should focus on building a relationship and establishing trust. If you are familiar with the person but you don't know about their current projects, legal needs, and challenges, your objective can be to learn about the types of projects that person is working on and the needs and challenges arising from those projects. If you are very familiar with the person, the work they are involved in, and their current challenges and needs, your objective can be to identify potential resources, connections and solutions that you have that you can share with them.

Keep in mind that you do not want to get ahead of yourself or make a request that is not appropriate to the level of your relationship with that person. Relationships take time and can't be rushed. They are built by first establishing familiarity and later, trust and understanding. A request to be introduced to the person's boss, for instance, may be inappropriate in the early stage of a relationship. At other points, that introduction may seem long overdue.

By setting clear objectives before your call, you'll know immediately whether you've accomplished your objective by the time you hang up the phone. The call will have been productive if you have established a clear next step, gotten the information you needed, offered a way to help the other person, or deepened the relationship in some meaningful way.

Planning Outreach Conversations

You've determined the number of people that you need to reach out to each week and know how to set an objective for each connection you'll be speaking to. While it may be tempting to spontaneously pick up the phone or shoot out a quick email, spending a little time preparing for the call, meeting, or email exchange will make the outreach much more productive. The more you do this informal outreach planning, the easier it will become, and the less time it will take.

You can develop a conversation plan for your outreach by asking yourself the following five questions:

Question 1: What have I learned about the person I'm about to contact and their company since we spoke last? Write down the new developments you already know about them and their company. Do a quick internet search to see what else you can find out. Read any articles or blog posts the person might have recently written, and review their LinkedIn profile for any changes. Check the company website for news, and take note of any relevant information you come across. Make sure you are aware of significant financial and market conditions that could affect the company.

Question 2: Based on all I know about the person and his or her company, what can I surmise about their needs and challenges? Think about their legal needs and challenges as well as their non-legal needs and challenges. That is, think about the business generally and the challenges it faces.

Question 3: Having identified potential needs and challenges, what do I have to offer that would assist them in this area? Review your master list of connections for people to introduce to them, identify articles and white papers that they might find helpful, or think about the advice you could offer based on your skills, experience, and knowledge. Think of the ways that you may be able to provide value to them.

Question 4: What new information do I want to learn? Your contact may have access to information that you would be helpful. They may have insights and perspectives that you don't. They may be able to give you a better understanding of their company or the work they are doing. Or they know things about your competitors or the industry that you'd like to know. Jot down the questions you will ask and the information you would like to get.

Question 5: *How will I personalize the conversation?* Ask yourself what do the two of you have in common that can help establish rapport with a newer connection or reinforce or strengthen the bond you have with them. Or, if you know something about the person's family life or activities outside of work, you might start the conversation by asking about that. Letting the person know that you remember these important details about their life will demonstrate your level of caring and the attention you paid in prior conversations.

This may seem like a lot to think about prior to a call so I created a short cut that you can use to make sure you have what you need for the call and help you to manage the conversation during the call.

Share, Care, Pivot, and Plus Up

As I said, I use a simple, somewhat quirky, phrase to remind me of the four parts of the conversation that I should mentally prepare before making the call. 'Care, Share, Pivot, and Plus Up' is a checklist you can use to plan and guide your conversations. The '*Share*' and '*Care*' steps help you establish or re-establish rapport quickly. The '*Pivot*' prepares you to move to a focused business discussion that points you toward your call objective. The '*Plus Up'* reminds you to bring value to every conversation by offering one small piece of *value* that leaves them feeling that they benefited from speaking to you. Preparing all four in advance will provide a roadmap for the call and help to ensure the call is productive.

Your 'Care' is information about your contact that you use to demonstrate your interest in them. Ask about something you talked about or know about them, whether personal or professional. The point of the 'Care' is to demonstrate that you follow what they are doing. The 'Care' can be about their family, work, hobbies, recent news, etc. Try to avoid politics, religion, or bad news or experiences.

Before you call, ask yourself: *'How can I show that I care about them personally?'*

199

Sharing personal information makes you more interesting, more approachable, and conveys trust to the other person. Your share can be about anything that's going on in your life, either personal or professional. Share about your quarantine experience, news about your kids or hobbies, recent concerts or arts programs you've attended, or about professional developments such as a new boss, changes in the organization, new projects, etc. Think about what would be interesting to the contact.

Before you call, ask yourself: *'What can I share about myself that can make me more relatable or interesting to this contact?'*

Note: The 'Share' and 'Care' can go in any order depending on how the discussion develops. The point is simply to be prepared with both as you prepare your call.

The 'Pivot' is how you transition the conversation to your call objective or to a business-oriented discussion. Hopefully, your research has uncovered a topic that relates to their business and for which you have additional questions. Your pivot can also be used to focus the conversation on advancing the relationship. The point is to be aware of how you will pivot the conversation from the small talk to a more substantive conversation.

.

The key is to get as detailed as possible on a topic the executive is familiar with or should have interest in or concern about. The more specific and relevant the topic is, the better. In your research, look for recent articles, speaking engagements, company developments, competitive developments, legal issues, etc.

Before you call, ask yourself: *'What topic will transition the conversation to a business discussion?'*

'Plus Up' is the delivery of unexpected or added value in the call. This may be an invitation, an introduction, new information or insights, a referral, or other resource that the contact didn't have before you called. Before making the call, think about what you can offer to deliver a small exchange of value.

Being a sounding board also provides value. Ask about their work and challenges and *actively listen* to them. Probe gently for more information and offer suggestions when the timing and their receptivity to your suggestion seems welcome.

Before you call, ask yourself: *'What can I offer that will leave them feeling good about the call?'*

Know Your Contact

You probably already know a great deal about the people in your power grid. Even so, before making a call, update your knowledge of them. Check their LinkedIn profile for any recent activity, comments, posts, and new professional interests. Google their name for any recent news. Check your CRM system notes to see whether others in the firm have recently contacted the person. Look at their contact record to refresh your memory of what you know about them.

Review past call notes:

1. If you keep call notes (and you should), review your past calls.
2. Make a note of personal information they may have shared that you can bring up.
3. If the contact is shared with others in the firm, review any updates made to the CRM record.

Check other firm relationships: Check whether your firm has done work for the company in the past. If it has, who did the work, and what is the history of those relationships and matters.

Know The Company

In competing for work, expertise and experience are the table stakes for playing in the legal services game. But a deep understanding of the business, its operational culture, the internal politics, its industry, and how decisions are made inside the company is the type of information that gives you an unfair advantage when competing for work. Before making a call to a prospective client, make sure you know the company as much as you can.

At a minimum, you should know the size of the company, whether it is public or private, how many years the company's been in business, the number of employees, their locations, and its top executives. If you have time, it can also be helpful to know about their competitors, their key suppliers, and their business model (how they make money and what sets them apart).

Google the company for any recent news. Check the news releases on the company website and review their financials (if they are a public company). Look for substantive changes in operations, new projects, new leadership or ownership, emerging company issues, pending legislation, regulatory changes, or other business-related developments you can use in your call.

Check for industry developments or emerging trends. Review industry news sources and professional association websites for issues the company may be dealing with. *Be sure to consider the problems that other practice areas in the firm can address.*

Privately-owned companies do not share much information about their financial condition or operations. Even public companies only share what is required by regulators. The most valuable information is usually gleaned through conversations with those who know the company well, either because they currently work there or recently worked for the company.

Take some time to get to know the business managers and staff who work for the company and ask them about their areas of responsibility. Ask others who have experience with the company, such as other lawyers, former and current clients, competitors, former employees, the company's suppliers, and analysts. In doing so, you'll learn new perspectives and insights that you might not have from the company's top leadership.

Set up Alerts and Notifications

There's no reason you shouldn't know what is going on with your connections. Today, technology enables you easy ways to monitor news mentions, website or blog posts, social media, and case filings and transactions. Make use of these systems. Follow them on LinkedIn to get their posts and publications in your feed. Set up google alerts for each company in your Power Network and enter notification requests in your firm's legal research systems. Get these weekly to coincide with planning your calls for the week.

Reasons to Reach Out

Having a compelling reason to call makes reaching out to others easier and more productive. Think about the needs and your relationship with your prospects and referral sources. If you have been monitoring news mentions, press releases, and the cases and matters of the connections in your power network, you should get a steady supply of reason to reach out to at least half a dozen or more each week. Call those individuals where you can congratulate them, ask questions, or put things together and provide additional information or insights to them.

If you follow a schedule of the people you want to stay in touch with each week, set news alerts for industry updates to coincide with whom you will call each week. The alerts you get can be filed away in your contact management system for use when their names come up in your weekly call schedule. But for the others, you may have to think of a reason to call. When you get stuck for a good reason to call, I've created a checklist of ideas to get you thinking of your options. Make this part of your call planning process.

Make Introductions

Your connections are a treasure trove of reasons to call prospects and clients. Introducing people benefits all three people, making it something that should be a regular part of your outreach. Go through your contacts list to see who might benefit from knowing others in your network. Avoid random acts of introductions. Make sure you have a clear benefit for each person you intend to introduce.

Share Interesting Information

Your calls to your network of connections inevitably will unearth new information about the market or the company's competitors. This information can be helpful to clients, prospective clients, and referral sources. Keep notes of interesting facts, challenges, and solutions you hear in your discussions and share that information with your other connections.

Share Engaging Experiences from Similar Clients

Similarly, companies value learning about the challenges and solutions experienced by similar clients in the same industry. Those lessons can help prevent those problems from developing in their company. They'll be interested in what happened and how the issue was resolved. They may also be interested in your analysis of what might have prevented the problem in the first place.

Breaking Industry News

Keeping your prospects and clients informed of breaking industry news demonstrates your awareness of the issues they face and the challenges unique to their industry. Track the emerging issues developing in the prospect's industry and prepare a summary explanation of the risks and consequences of these issues.

Recent Results and Similar Situations

Every case and matter is different. Similarly, clients believe their business is unique. However, most of the cases and matters you'll work on have many similar aspects. You can share recent accomplishments and use them to learn more about the target's business. Focus on how the matter may relate to their business or the unusual issues you encountered. Describe how the issue came to be and how the company handled it. If the company has changed how it operates, describe the changes it put in place. Then, ask them how that issue or matter might have developed in their company. Would the same contributing factors be at play? Use similar situations to understand better the business of your prospect's company.

Upcoming Nearby Events

For clients and prospects in your geographic area, call about upcoming events that you think they'll find helpful. If they are going to the event, try to coordinate driving together or meeting up at the event.

Upcoming Online or Televised Events

Found a good training webinar or CLE source? Share it by calling your clients or prospects to let them know about the event. Invite them to your office for lunch or drinks and make it a watch party. See if others in the company will join you to create opportunities to meet new people in the company.

New Resources

Share the interesting online resources you find. Have you found a useful checklist or guide that you think your connections will find helpful? Share the new resource. Then call to get some feedback on it so you learn more about them and the types of resources they find beneficial.

Recent Publications

Lawyers and their firms regularly put out newsletters, case summaries, and client alerts. Rather than just emailing the information to them, make the call to ask whether you can share the information with them. Be prepared to explain why they should be interested in the information.

Recognition of a Significant Interview, Promotion, or Accomplishment

Has your client been mentioned for a recent promotion or achievement in the news? Have the newspaper clipping framed and give it to your client. Sending the framed news clipping can leave a lasting impression, one that they may see every day if they hang it in their office. Better yet, schedule an appointment to deliver it in person.

New Research or Statistics

Business people love facts. Research and statistics help managers make better decisions. Share the results of research and statistics you find relevant to their business or challenges. Consider doing your own research project on a topic important to them and their industry. Or you can report and comment on the implications of research from another source.

Changes in Pricing or Fee Arrangements

Changes in billing rates and new fee arrangements provide another good reason to connect with clients and prospects. If possible, always communicate these changes in person rather than informally through email or a letter. The inevitable questions can provide surprisingly fertile ground for new business development.

New Practice Area or Service Offering

Use the introduction of a new practice or new capabilities as a reason to connect with clients and prospects. Find out which firm handles this area for them today, what they value most in their offering and the most pressing issues in the business area. Be prepared to say how your firm's offering is unique and valuable.

New Feature or Procedure

New features of the firm (such as a client extranet service) or new procedures (such as a legal matter management process) can provide a good reason to reach out to clients and prospects. Learning the value that they put on these developments can provide insights for future negotiations while demonstrating the firm's commitment to improving its operations.

Value-Added Offering

The value-adds that you do for your existing clients (such as the complimentary review of an employee handbook) can be offered to prospects. Having done them for your current clients, you'll be able to provide them efficiently and at little cost to you. Leverage these services to build new relationships.

Seek Input or Advice

There are many parallels between businesses and professional services and much to learn and apply by observing and getting input from well-run businesses. Gain a new perspective on a project by seeking the advice of your connections on the changes in the firm. Letting clients and prospects in on how the firm operates can subtly garner commitment to the firm's success.

Request to Tour Operations or Visit Offices

Learning about your clients' and prospects' businesses can't be done from afar. You have to experience the environment to get a sense of the culture, the level of activity, and how things work. Most business managers and owners take pride in their business and make time to show off the offices or operations. Demonstrate your interest in their business by calling to ask for a tour, use their products or services, and ask to meet key business managers.

Pre-Publication or Speaking Input

Preparing an article or presentation? Ask clients and prospects about their experience in the issue, what advice they would share, and the examples they have experienced that can illustrate your points. Seeking advice is an excellent way to build relationships and gives you a good reason to follow up to share the results of your presentation.

Feedback or Client Satisfaction Survey

You probably think you know how the client feels about you, but unless you take the time to walk through all aspects of your service delivery, you are not likely to have a detailed understanding of how you can improve service levels to your client. If it is a prospect, a reverse client satisfaction call, in which you inquire about the various aspects of service levels that they have experienced with their current providers, can give you insights into how to position your services better. It may even sow the seeds of doubt about their current provider.

Changes in Firm Operations

Firms are constantly evolving in ways that add value to their client relationships. New leadership, changes in procedures, new technology, new training, and other internal developments will demonstrate that the firm is client-centered and adapting to marketplace changes.

New Attorneys

When you hire a new attorney, you've expanded your team. Most clients and prospects find this information valuable, especially if the lawyer brings unique expertise, new skills, adds to the reserve of talent, or gives access to new connections, similar companies, and influential people.

End of Year Call

The end of the year is a time when many businesses are reviewing their performance and trying to figure out what changes in personnel, projects, and budgets should be made for the coming year. This makes end-of-year calls an excellent time to learn about the company's most significant challenges and new initiatives.

Beginning of Year Call

The new year's start often brings new projects, new investments, and fresh resources for companies to deploy. Calls made at the beginning of the company's financial cycle can be timed to take advantage of a new list of projects and activities.

Mid-Year Call

Midyear is when many companies are reviewing and adjusting their plans and financials. It's a good time to discuss how the company is doing against its goals.

Update on a Competitor

If you monitor developments with your client or prospect's competitors, share what you learn from your monitoring with your clients and prospects. Provide analysis where possible and appropriate.

Permission to Add or Join

Call prospects and clients to get their permission to add them to your mailing list, join member-only online groups, or connect with them on social media. A quick phone call shows your personalized approach.

Opportunity to Co-Publish or Co-Present

Call clients and prospects to co-publish or co-present at seminars and conferences. Not only will you build a relationship working on the presentation, but you'll build credibility by presenting with a client.

Community Involvement

Reach out to prospects and clients to find out the important community or charitable issues for their companies. Then find a role, volunteer, or contribute to the cause to build a relationship with the target.

Follow-Up Strategies

"Fortune is in the follow up."
– Toya Powell, U.S. Black Chamber of Commerce

Consistent follow-up is critical to establishing a reputation as someone who gets things done. Doing what you say you'll do and doing it quickly makes a positive impression on others. Done consistently, you will be perceived as more reliable and more trustworthy. That reliability will lead to more opportunities and the chance to win new engagements.

More importantly, follow-up is required for business development success. You will not win a new client or get the engagement on your first and only contact with a prospect. (It may happen, but it is rare.) For many practice areas, it takes as many as eight to ten calls and meetings to land new business. With this level of contact required, follow-up from one conversation to the next is essential.

Follow up quickly

Anytime you commit to doing something, do it as quickly as possible. If you can't do it immediately, keep a record of it. Jot it on your calendar and put a tickler on it to remind you to follow up and what to do. It is best to follow up quickly while the situation is fresh in your mind. The better you become at follow-through, the more you position yourself as someone who gets things done.

Seize Clear Opportunities Boldly

People often hesitate to follow up on new opportunities. For instance, you may get a suggestion to approach someone influential in an industry. It's not uncommon for people to hesitate before pursuing a 'cold outreach' even though that new connection would be valuable. They ruminate and deliberate about their approach, what they'll say, or how the other person might perceive a cold approach from them. And in that time, the zeal to pursue that opportunity melts away. Taking action is a characteristic of great entrepreneurs and rainmakers. They seize opportunities boldly and confidently. It's better to take action and follow up on clear opportunities, even if it means being less polished than you'd like to be.

Send Hand Written Notes

Handwritten notes differentiate you from others by positioning you as a thoughtful and appreciative person that takes the time to go the extra mile. Notes are capable of engaging people on a deeper level than other forms of communication. They remind clients why they work with you and convey confidence about their future relationship with you. Handwritten notes establish connection by demonstrating a deeper level of care based on your willingness to take the time to write. People like to know they are thought of and valued. Handwritten notes not only accomplish this, but they also take it a step further by laying the foundation for a lasting relationship.

Research shows that even a handwritten Post-It note can make a big impression. In one study, researchers distributed three sets of questionnaires around the office. The first set included a handwritten Post-It note requesting completion of the survey. The second set got the same survey, with the request to return it handwritten on Page 1. Third group got the same survey with their name mentioned (in type) on page 1 of the survey. Response rates? 75%, 48%, 36%. People appreciated the personalized approach, and somehow even a Post-It note highlighted the extra work that someone did before sending out the survey.

Send Small, Uniquely Personalized Gifts

When you know your connections personally, it is easier to find ways to enhance that relationship by giving small, unique, personalized gifts. Small, inexpensive gifts that demonstrate how well you know an individual leave lasting impressions and build the foundation for stronger relationships. Make sure the gift reflects an interest or hobby, or otherwise connects you to them by relating to how you met or a common experience you have had together. Don't spend much money on the gift. You want to convey that you were thinking about them. The more expensive the present is, the more the gesture can be misinterpreted or cause your motivations to be questioned.

Here's an example. I'm a big Dave Matthews Band fan. So is someone I know in my industry. I'd really like to do work with his law firm. We've talked about the band and the concerts. So, when he wasn't expecting it, I sent him a 'Fire Dancer' car sticker with a handwritten note. In my note, I said, "I thought of you when I was getting souvenirs for my kids at the merch tent. Fantastic concert!" That's all. No selling or promises or requests. It was a simple, kind gesture for a person with whom I share a DMB love. It cost me a couple of bucks but was well worth it. Plus, it felt good to do it.

Following up consistently and, where possible, creatively is a core skill needed for building the value in your power grid. Pay attention to when and how quickly you follow up on things you commit to. Then look at how consistently you follow up to stay in touch with people in your network of connections. And lastly, think about how often you've sent gifts or done something creative to make a larger impression. Actively look for ways to make deeper impressions on the people in your power grid. And, of course, develop a system to ensure you follow up consistently any time you make a commitment.

7

Building Your Value Arsenal

Strive not to be a success, but rather to be of value.
-     *Albert Einstein*

Focus on Providing Exceptional Value

Value, like beauty, is in the eyes of the beholder. Your clients define what exceptional value means to them. That definition will change from client to client. Sometimes the client's perception of value is clear and well-defined and they can easily describe what value looks like to them. But more often, what clients report as valuable or good service is described in broad terms, such as 'they know my business,' 'they are proactive,' or 'they provide better service.' Those broad descriptions rarely give you the specific guidance necessary to deliver 'exceptional' service and value.

Clarifying what clients expect regarding service levels and what they might see as 'exceptional' service or value goes to the heart of delivering exceptional service. Consider including in your onboarding process steps to clarify what clients consider an expected level of service. Then, adjust the delivery of your services, if necessary, to exceed those expectations. These steps should be standard operating procedures for most lawyers. I don't think it is. In my experience, most lawyers assume that they deliver good service and never ask their clients what an exceptional level of service looks like to them.

There are four types of exceptional value. Clients will pay a premium for services when you deliver one of four following value drivers:

1. An unrecognized problem is identified
2. An unanticipated solution is determined
3. An unseen opportunity is revealed, or
4. The service provider serves as more than a provider of services but also as a broker of capabilities.

Delivering any one of these four drivers of exceptional value requires a deep understanding of the client's business and industry. That is, it requires an exceptionally thorough understanding of the client's business operations, financial and competitive environment. Lawyers today are just beginning to understand the importance of this level of understanding of their client's business. But analysts and investors have known the importance for a long time. They have developed monitoring systems, in fact, to watch for changes in the value drivers of a business in which they have invested. Law firms would be wise to do the same.

Ways to Provide Value to Your Network

Your outreach program should be designed to help others. That means you are constantly scanning your network for ways to deliver more value. Although we've discussed the importance of giving without the expectation of receiving anything in return, the fact is that when you reach out to your connections to provide something of value, it will very often create opportunities for new conversations, collaborations, and ultimately new business.

You may not have contemplated all of the ways that you can add value to a relationship. In this section, we'll look at the various ways, large and small, that you can add value to the connections in your power grid. Give these careful considerations to see how they might apply to your practice. Where appropriate, start a list that you can refer to as needed.

Information

The first way is by providing information that your connection may not have access to or know about. What you send should be relevant to them, it should be current information, and where possible it should provide a unique perspective. If possible, send the information along with your prediction of how an issue will likely develop over time. Project out the possible problems the issue could cause. Sending out projections enables business people to think ahead and avoid problems. They are conversation starters too because everyone can give their ideas about how the issue will develop and the problems that could be caused.

Another effective information strategy is News jacking. News jacking is just like what it sounds like it is. You monitor the news and hijack the topic for your own use. Choose topics that are business-related or relevant to their organization. Avoid political news, world events news, religious news until you know your connection exceptionally well. Create a news feed made up of the top publications in the industries that you serve and review it weekly for subjects that could spark conversation.

With a little thought, you should be able to identify the types of information that they will appreciate. This could be information that you or information taken from articles, books, or other writings that you can forward to them. Industry associations and professional consulting websites usually have a section where you can find the current thinking about various issues. You can search among adjacent industries, industries which are closely related or part of the same supply chain, to find more ideas for information to send to your connections.

Sometimes you'll provide information or content that your connection already has. That's OK. The mere gesture of offering information that you think the person would find helpful shows the person they are important to you and that you are looking out for them.

Insights

You can add value by offering your insight into various issues or problems based on your experience and expertise. Insights helps them better understand the dynamics of situations or issues and enable them to see them in a new way. These insights can be drawn from either professional or personal experiences and expertise. Your connections may not ask for your advice, but you may find opportunities to offer your insight if you listen attentively and ask the right questions.

Where appropriate, ask them what they are currently working on. Consider offering to review their draft or help them edit a document. Or give your thoughts on an article, speech, blog post, or another document they are working on. Most people will welcome the help and appreciate your interest in helping them look good!

Referrals

Providing referrals to other people in your network is another way to add value. If you hear of someone looking for a particular type of service, you can review your master list to see if you have a connection in that field and offer to make an introduction. Your referrals shouldn't be limited to professional pursuits. Consider making referrals that will help them personally as well. Keep a list of the people you know who provide common services, such as mechanics, realtors, physical therapists, accountants, doctors, etc. These referrals can be a tremendous help and can help strengthen your relationship with that person.

Introductions

Similar to referrals, you can introduce people within your network that share common interests or goals. Introductions cause more connections, which multiplies the value of your power grid. The more that the people in your network know each other, and create their own mutually beneficial relationships, the more powerful the network becomes.

There are other ways that you can offer value. The key is to think carefully about how your experience, knowledge, skills, interests, and relationships can benefit others. Then take the initiative to share what you have to offer to those you want to build strong relationships with.

A powerful network of connections is one of the most valuable assets you will develop both in your professional career and personal life. The more value you build into your network, the more it will produce solid results for you and your most important connections.

Create a Value-Add Inventory

In a competitive market, companies seek greater value. So do your connections. They seek new ways to approach solutions, greater competitive and market intelligence, and ways to make their jobs easier. Value is the great differentiator. But value is often a murky and misunderstood concept. To be sure, 'value' is in the eyes of the beholder. So, asking your clients what they value most will help you identify the levers of value in the relationship.

Know the People in Your Network
The most practical value you can inventory are the people in your network. The connections to people provide a tremendous value that you will draw on consistently. Knowing the people, where they work, which of your contacts are subject matter experts, their hobbies and passions, and their connections to other influential people will be useful.

Make Productive Introductions
Introductions are a win-win-win connection activity. The people being introduced win because they are making valuable new connections. And you win because you get the benefit of having connected the two. Your introduction of another person should prepare both people with what they need to know to move forward without you. They should have enough information that finding something to talk about is relatively easy. That means, a good introduction gives a person's name (duh), where they work or the role they play, how you know them or the history between the two

of you, and what is unique about each of them or what they offer in terms of a resource.

Here's an example:
"Bob, this is Sally Fricksen. Sally and I worked together at Cosmo Labs where Sally was my 'go to' person for anything related to artificial intelligence. She knows more about AI than anyone I know and she loves to talk about it.

Sally, this is Bob Craft. Bob and I were friends in high school and he did all he could to lead me down the wrong path, but man, was he fun. Bob is now the lead programmer at Border and Batch, working on Bio Metrics and eye scan technology. He has an uncanny ability to simplify the most complex issues so that anyone can understand them."

Obviously, making introductions of this level of quality requires you to know both individuals. But that's what good connectors do. They take the time to know people in their network well.

Invite Them to Entertainment, Meals, and Events

Sharing experiences and meals together builds strong bonds. Most people welcome the chance to meet new people, get to know each other, or enjoy sharing a hobby or interest together. These types of offers of value have numerous lasting benefits. Consider forming groups for regular get-togethers around poker, golf, crafting, wine tastings, or other shared interest. Consider trips, movies, or performances that combine entertainment and networking opportunities. Be creative.

Provide Training and Instructional Guides or Opportunities

Lawyers that provide ongoing Continuing Legal Education (CLE), training programs, and instructional guides provide value by shifting the task of providing this from the client to you. The training can be done by webinar, onsite at the client's offices, or in written form. Some lawyers provide training videos on a client extranet, ensuring the client gets the custom-designed training program's exclusive benefit. Learning Management Systems

(LMS) can be configured to deliver training to a company's personnel, allowing for easy reporting and management.

Share Competitive Intelligence

Lawyers often have access to resources and information that their clients do not have. You can draw on the experience you gained through years of working with similar, even competitor, companies. Identify the key competitors of your clients and do research on them to understand their strategic direction and competitive advantages. Monitor the media for updates about the competitors and provide regular updates to your clients on their activities, legal issues, and changes in financial position or personnel.

Provide Analysis or Research

Custom analysis or research can provide significant and unique value to a client. Use legal analytics to reveal the behavior and history of judges and their ruling tendencies and insights into opposing counsel, prospects, and clients' litigation history. You can leverage state trial court and verdict data to be more efficient, more proactive, and achieve better results for your clients.

One law firm undertook a national analysis of all the wage and hour decisions in the U.S. circuit courts and an analysis of each judge's historical decisions. This gave the national retail client an exceptional tool to evaluate each jurisdiction, make better venue decisions, and prepare for each judge's tendencies and litigation history they had cases before.

Research can also set you up as an authority in a topic. When you produce research or a white paper that delves deeply into a subject, you can share parts of it with the general public and keep the more significant findings for the exclusive benefit of your best clients.

Spot Issues for Them

Businesses are constantly on the lookout for issues that could present challenges or opportunities for the company. Issue spotting is the process of monitoring industry news, legal matters, and business trends to identify emerging issues and opportunities that could affect a client's business. Set up Google alerts to monitor when the issue's keywords are mentioned on the internet. You can also gain insights into emerging issues through conversations with the partners in your firm who have clients in the same industry.

Offer Process Improvement

There's no question that clients are focused on increasing the efficiencies in every aspect of the business. This is no less the case in their management of litigation, large transactions, and the handling of their legal issues. Checklists, guides, and tracking systems can help improve the effectiveness of a department and the efficiency of the work. A checklist or guide developed for one client can often be revised and offered to other clients, making the initial effort to create the checklist more productive.

Conduct Planning Sessions or Provide Plans

Well-crafted plans provide exceptional value. Plans demonstrate to clients a commitment to accomplishing the client's goals on time and on budget. Many lawyers meet annually or quarterly to look at the upcoming year or quarter and help clients plan for the anticipated work. Plans come in many varieties and can be done for training, legal work, talent onboarding, expenses, and many other purposes.

Help with Recruiting and On-Boarding

Finding the right fit for a position can be a challenge. In the legal area, outside counsel can be particularly helpful in finding and introducing potential candidates to fill open positions. They can also help write job descriptions, interview or vet candidates, assist in orientations, or help with onboarding the new hire.

Offer Secondments and Reverse Secondments

Secondment is the assignment of a member of one organization to another organization for a temporary period. The employee typically retains their salary and other employment rights from their primary organization but they work closely within the other organization to provide training, a liaison between the two companies, and the sharing of experience. Reverse secondments are similar but place the client's executives at the law firm.

Business and legal departments often face a temporary shortage of help. Law firms can provide exceptional value to their clients (and themselves) by temporarily placing staff in the client's business. Both strategies provide experience for the individuals being placed. The practice adds lasting value because the placed executive learns new systems and processes, understands the culture and business imperatives of the client better, and often expands the relationship within the host firm. Even one day spent in a client's office can add significant, lasting value.

Share Technology and Software Tools

There are many ways to use technology and support personnel to add value to a client. The firm's technology can assist with regulatory compliance, patent filings and renewals, and data and case management. You can configure Learning Management Systems (LMS) to deliver training to client personnel, monitor progress, and report results. Some also have the ability to deliver webinars to co-teach CLE with clients. Some firms set up extranets and war rooms for large projects, and the Firm's CRM systems and mailing systems can help manage contacts and email programs. Think broadly of how you can use the firm's resources to deliver more value to your clients.

Use Their Products or Services and Promote Them

Businesses are always on the lookout for ways to market their company. And you could be an avenue for them that they hadn't considered. Whether using your client's products or services, developing a co-promotion, or simply promoting your client's business, aligning their sales and marketing goals with your own can be a win-win.

Provide Insights and Thought Leadership

Some insights and thought leadership can be shared to add value to the client relationship. Once you know the issues your client is most concerned about, you can develop thoughts about how your clients can better understand what the future holds for them. You can also provide competitive intelligence to your clients and prospects to help them better understand competitive trends, strategic moves, and changes in locations or executives. Consider sending articles you've found on both personal and professional shared interests. Catalog all of the issues the client will likely face and develop an editorial calendar to regularly address each issue in client alerts and memos.

Provide Investigative or Research Services

Law firms are well-positioned to provide investigative or research services for their clients. That could be things as simple as basic legal research or conducting surveys and studies to full-fledged investigations and research projects to help inform company decisions. It could be as simple as interviewing a candidate for an open legal department position or offering to provide reports using the firm's research technology.

Give Them Anonymity

Sometimes companies need a way to interact in the marketplace without their competitors or customers knowing who is behind the request or inquiry. Law firms are unique in their ability to protect or shield the company's name in situations where anonymity may be desirable. Whether receiving resumes for top executives, conducting research, or requesting public records, law firms can provide the anonymity clients need to accomplish their goals.

Curate Content for Them

Who can read everything they need to read on every subject they need to monitor? No one. So curating content on topics of high interest to your clients is a way to make their jobs easier and their loyalty to you more secure. The more customized the content to your contact's personal and professional interests, the better. Use a Kiplinger's Report approach by summarizing each news article to make it easier and faster to read.

Support Their Community Initiatives

Your business clients have charitable and community causes that they feel strongly about. Align a portion of your community involvement and charitable giving to fulfill your client's community objectives.

With a little thought and effort, you will be able to select several items that you can have to use in your calls each week.

8

Tips for Connecting Effectively

"We cannot seek achievement for ourselves and forget about progress and prosperity for our community... Our ambitions must be broad enough to include the aspirations and needs of others, for their sakes and for our own."

– Cesar Chavez

Tips for Productive Conversations

Your outreach should be done with purpose. Every call, every visit, every interaction with your power grid connections should have an objective and be done with intention. Calls that do not have a specific purpose may be perceived as unnecessary or waste your connection's time. Use these tips to help you improve the quality and productivity of your outreach efforts.

Master Small Talk

According to Wikipedia, small talk is defined as 'polite conversation about unimportant or uncontroversial matters.' Small talk warms people up for more weighty discussions. It enables people to talk and get a sense of the person's mood and their conversational aptitude. It gives people a chance to gauge another person's reception to having a dialogue.

Small talk helps to establish the tone and vibrancy of the discussion going forward. The setting can be determined quickly, within a few back-and-forth exchanges. For time-constrained executives and busy lawyers, try to keep the small talk to a minute or two. The best topics for 'introductory small talk are the weather, holidays, and traffic, mostly because those topics are generally safe subjects for everyone to talk about.

Some small talk can also help gather information about the other person. Discussion topics may venture more deeply into family events and activities, travel interests, sports, or musical interests. But don't be afraid to be more creative in how you engage people in conversations. If you've done a good job keeping track of your contacts family, friends, hobbies, and activities, you should also use those for making small talk.

Keep in mind the meeting after the meeting. There are small talk opportunities available after the meeting has ended. Post-meeting conversations can be an excellent time to get more personal information, confirm how and when you will follow up on the meeting, and suggest next steps or social get-togethers.

But the best topics for small talk are those that bridge a person's thinking with their work. Business trends and perplexing issues are also good ways to engage people in discussion in more engaging areas than the normal domains of small talk. You can say something like, 'I was listening to an NPR broadcast on artificial intelligence. Which parts of your work could be done by robots?' As you listen to the news, your favorite podcasts, or read the community paper, ask yourself which topics might make for good conversation starters. Look for mildly controversial, interesting topics that won't implicate a person's political or religious beliefs.

Play the Name Game

Most people forget names almost immediately after being introduced. That can be embarrassing for your new friend making them uncomfortable and often distracting them from the conversation. You can make it easier to remember your name by anchoring it to a mental image or familiar phrase. For instance, I introduce myself like this: 'Hi I'm Eric Dewey, Like Huey, Louis, and Dewey'. By mentally connecting it with something they are already familiar with, they have a second tool to retrieve your name later on. If it's a complicated or hard to pronounce name, offer a shortcut or nickname. Sometimes you can even make a joke of it, which also helps provide access to your name later on.

Never assume people remember your name no matter how familiar their greeting. Try to work your name into the conversation a second or third time in the first conversation with them. After that, remind them of your name the first two to three times you meet them again later.

Remain Present
It's easy for our minds to wander when someone else is speaking. There are many things to distract us when we are talking with others in public spaces. Activity in the room, loud noises, and even our pressing to do list can divert our attention from the speaker. Even in private conversations, we can become distracted and stop being engaged in the conversation.

The human mind picks up on other humans' expressions, sounds, and body language in ways that are hard to comprehend. We don't miss a thing. We form impressions almost immediately and confirm those impressions throughout our conversations. That often happens at a subconscious level. When you are no longer 'present' in the conversation or become disengaged, your body and facial expressions speak loudly. You want the person to leave your conversation feeling like they were heard, appreciated, respected, and that you were present throughout your discussion.

To stay present and engaged:
1. Look the other person in the eyes.
2. Respond to what they are saying by nodding and affirming their words. If you're distracted by something going on in the room, acknowledge the distraction.
3. Re-engage with the person.

Sprinkle In Personal Information
As the Share, Care, Pivot, and Plus Up call formula indicates, sharing something personal about yourself helps to humanize you

and makes you more authentic. Most people have hobbies, interests, or enjoy sports and travel. Any of these activities are good areas to share about yourself.

As an example, I'm a musician and am very involved in bringing music to my town. I've met more musicians by finding ways to mention my interest in music in all types of conversations. Slipping your interests into the conversation reveals tidbits that they can bring up later. And it shows that you have other interests outside of work.

Of course, you do not want to share information that is too personal or might make the other person feel uncomfortable. You should avoid discussing marital problems, health issues, politics, religion or spiritual beliefs, anything that might be negatively perceived and anything that discusses race, ethnicity, and other sensitive topics. Hold off on these topics until your connection is strong and you understand each other's characters and values.

Forget the Elevator Pitch

Do you have a 30-second elevator speech? Too often marketing professionals teach lawyers to sell themselves with brief, crafted and rehearsed statement about what they do for a living or how they solve the world's problems. Often, they are instructed to insert this in the first few minutes of meeting someone or anytime they are asked what they do for a living. They want a crisp and compelling description of their work that they can deliver in the short time it takes to rise to the next floor in an elevator – hence the name. I disagree with this. It strikes me as odd when it has happened to me. They came off as fake, or at least overly coached.

How many times have you used it if you've been through the elevator speech boot camp and developed an elevator pitch? How many truly good rainmakers do you know that have learned to pitch their services in three sentences or less? The complexity of legal advice and counsel can rarely be reduced to a few well-crafted sentences. And anyway, if you are speaking to the type of sophisticated buyers who can retain your services, they don't need your elevator speech.

So, you ask, how do you respond to 'What do you do for a living?'
Simple. "I am a lawyer. I help people and companies by
_____." Enough said. Keep it simple.

Avoid Creating Pressure

It doesn't take much to be perceived as 'salesy'. A poorly-timed
question, over-confidence, or too much enthusiasm can sour your
prospect on you. Being perceived as 'salesy' can create obstacles to
winning the engagement. Fortunately, it's easy to avoid being
'salesy'. Simply, avoid creating sales pressure.

Sales pressure (also called selling pressure) is often the result of
manipulative tricks designed to increase the pace of the sales cycle.
It is that uncomfortable feeling buyers get when they feel
manipulated, not heard, or pressured. A buyer who says, 'I feel like
I was being sold' is a sure sign that the prospect experienced sales
pressure.

Sales pressure is created when salespeople use conventional sales
techniques to persuade prospects to buy their services. Most
lawyers do not intend to create sales pressure. Sales pressure is
experienced by the buyer, most notably when they feel pressured
to do something or commit to an engagement. It rarely achieves its
purpose but almost always makes relationships feel adversarial.

You can avoid creating sales pressure by learning to avoid these
common mistakes.

Too Many Discovery Questions.
While discovery questions are necessary, too many inquiries can
feel overwhelming, especially if they are asked in rapid succession.
The tone of your questioning is also important. You want to avoid
the prospect feeling interrogated by the questioning. Discovery
conversations should be balanced and interactive. You should
listen more than you ask and watch for signs that the prospect is
growing uncomfortable. Avoid asking questions that are too

intimate for the level of your relationship. Your questioning style should make the buyer feel relaxed and comfortable.

Using Leading Questions.

Leading questions are used to establish a position that is difficult for the prospect to reverse. It is a question that prompts or encourages a desired answer. They sometimes come in sequences of questions that are strung together to get the desired result. Once the prospect senses the path of the leading question, it creates a sense of manipulation. Even if you are successful, prospects will resent feeling cornered and manipulated. Avoid using leading questions.

Asking to Meet with Higher Ups Too Early

It may be necessary to include superiors in your discussions. However, asking to meet with them too early in the relationship or before the prospect trusts you will create sales pressure. Let the person initiate introductions to others in the company. To encourage these introductions, say 'At some point, when you feel its best, I'd love to meet some of the others in your department.' Your contact in the company will introduce you when the time is right.

Overly Persistent Contact

Persistence is a quality of the best salespeople. However, dogged persistence creates sales pressure and feels 'salesy'. The frequency of contact you make with your prospect can influence their perception of you. Contacts made too frequently can create an impression that you are not busy or not in demand. It may even create the erroneous perception that you are desperate for work. Be respectful of your contact's workload and pressures. Make sure you have a good reason to call – one that your contact will also think is a good reason- and call when it is most convenient for your contact. Ask them, 'when do you prefer to be reached by phone?'

Unreasonable Demands or Deadlines

Prospects have their own schedules for the time it takes to make decisions. As much as we'd like to think that setting a deadline for someone else is helpful, most people prefer to work within their own timeframes. Arbitrary deadlines create pressure. Instead, ask how much time they need before you should reach out again. Let them set the pace for the conversation.

Asking the Wrong 'Why' Questions

Be careful when asking 'why' questions. Why questions tend to examine the rationale of decisions. They can carry the implication of personal responsibility that is not helpful in a sales discussion. It may be important to understand why a decision was made or why a course of action was taken. But when so, couch the question as a decision by the company rather than the individual. Ask "Why did the *company* decide not to include consultants in its training program?" rather than "why did *you* decide not to use consultants in your training program?" Try to avoid implying blame or responsibility in discovery conversations.

Fortunately, most lawyers don't come off as 'salesy'. But you don't have to be a salesy type to create sales pressure. Reducing sales pressure can help you build relationships and trust more quickly. And that will lead to new engagements.

Connecting in Conversation

Building rapport in conversations is not something most people think about. But success comes from planning and practice. That advice is no less true for your conversations. When you act intentionally, authentically, and stay present in the conversation, you will build rapport. And those positive and memorable conversations will lead to behave the part you want, and believe in yourself great things happen.

Be Creative in Describing What You Do

Don't just tell people, engage people in what you do for a living. Be creative. For example, one attorney I know describes his M&A practice this way: I re-design companies by co-mingling cultures, financials, and products. Or, a state tax planning lawyer I know jokes: 'I ensure my clients only feed the state its recommended daily dosage'. People only know generally what lawyers do. They don't know the specific details of the legal work. And a lot of them won't be interested in that level of detail. Don't confuse them and bore them to death in your explanation. Keep it light and memorable, and use humor when appropriate.

Learn to Pause

There may be nothing in speech as powerful as a pause. Silence adds emphasis. It encourages others to speak. Most people can't bear more than a couple of seconds of silence in a conversation. And a pause can demonstrate that you are listening actively and considering your response carefully. Pauses can be used by both speakers and listeners in conversations. They can slow the pace of the discussion, help you to pivot to new topics, and prompt the speaker to clarify their statement. Pauses that create uncomfortable silence are an effective conversational, and even negotiation, tool. Think about how you can use a pause in conversations and presentations. Practice using them until you become comfortable and can use them to great effect. You'll quickly see how useful a pause can be.

Be the Last to Speak

Have you ever found yourself among a small group of people talking about a topic that everyone seems to have an opinion about? In this situation, allow others to weigh in on the topic first. Those first with an opinion often times will appear dominant or like know-it-alls. Speak last or even wait to be asked your opinion. Waiting to be asked your opinion creates anticipation. And it can focus the other listeners on what you are about to say. Not only will you have had time to formulate your thoughts and opinions better, but it will carry more weight and appear more reasoned and thoughtful.

Pupils Are the Windows on The Mind

A person's pupils expand and contract depending upon their thoughts and how engaged they are in a conversation. When a person's pupils are large and remain large, they are interested and engaged in what you are saying. Conversely, when the pupils get smaller, the person has lost interest, their brain is overloaded, or their mind may be wandering.

But don't stare at your prospect's pupils too long. Looking into someone's eyes for longer than 5 seconds will make most people feel uncomfortable.

Don't 'Phub' Your Partner

Looking at your phone, even having it within reach on the table, can impact the quality of your conversations. Researchers looked at the impact of snubbing your conversation partner to look at your phone. It's called 'Phubbing.' (Yeah. They have a name for it).

A study of 145 married and partnered couples found that 46% had been 'phubbed' by their partner. And 23% said this phubbing caused conflict in their relationships. If phubbing affects the relationships of married people, surely it has an even greater ability to sour fledgling business relationships.

Examples of 'phubbing' include:

- My partner places their phone where they can see it when we are together.
- My partner keeps their phone in their hand when they are with me.
- My partner glances at their phone when talking to me.
- If there is a lull in our conversation, my partner will check their phone.

We're probably all guilty of phubbing conversation partners at some point. But some people do this much more than others. Unlike with a spouse, the problem is that you're not likely to hear about it from your conversation partner. They will make a mental note of your rudeness. It will make it harder to build a good relationship with that person. Looking at or picking up your phone while in conversation signals that you are not engaged in the conversation or interested in the topic. Whether or not that is true, you don't want to create that impression. Leave your phone in your pocket or purse, turn it on vibrate, and be present in your conversations.

Keep Epic News to Yourself

It's tempting to open a conversation with a prospective client with a tale of your vacation to Tahiti. You had a wonderful time, the weather was beautiful, and Tahiti is an exotic place few people get to visit. Who wouldn't want to hear about your epic vacation?

It turns out that most people don't. Epic tales (a large purchase or exotic vacation, for instance) are extraordinary. To be extraordinary is to be different, and social interaction is grounded in similarities. This may seem counterintuitive but social research backs this up. Participants in a recent study thought that sharing their extraordinary experiences would make for an engaging conversation. But in fact, the opposite happened. The people being told about the extraordinary experience felt more distant and less able to relate to them.

Do Not Over Polish

Promote yourself sparingly. And when you do, be authentic. Make sure the achievement you are promoting is truly significant and substantively adds to your reputation. But keep it short and specific. Long, drawn-out explanations of your accomplishment run the risk that you'll bore your listener or create the impression that you are self-absorbed. Let them ask for more information if they are interested in hearing more.

Make Your Accomplishments About Them

Strike a balance between sharing meaningful accomplishments with 'wearing out your welcome' by adopting the client's point of view when deciding whether or not to promote an accomplishment. Do this by asking yourself, 'What value, benefit, or new capabilities does this accomplishment convey to my clients?' It is most likely just empty self-promotion if you cannot think of how your client would benefit from this information. If you have an accomplishment you want to share, make sure you explain the benefit to your clients.

For instance, if you were named a Super Lawyer, you can mention the award and add, 'which means others in your company will have objective evidence that you are using top legal talent.' Find a benefit for the client so that you are not just promoting yourself but promoting the benefits to your clients.

Never Poke an Open Wound

Gossip, innuendos, rumors, or unsubstantiated claims are like open wounds. Each person who passes along the information pokes the wound and irritates it more. Wounds take a long time to heal when they are constantly poked, prodded, and kept raw. The reactions to poking a wound and passing along gossip are the same: It is fascinating to watch but the respect you feel for the poker is diminished. One can't help but wonder if you had the wound, would the poker poke it too. Poking leaves a bad impression. Avoid poking open wounds.

Stay Positive

The world is full of negativity. The news and our culture seem to exist on a diet of fear, gossip, rumors, and conspiracy. Negativity gets the headlines. But it also brings the spirit down. Never say anything negative about the competition, former or current employers, peers, friends, family, politicians, or religious people. Instead, always look for something positive to say. Maintain a positive, upbeat attitude and people will be attracted to you. The rarity of a consistently positive outlook attracts people and can be contagious.

I worked for a managing partner once who was relentlessly positive - almost to the point of it being ridiculous. When you asked him how his day was going, he'd say, 'It's perfect. 'How are you doing, Ed?' 'I'm perfect.' Or, 'how was your evening, Ed?', he always responded the same way, 'It was perfect'. We joked about his insistent, sunny disposition, but it was infectious. And we loved him all the more for it.

Peel The Onion

Clients don't buy services. They buy solutions. Finding the root cause of a problem is critical to determining a comprehensive solution. While many will say that the solution is winning a case or successfully completing a transaction, the 'value creating' answer is often not so obvious. Providing true value to clients means that you are looking out for their interests and understanding the circumstances and factors that contributed to the situation. Legal solutions should not only solve problems but improve how the company operates, serves customers, or gets better results. Make your solution a total solution, not just a technical one. Learn how to ask questions that uncover company needs, risks, and the various ways problems affect the company's operations, culture, or clients.

Refine Your Questions

The prevailing wisdom in legal sales techniques is to compile a list of questions to ask clients or prospects about their companies to learn their 'pain points', what's important to the company, and the industry trends that are 'keeping them up at night.' They are presented as 'discovery' questions designed to learn how you can best help the company. But, are these questions really the best way to discover needs? Do they communicate interest in the company and demonstrate respect for the prospect's time? I don't think they do. I believe that what makes the best impression is questions that are developed from researching the company.

Routine Versus Relevant Questions

I've been on the receiving end of generic, routine questions. From experience, I can tell you that routine questions lead to poor impressions. Standardized and rehearsed questions create the feeling that you are just a sales target. Not a unique, complex, and dynamic organization. It quickly becomes evident that there was little time spent researching me, my company, or my industry. My fear, and this is a compelling fear, is that I will have to educate this salesperson in order for them to sell me better. The more of these types of questions asked the quicker I begin to fidget and look for ways to get out of the meeting.

What prospects respond to best are questions designed to clarify the research you've conducted on my business. Instead of asking questions that can apply to any company's business, ask questions specifically relevant to your prospect's business. That requires research and analysis of the client's business. But these questions are more likely to lead to real issues that the company faces.

Here's an example to clarify the difference between routine and relevant questions.

Generic question: "What types of patent issues are you most concerned about today?"

Company relevant question: "Your competitor has had difficulty in getting patents protected in several foreign countries. What are you doing to protect your intellectual assets in Malaysia, China, and Taiwan?"

The more customized the questions, the more the prospect is likely to get something out of the discussion and the greater the impression you make that you understand their business and are ready to hit the ground running if they award you work. Demonstrate your investment in understanding their business and you will gain credibility and trust more quickly.

Probe Effectively

Probing for more information is an important skill to learn. Probing with effective questions can reveal information and insights that you can't get in any other way. It encourages people to share more detailed information and reveal issues that they may not have thought about.

Probing techniques can be simple. A favorite probing technique of mine is to ask the AWE question. AWE stands for 'And What Else?' Once you've established the cause of the issue you are examining, ask 'and what else' two or three times to probe for more details. That will prompt your partner to think through more of the issues and implications and give you a richer body of information to work with. You can also ask, 'is there more I should know or that may be relevant?' You'll be able to sense when you've probed enough by watching their body language and listening carefully to their responses.

Talk to Strangers

On a one-hour flight I met one of the most successful plaintiff's attorneys in the state of Florida. At the bar of a Colorado restaurant, I met the first female managing partner of a large Denver law firm. In the subway, I met the head of the litigation department for a large global law firm. You never know who you will meet if you don't talk to strangers. Strike up a conversation. Be curious about people. Interesting people are all around you. Take the time to notice them and inquire about them.

You also can't tell a person by how they are dressed, their jewelry, or game they are playing on their phone. I've met senior partners in law firms that had long hair, leather bracelets, and smelled for pot. But conversations with them ended up being fascinating. I've never regretted talking to a stranger. And you won't either.

Connecting Inside the Law Firm

For most lawyers, connections inside the firm are the most significant source of new work. Typically, three to five lawyers will send you work or ask you to work on their matters. But many firms today are spread across a large geographic area. Practice groups can become siloed and insular. Regardless, the partners in your firm are a rich source of potential referrals. Developing the broadest network of connections inside the firm is well worth the effort. Your partners are also a force multiplier for your practice.

It's not difficult to develop relationships with the other lawyers in your office. You are around them enough that those relationships can develop naturally. But developing strong relationships with lawyers in different offices can be a bit more difficult. It takes more of an effort on your part. But, again, it's worth the effort.

Hunting Parties

One strategy is to create a core business development group of partners from complementary practice areas with whom you collaborate to build your collective practices. By collaboration, I'm describing a support group in which you meet regularly, share information, and help one another improve each of your practices' marketing and business development. While the result may end up being cross-promotional opportunities among your respective client lists, set the expectation early on that the greatest benefit is in the accountability, creativity, strategic group thinking, brainstorming, and camaraderie that this type of group offers. Everyone can deliver on that, and everyone will benefit from that.

Identify partners in synergistic or complementary practices to your practice that reside in other offices, preferably in your time zone. Synergistic practice areas are those groups in which a typical company's everyday needs often overlap or complement the practice areas.

Identify attorneys in those practice groups who have growing books of business but do not have your practice area represented in their officers. If that's not available, look for attorneys with significant client relationships with the types of companies in which you would like to work. Reach out to them, explain what you would like to do by forming a business development group, and ask them to whom they typically send your type of work. If there is no one, or those relationships are not strong, ask about their interest in collaborating with you.

Look for partners in other practices who don't have someone like you easily available. If they don't have someone, focus on building a relationship with them, explaining your practice, experience, and value proposition. Explain to them that you are developing an informal referral or business development group and that you'd like to meet for 30 to 60 minutes once a month (or once a quarter) to share information about your clients, new developments in your practice area, and share market intelligence with them. Most lawyers will be amenable to joining an informal group of six to eight lawyers to talk regularly about client development.

Creating a Practice Highlights Cheat Sheet for Your Partners

No one knows your practice as well as you do. At the same time, it's hard to be objective and see your practice from a potential client's perspective. Moreover, companies value different things when they consider new counsel to bring in. And there is no way to know what a company values working two degrees away from them through your partner. The best you can do is to give your partners compelling bullet points describing your most impressive work and the value you deliver in the various aspects of legal services.

The Practice Highlights Cheat Sheet summarizes your experience, service, and client work with a few memorable, relatable examples that your partners can use to spark interest in you. The objective is to identify the buying triggers that a client might say and the associated response you want your partner to give. In writing this for your selected partners, remember this 'call and response' objective when describing your experience, benefits, and expertise.

Answer every question in the highlights cheat sheet. Be brief and concise. List only the most impressive or substantial pieces of information. This is different from your bio or CV. You will use the information to create a referral or pitch script. Fewer, more powerful points are more memorable and more likely to be used. Think about how a conversation might evolve and what words or activities should trigger your partner's suggestion that you be brought into the conversation.

Once completed, go back through and prioritize each entry in terms of which are the most impressive. Force yourself to rank each one. Where two seem equally impressive, consider how the client might view them. Make number one the most impressive from the client's perspective. Stay objective. Once you have prioritized each entry within each section, go through the entire document and prioritize each section to come up with the two or three items that are the most impressive of your highlights.

Next, write a referral script for your partners. Keep it to two or three of your biggest achievements, and keep it concise. Don't worry about qualifying any achievements or explaining the circumstances. Explanations can come later. You want to generate interest in yourself. The referral script's only purpose is to get your client's agreement to meet your partner.

Follow this format:
- Introduce yourself
- Briefly describe your most exceptional case or matter. Name the clients if possible and if they enhance credibility.
- State what made this case note-worthy.
- Give an example of a value-added service you have done for your clients.
- Describe the attorney's most impressive influence, position or thought leadership
- Conclude with a choice of three dates and times that the client can choose from for a meeting.

Example:
[Attorney name] is an IP lawyer who recently won a $2.6 million verdict against [name company] for infringement on a chemical component of their bug spray. Two other firms failed to win an infringement decision on that same issue. She also recently re-organized [name company] 's international trademark monitoring portfolio, saving them 35% and speeding the renewal process by six weeks while ensuring there's no lapse in fillings for the company. She is a former Patent Office Regulator and chairs the ABA's IP section. I think she'll have some great ideas for your company and she'd be an excellent resource to know. I want to introduce her to you.

Lastly, share the completed cheat sheet with select partners to familiarize them with your practice and marketing.

Brevity is the key to writing your highlights cheat sheet. Keep your answers brief, compelling, and prescriptive. For example, matter experience should be kept short like this: "Mike led due diligence on Pfizer's $11.6 Billion acquisition of Biohaven Pharmaceutical" versus broadly stated like this: "Michael has represented several different private equity clients in numerous acquisitions in the energy industry, as well as in the food, restaurant, beauty care, and other consumer categories, as well as in the subsequent follow-on acquisitions, public offerings, and dispositions; and he has worked as lead counsel on many equity and debt public offerings on behalf of issuers and underwriters."

It may seem obvious, but attorneys write differently than they speak in casual conversations. Write your responses as if they were being spoken. Read your final draft out loud and listen to how it sounds. It should feel conversational and understated.

Remember, the highlights cheat sheet is meant for personal one-to-one conversations with existing clients. Trust your partner's discretion in whom and how much of this information to share with their client.

Practice Highlights Cheat Sheet

Introduction:
Describe your work style and practice in two to three sentences. This is an introduction to you and should include the most notable highlights of your career to date.

Value Proposition Statement:
(If you do not have a value proposition statement, see chapter four for an exercise to build your value proposition.) This statement captures in one to two sentences the essence of your practice and how you provide value to clients.

Areas of Special Expertise:
List any niche practice areas or legal specialties—the fewer and more specific, the better. Describe the unique solution you offer and what conditions a partner should look for among their clients to recognize the challenges you can help them with.

Key Clients and Industries:
List your top two to three clients and the top two to three industries in which you have significant experience or substantive knowledge.

Desired Client Profile:
Profile your ideal client by listing the company size, phase of growth, number of employees, industry sector, regulatory issues, capital needs, technology use or needs, issues faced, etc.

Buying Triggers:
List the words and phrases that attorneys should listen for in their conversation, which may indicate client needs in your practice area. These are the buying triggers. List a company's activities, events, or problems that indicate a need for your services.

Personal Service Commitment:
Describe your commitment to client service in one to two sentences. It could include accessibility (even after regular business hours), a commitment to responsiveness within a specified time frame, returned calls/e-mails, a commitment to staying within budget, or other service-related commitments.

Key Client Results and Case Studies:
Give brief examples of the results you have achieved for clients, including those resulting from service delivery, legal strategies, operational efficiency, and other results. Where possible, assign a monetary value to the results. Who are the most impressive companies or roles in companies that rely on your expertise and experience?

Thought Leadership:
1. List two or three topics in which you consider yourself an expert or highly knowledgeable.
2. Make a note of the most-read publications and the channel where they can be found.
3. List the publications and articles written in the past year, speaking engagements, and other evidence of thought leadership.

4. Choose articles that demonstrate a unique area of expertise and published in the most respected journals.

Unique Access, Influence, or 'Clout':
List the relationships, organizations, past positions, associations, or clubs that grant you unique and exclusive access to individuals who can influence or assist in some issues. *Previous work inside regulatory agencies, inside companies, and with influential judges can have an overweighted influence on the outside counsel selection process.*

Unique Value-added Services Offered: Describe ways you add value to client relationships. These could be training programs, complimentary services, special publications, special industry knowledge, project management, or unique activities that provide additional value and build client loyalties. Think about your participation in company activities such as training programs, attending board meetings, meeting with department heads, doing research, helping with onboarding new legal department staff, and sharing these in your cheat sheet.

Online Presence: Describe your online presence and exposure. Describe how you can cross-promote your partners among your social media or Internet channels.

1. Firm, personal website, and/or blog addresses: List the addresses of any personal websites, blogs, or other microsites you maintain.
2. Social network site address: enter your Facebook, LinkedIn, Twitter, or other social networking site address.
3. Participating sites: List the groups in which you actively participate, including bar associations, special interest groups, LinkedIn groups, and industry groups.

Communicating Accomplishments Internally

Some lawyers have expressed concern to me over the years that sharing personal accomplishments is a form of self-promotion – something they believe is frowned upon in their firm or practice group. I always ask how they have come to believe that.

I've never seen or heard anything that would lead me to believe any law firm that I have ever worked with discourages this type of promotion. When asked, it's usually described as 'not being a part of the firm's culture' or that it would be 'counter to their collegial nature to talk about one's accomplishments.' Fortunately, that cultural folklore is fading. That's a good thing because communicating your accomplishments is a vital part of marketing your practice inside the law firm, the place where you'll get the majority of your referrals for work.

In thinking about sharing your accomplishments, your mindset should focus on how your accomplishments can help the clients of your other partners. Couch your achievements in terms of the benefits that other companies will get from your experience, and it becomes a desirable activity inside the firm and something to be embraced. Share what is meaningful to the clients of your partners. If you can't describe your accomplishments in a way that benefits the firm's clients, think twice about sharing them. If it is only meaningful to you, you might want to get another person's input on whether or not to share the information.

There are many ways to share the news of your practice. Most firms have internal newsletters which help keep everyone informed of recent matters, new clients, recent publications, awards, and recognition. You may also be able to attend and get on the agenda of other practice group meetings. Meet with your marketing professional inside the firm to explore the best ways to communicate the information. But at the very least, share the news with your core business development group. And ask that they share their accomplishments with you.

Connecting While Breaking Bread

Food connects people. Sitting down to eat together means you're not only sharing another person's company, but you're usually eating the same food as the other person. Apparently, there is something about eating the same food that bonds people together and makes them more collaborative.

Family meals are widespread and commonplace in all cultures, and inviting friends or visitors to dine remains a regular social activity in most societies – with communal eating with guests widely regarded as both the height of hospitality and an important way of getting to know people.

Eating is believed to be an act of pleasure and sparks the production of endorphins in our brains. Therefore, the very act of eating might promote bonding, since we tend to bond with those whom we experience other endorphin-inducing activities such as laughing, dancing, singing, and exercising with others. Much of the science points to the theory that people who often eat with others can be expected to have more extensive social networks and be happier and more satisfied with their lives and be more engaged with their communities.

I'll Have That, too

There's evidence that not only is it beneficial to eat meals with other people, but there may also be a further bonding effect when you eat the same foods together. "People just feel closer to people who are eating the same food as they do. And that shared activity builds trust, cooperation, and other positive consequences of feeling close to someone," reports Ayelet Fishbach.

She should know. Fishbach and her colleague, Kaitlin Woolley, at the University of Chicago ran an interesting study that included a series of experiments. They tested the effects of eating together and what happens when people either eat the same food or eat different foods. In one of their experiments, they had volunteers play the role of a manager and a union representative.

The two had to agree on the hourly wage that management was willing to pay and that union members were to receive. Pairs of volunteers were sometimes given candy to eat together or sometimes given salty snacks. And sometimes, one of the volunteers was given one kind of food and the other was given the other kind of food. When the volunteers ate the same kinds of food, they reached agreement much more quickly than when one person ate the candy and the other person ate the salty food.

It took them 3.6 rounds to reach an agreement when they're both eating sweets. When one person is eating salty food, like potato chips and pretzels and so on, while the other person is eating sweets, then it takes them on average 7.3 rounds of the game until they finally settle on their hourly wage.

In another part of the study, the researchers had volunteers listen to someone offering a product testimonial. The person offering the testimonial was also eating something. When volunteers were given the same kind of food to eat, they were more likely to trust the information in the testimonial.

The bottom line is that you can use food to build trust. Don't just aim to eat together with your connections, try to ensure you're eating the same food. Tell the waiter, 'I'll have that, too.'

Manners Matter

I remember meeting with two salespeople in a fairly nice restaurant. I don't remember what the meeting was for, or which company they represented. I only remember how one of them chewed with their mouth open and slurped his soda. He made more gross sounds than a cow giving birth. It was so distracting I couldn't focus on the conversation and I'm sure it showed in my face.

Good manners matter. Bad manners signal an insensitivity to others, a lack of education, and a person who lacks self-awareness. If you haven't read an Emily Post book, it's time to get one. Know which silverware are for which purposes and where to put your bread and butter. Stand up when an older person or woman comes to the table. Open doors for others and offer to carry things for women. Don't smoke or smell of smoke, especially in confined spaces. Say please and thank you. Show genuine interest in others and listen when others are speaking. Don't interrupt. Don't meet with others when you have a cold. Be on time for meetings.

Leave your phone in the car. If you must have it with you, silence it and leave it in your purse or pocket. Checking your phone sends a strong signal that you don't feel the person you are with is as important as what might be happening on your phone.

You'd wish I didn't need to include this in a book about building relationships with connections, but I did. Because I see it all too often that people lack basic courtesies and manners. You won't be successful without them. You won't get to spend time with the power brokers if you can't eat a meal without grossing people out. And how you treat the waiter really does matter. People notice. Don't let them notice bad manners in you.

Have Them Face the Wall

When you take a client or prospect out to eat, try to control distractions. If they can view the entire restaurant, they will often be distracted by others in the restaurant. It's human nature to divert your eyes to see who is coming into the restaurant, look around for where the waiter is, or watch people when the discussion gets boring. Few people are so engaging that their lunch partner doesn't occasionally drift off during the conversation. But if you sit with your back against the wall and them facing you, they will be distracted less often by the other people in the restaurant. Select a booth if that option is available. This can help you keep their attention on you and what you are discussing.

But Sit Next to Them in Presentations

Sitting next to someone has the tendency to encourage collaboration and agreement. Sitting across from someone tends to reinforce feelings of competition, making them more likely to be adversarial and disagreeable. If you expect a conflict or opposing views, sit beside the person you think may disagree with your position. Sitting side-by-side promotes feelings of camaraderie and cooperation. You're more likely to get agreement from those you sit beside than those you sit across from.

Meet for Breakfast

Morning meetings are the best times to meet with prospective clients. Breakfast meetings catch clients before they get into the office and get dragged in to their hectic days. It's a time when most people are thinking more broadly about what needs to be done and are often more receptive in the mornings to ways in which they can accomplish their goals and get projects underway.

But remember. You are not at breakfast for the ham and eggs. Breakfast meetings are not about eating. They are about talking with clients about their business and their challenges. Keep your meal light and simple. A fresh fruit bowl is ideal. If possible, avoid coffee on the drive to the meeting and at the meeting- you don't want a spill to ruin your presentation.

Lastly, always treat the waitress and hostess with the utmost respect and friendliness. Clients will notice if you are disrespectful, rude, or lack compassion. Clients know that how you treat the waitress or waiter is how you will treat the client's secretary. Treating a secretary poorly will take away your chance to ever work with that client. It's practically guaranteed.

Connecting at Conferences

Conferences are a great way to expand your network of connections, learn best practices and gain valuable insights into emerging issues affecting your industry. The energy created by hundreds of industry insiders meeting for several days delving into the day's challenges can recharge your batteries in ways few other marketing activities can. But they can also be expensive endeavors that need to be carefully managed and executed to reap the greatest rewards from the investment.

The following is a checklist of tips and techniques that can help you get the most out of your next conference or seminar.

Determine What You Will Accomplish

Any marketing initiative should begin with clarifying your objectives. Business development funds are limited. It's important to contribute to the firm's growth by ensuring your use of funds is directed at the highest and best use of its resources. Conferences can be expensive when you add together the cost of travel, accommodations, conference fees, meals, client entertainment, and lost billable time. What are the alternative uses of those funds, and would that be a better use of your time and investment of hours?

Knowing what you need to accomplish will help determine the type of conference that you need to attend. You may need to learn more about an industry. It may be that you are looking for better connections to prospective clients. You are attending the conference with a client to deepen the relationship. Or, you are going to increase your knowledge about a subject area or industry. Be clear about what you need to accomplish to be sure to attend the right kind of conference and plan your time accordingly. There may be several reasons to select a conference. If so, prioritize the reasons to clarify which are the most important. These top reasons should be your vetting process for choosing the most appropriate conference and topics.

Choose the Right Conference

Depending upon what you are trying to accomplish, the selection of where you go can make a big difference in the results you get from the conference. Consider the subject matter and the level of expertise the conference offers. Consider who the people who speak at the conference and attend the conference. Are these direct buyers of your services or referral sources? Or are they mainly in the same boat as you? Some attorneys spend a lot of time at Bar Association conferences to build referral sources. But they don't need referral sources as much as they need to better learn about the dynamics of their client's industries.

Prepare to Attend the Conference

Preparation is essential to a successful conference however it is also the most often overlooked step. Good preparation can make the difference between a mediocre conference and one that produces solid results for you and the firm.

Plan Each Day's Activities

Develop a plan of action of what you want to learn, who you want to meet, the activities you will participate in, and the steps you'll need to take to fully prepare for the conference. Review the speakers, the subject of their presentation, and their bios. Decide which of them you would like to try to meet. Think about the questions you will want to ask during the Q&A portion of their talk. Plan out your attendance to know in advance which presentations you will attend, who you want to meet, and what you want to learn.

Get a List of Attendees

Call the event organizers and try to get a list of the attendees in advance of the conference. Some conferences publish this along with summary information such as each attendee's company, title, and geographic location. Get whatever they have available. It won't be a complete list as there are always those that sign up last minute or change plans. But it will give you about 70% to 80% of the attendees. Review the list and mark those that you'd like to meet.

Review the list of speakers and identify ones that you would like to meet. Do some research into each by googling them, checking out their website, and looking at their LinkedIn profile.

Reach Out to Learn What to Expect

If you've never been to that particular conference before, get a list of past attendees and reach out to them to ask what you can do to make the most of your conference experience. Ask their opinion on who the most influential or most connected people you should try to meet and any inside tips they might give you to make the most of the conference. Often there are 'not to be missed' parties, specific presentations that everyone goes to, or insider tips that are good to know as you plan your conference strategy.

Make the Most of Your Time at the Conference

Attending a conference is not a vacation. It is work. If you execute your conference experience correctly, you'll find you are more tired than on a typical workday. At a conference, you are constantly 'on.' That takes energy and discipline to stay focused like that for 10 – 15 hours a day for several days in a row. So be sure to eat healthy foods in moderation, get plenty of rest, and don't drink too much while at the event.

Arrive Early and Stay Late

Arrive early and be prepared. Have a way to take notes, bring business cards, an extra pen, mints, the conference schedule and attendee list, your nametag or badge, chargers, and anything else you think you might need during the day. Getting to sessions a few minutes early enables you to get a good seat, speak to others beforehand, and sometimes get time with the speaker before they go on.

Offer to be a Question Plant

An effective way to establish a relationship with a speaker is to get there early and ask the speaker if there are any questions that they hope will be asked during the Q&A portion. Speakers often dread the idea of no one asking any questions. You can offer value to the speaker by suggesting that you can ask a question the speaker would like to have asked. Not only does it give you an easy way to meet the speaker, but after the presentation, they will be grateful and more willing to speak to you.

Stay Off the Smartphone

You can't meet people if your head is buried in your phone. Studies show that most people check their phones about every 6 minutes. Look around the room during a presentation, and you'll see just how tied to their phones most people are. But the time you spend on your phone is time you are not spending making new connections. Sure, there are times when you have to take a call or answer an e-mail. But these are pretty rare instances. Set up your out-of-office message to explain that you will only have period access to your e-mail and then live by that. Check your e-mail no more than three times a day.

Introduce Yourself Effectively

When you meet someone for the first time, greet them with a smile, look them in the eyes and show genuine interest in meeting them. Avoid talking about yourself until you are asked. And even then, keep it brief. The less you say about yourself and the more you ask about them, the more curiosity is built to learn more about you. Ask easy questions that anyone can answer. Listen to learn what they like, where their interests lie, which aspects of the conference are most intriguing, and why.

Socialize with People You Don't Know

At all types of events, it is human nature to gravitate toward those you know well or in whom you have things in common. Resist the temptation to (what one of my managing partners used to call) "clump with your buddies." One of the greatest values of a conference is the opportunity to meet people you might not otherwise meet. These opportunities don't come along often, so make the most of them. Go out of your way to strike up conversations with strangers.

Initiate Conversations

To establish a new relationship, you have to find common ground to start building the relationship. You don't have to find someone that likes your hobby of skydiving. Simply being at the same conference is enough common ground to start a relationship. While you are mingling in the halls or before the start of the presentation, is the perfect time to initiate meeting someone.

Be matter of fact and ask simple questions that anyone can answer. Did you travel far to get here? Is the hotel what you expected? Is this weather a break from what you have at home? Once you've broken the seal, offer something of value, such as an interesting session you attended, news of recent development in the industry, or the best ideas you plan to take back to the office. Watch their body language and be prepared to exit the conversation politely if they don't appear interested. Follow the flow of the conversation and stay focused on what they are saying.

Stay in the Flow of Traffic

People who hang out in the corners signal that they don't want to engage with others. It's not typically accurate, but people who are not proactive connectors won't approach someone standing by themselves. If you see someone standing by themselves, do yourself and them a favor, approach them, and start a discussion. Everyone is there for the same reason, and most people will appreciate the chance to talk to someone and not look like they are by themselves. If you have time to kill, stand near the food or beverage tables or where people are congregating. Gravitate toward where there is activity. That is where you'll most likely find natural connectors.

Introduce Others

Adding value to a new relationship leaves a strong impression. One way to add value is to share your network with others. You never know how others will benefit from knowing one another. More often than not, especially at conferences, the people you introduce will benefit from the introduction. If they do, you will as well. Make an effort to invite others into your conversation, introduce them to one another and mention how you know each other. If you can, say something interesting about both people, such as hobbies, recent trips, or work projects. Often, others will find something in common, and it can provide energy and interest for the conversation to develop.

Watch Body Language

Before approaching a group, be sure to check out their body language. Groups of two or three facing each other may be in a private discussion. If they have a more open stance, they are in a casual conversation and will typically welcome another person to the conversation.

Take Notes

You'll meet dozens of people during the conference if you are good. Recalling the particulars of the conversations you had, their interests, information on their family, or other key information will be difficult in the days after the conference if you don't take good notes immediately following your discussion. Always ask for a business card and write notes on the back of the card. You may even feel comfortable writing a note while speaking to them for some that you meet. It's flattering. It shows that you value meeting them and want to continue a relationship. Record as much information to make a future contact easier and show that you were listening.

Be Present and Listen

Once you have engaged in conversation with someone, be 'in the conversation'. There's a lot of activity at conferences and most people tend to keep one ear on the discussion and one eye on who is walking through the room. That sends the impression that the person you are talking to is not that important. And it is off-putting. You will set yourself apart by being present in the discussion, looking them in their eyes, and genuinely listening to what the other is saying.

Follow up After the Conference

If you had a good conference, you most likely came home with several dozen business cards or names of individuals with whom you will want to follow up. Initiating contact within the first week or two is essential. Plan your schedule to be able to accomplish this. Any longer than two weeks and people's memories begin to fade. The glow of meeting you will have worn off.

You'll also want to follow up with those you were unable to connect with at the conference. Plan time to send notes to these individuals as well. Apologize for not connecting with them, offer your insights on the conference, and offer to meet them at a future date.

Lastly, add the new contacts to your address book and plan out on your calendar when you will reach out again to them. Make sure you qualify the people you add to your power grid.

Everyone in the firm should benefit from the knowledge you gained at the conference. Write a summary of the most important information gleaned from the conference and share it with others in the firm. In addition to key learnings, share the names and positions of the people you met at the conference. Often, others will know the people or companies you met and new opportunities will develop through these conversations.

A successful conference takes effort. But those that put the time into it will reap the rewards.

Connecting by Video

There is no question that the pandemic has changed how we work and where we work. Today, staying in contact with your connections requires mastery of virtual mediums such as video conferencing and social media platforms. There seems to be an ever-expanding choice of mediums and tools you can use to communicate with others. Regardless of what you choose and where your communications happen, real-life rules still mainly apply in the virtual world.

Video

Video conferencing is here to stay. Whether you like to see yourself on camera, it is unavoidable today. A large portion of your conversations will be virtual. Virtual mediums require the same attention to detail as you would in an in-person meeting. To get that in-person feel, use an HD quality camera. Most computers come with HD quality cameras today, but if yours didn't, or you are using an older computer, consider buying an HD camera for video conferencing or webinars.

Also, think about the height of your webcam and where your image shows up on the screen for others. Try to position your webcam to be on the same level as your face. If it sits below your face you will look like you are looking down on the other participants. If it is above you, they are looking down on you. It's best to position your webcam or laptop level with your face.

Lighting

Lighting is one of the crucial aspects of getting a good look on camera. Try to face a natural light source. Natural light gives the best appearance. If you can't face a window, consider using a ring light or a natural daylight lamp. Set it up to face the light, preferably directly behind your webcam. Most versions have several types of lights that you can adjust your appearance using. Test out the ones to get a light that looks best for your complexion and ambient lighting.

Audio

It's best to plug an external microphone into your computer or laptop. External mics are designed specifically for recording and give a much better-quality sound. You can also get the mic closer to your mouth, reducing the background noises picked up. Be sure to test the microphone, make sure you like the tone of your voice, and check to make sure the audio is picking up clearly.

Turn off the notifications on your computer and your phone. These can be heard when they ping in the background. And don't forget to minimize noises in your office or home. The fewer distractions, the better.

Your Background

You have basically three options for your background: a green screen, a prepared background, or the actual background that shows up behind you while on camera. The advantage of a greenscreen background is that you are able to put any image, including your firm's name, in your background. This is the option I suggest you use. A prepared background enables you to blur or colorize your actual background to reduce the acuity or focus of what others see. Most video conferencing software enable you to adjust the sharpness of your background.

Lastly, you can go au natural and leave your background to display for others to see your office or workspace. One advantage is that people get a glimpse into your office, home or workspace. You can strategically place things in view that prompt questions, entertain those on the call, or reveal your hobbies and interests. That can be a fun way to start your meeting.

If you go the actual background route, be sure to limit any activity in your background. Avoid traffic routes to where kids or pets walking by will be in view. Pay attention to what is in your background and set the view to be a positive reflection on you.

You

First and foremost, always be professional and act and dress as you would be if you were meeting in person. While the world has gone much more casual for work dress, never dress more casually than the people you are meeting. Stay present in the conversation and avoid answering emails, checking messages, or texting others while on the call. Turn off notifications, so you aren't distracted by incoming emails and messages.

Connecting on LinkedIn

LinkedIn is the most important social media channel for professionals in any field. More and more of us are working at home, making connecting through LinkedIn more critical. You should be leaning into social media and using it to enhance your relationships both personally and professionally. Social media enables you to meet and connect with people you might not have met otherwise. It affords a unique view into the lives of the people you know, their interests and hobbies, and their thoughts and viewpoints. That more transparent view of your contacts can be both good and bad. But it is here to stay, thanks to the exploding ubiquity of social media.

There is no shortage of advice on using LinkedIn to build your practice and grow your network. I won't go into the topic in much detail. But not including a basic overview of how to connect through LinkedIn would be a grave oversight. The following is a brief explanation of what you should do, at a bare minimum, to maintain a professional presence on LinkedIn and connect with others.

Lasty, whether or not you are an expert in social media, keep an eye on the developments across all platforms. Watch for new platforms and new technologies that promise new ways of connecting with others. The metaverse and our real worlds are merging. Those that don't keep up with the changes will find it an overwhelming challenge to learn it quickly and catch back up.

LinkedIn Basics

To begin with, you should complete all areas of your profile. This includes the headline, summary, contact information, friendly custom URL, past experience, and education sections. Completing each section will enable you to reach "All Star Status."

Your Headline

Your LinkedIn headline is one of the most visible sections of your LinkedIn profile. Not only does it stretch across the top of your profile page, it also introduces you on newsfeed posts and the "People You May Know" section. Your LinkedIn headline is key to making a positive impression and explaining *exactly* what you bring to the table.

It's also one of the most important fields for LinkedIn's search algorithm. Your LinkedIn headline should portray you professionally. Include the keywords that help you appear higher in LinkedIn searches. Key words are the words that people search for on LinkedIn and that show up on search engines. Your headline is pulled into both LinkedIn and Google search results.

If you don't create a headline, LinkedIn will automatically pull in your most recent job title and company and use that for your headline. Think about who you want looking at your profile and appeal directly to them in your headline. Type in exactly what they need to know before anything else. Look to your most influential peers for some ideas.

Profile Summary

your summary should speak to your skills, experience, and professional interests. It should summarize your professional expertise and highlight your most significant achievements. Try to find an interesting and genuine way to describe your professional background, but don't stray too far from your expertise. If you've developed an expertise in a specialty area of the law, include that and make sure your posts and articles provide evidence of this expertise.

Contact Information

The Contact Info section is located in the introduction section on your profile. This section displays your contact and personal information. By default, your email address is pre-filled based on what you entered as your primary email address during sign-up. You can manage this section by filling in the other fields in the Contact info section, such as:

- Direct link to your LinkedIn profile
- Email address
- Phone number
- Website
- Instant messenger accounts
- Your birthday

I recommend adding your work phone number and work email address to your contact page. You want to make yourself accessible to others.

Photos and Cover Image

Make sure to upload a professional profile photo that shows you smiling with a welcoming expression. Avoid the angry litigator look. You're a lion of the bar in court, not when you are trying to attract clients. Use a cover image that complements your area of the law. Avoid cliche images like the balance of justice, lady justice, or shelves of law books.

Avoid grammar, punctuation, and spacing mistakes. Have someone else review what you've written—we can all use a second set of eyes before we hit the publish button. Keep your profile up to date with your latest awards, featured content, and publications.

Posts and Content Marketing

Share an update from your LinkedIn homepage at least once a week. It's simple to do. Copy the link to an article and hit "Share." Share articles and blog posts that you've written, articles that other attorneys have written at your firm, and even articles written by your clients. If you follow influencers and thought leaders on LinkedIn, share their content as well.

When you find something you like, share it with a comment about what you liked about it and ask for input from your readers. Focus on general business or economics articles that suggest solutions to the emerging issues or industry changes on the horizon. Focus on articles and posts that will help your readers avoid problems.

Always think "insights over hind sights." Show readers how issues impact their business and guide them on how to address their challenges. Give them insights rather than simply reporting on the development. Talk about resources available (either through you or through others) to help with various issues. Think about your article topic from your client's perspective: What are their challenges? What problems might they be dealing with? What unintended consequences could result from the issue? Create content and social media posts about the timeliest issues and write about them in the business manager's language, not in legalese.

Post content about others in your network (and tag them in the posts). It can help to build stronger relationships as they will appreciate the added coverage into your network of followers. Take the time to like, comment on, and share the posts of connections in your power grid. It builds relationships and keeps you on their radar.

Try a mix of mediums to engage with your target audiences (video, written content, podcasts, etc.). Videos and podcasts do not need to be professionally done. You can use your phone's camera or the webcam on your computer. A more low-key approach is in vogue. Using your mobile device or computer to capture your video or audio recording is the new norm and makes you more relatable.

Visual content greatly outperforms posts with just text on every social media platform. So use imagery to accompany each of your social media posts, such as headshots or practice images, or use a site like canva.com to create free custom graphics.

Cultivate Your Network

While quality is always better than quantity, most people should increase the number of connections they have on LinkedIn. Here are some ideas on how to create a strategic connections plan to find contacts and maximize your network:

Join LinkedIn alumni groups of your former firms and educational institutions. When you make new connections through these channels, send personalized notes to key contacts asking how they're doing. Utilize the "People You May Know" feature. The more you use it, the more targeted your future connection suggestions are.

Beware of LinkedIn's mass "Import Your Contacts" feature. Clicking on this brings every contact in your address book with a LinkedIn profile into your LinkedIn connections. As you saw when you put your master contact list together, not everyone in your address book is someone you want to connect to on LinkedIn. Build your LinkedIn connections organically, taking the time to pursue the most appropriate and meaningful connections for you and reflect well on you.

Strengthen Relationships

One of the biggest mistakes I see on LinkedIn is when a client makes a valuable connection and doesn't do anything with it. The follow-through required to move those relationships from social media acquaintance to a powerful connection is not much. Here's what you can do.

Curate new relationships with your connections to maintain and deepen them in a planned way. Have something of value to offer new connections. Post updates and share frequently. People are more likely to remember your interactions, comments, and posts when they regularly see them. You want to be seen as a valuable resource with something to offer, authentic and trustworthy, and smart and interesting.

Send personalized messages to your connections to acknowledge their work anniversaries or other accomplishments. Share and comment on their content that resonates with you.

Deciding Which Connection Requests to Accept

LinkedIn is designed to act like one great Rolodex for the business world. You'll get lots of requests to connect. How do you know who you should connect with and who you can ignore? Make those decisions based on what you want to accomplish.

Many connection requests are from salespeople, consultants, coaches, and investors, all of whom benefit from large networks of connections. Their motivation to connect with you may be to sell you their services, tap into the network of people you have cultivated, or simply follow your posts. It's hard to know for sure.

Ideally, you want your network of LinkedIn connections to be similar to your personal power grid- though it will be larger. Keep the same principles in mind when accepting requests to connect. Look for people who are well-respected, trustworthy, have something to offer, and have a giving mindset. These things are sometimes hard to determine just from their profile. But try to vet people the way you would for your power grid. Remember, quality is better than quantity.

9

Putting Your Network to Work

"The new form of networking is not about climbing a ladder
to success; it's about collaboration, cocreation, partnerships,
and long-term values-based relationships."

-   Porter Gale

While most of your efforts should be put into helping others, there
will be times when you will need to make requests of your
connections. This chapter discusses ways to put your network to
work for you.

Making Requests of Your Connections

As we've discussed (perhaps ad nauseum), your power grid and
secondary connections represent a wealth of resources,
information, and people to tap. Making those requests, however,
should be strategic and intentional. They should have purpose and
be appropriate for the level of the relationship. The following are
some tips and techniques for making requests for the people in
your network.

Start Small

Small requests are easier to agree to than are larger requests.
Surprisingly, however, small requests also lay the groundwork for

accepting larger requests. The technique, called the 'Foot in the Door' technique, works by creating a connection between the person asking for a request and the person being asked. When a minor request is granted, the person who agrees to the request tends to feel obligated to also agree to larger requests in order to stay consistent with the original decision. Numerous studies have born out this phenomenon. The small request before a larger request is now commonplace in fundraising, sales, and marketing.

Make Sure it's Appropriate

Make sure the request is appropriate to the person. It should be something they can do with their existing resources and schedule. Most importantly, be sure that the request is relevant to the level of the relationship you have with the person. Ask yourself: Is the request appropriate to the person, the company, the situation, and the level of the relationship I have with that person? Be more cautious in the earliest stages of a new relationship. Wait until the relationship is strong and there is a good understanding and strong familiarity before making requests.

Be Reasonable

Don't ask for the moon. Ask for reasonable things. Asking someone to read, edit, and comment on a 200-page manuscript may be a bit much. But sending an email to check out and give feedback on your new website is reasonable. Think about how you would react were you requested to do the same thing. For your closest relationships, you'd probably do whatever was asked, regardless of how large or small the request. But you will probably think harder about a large request from someone who you are not as close to.

Make it Easy

Try to couch your request so that they will perceive it as easy to do. Anticipate the questions they may have or the additional information they may need. Think about your request from their point of view and assume they are busy and must fit your request in. Make it as easy as you can for them.

Make the Value Clear

Can they see how you will benefit from your request of them? Make sure your request has an obvious connection to a worthwhile objective. People want to help others when they know their assistance will have real benefit. Try to clarify how the request will help you accomplish a larger goal that is meaningful and worthy. Give people a good reason to help you so that, in helping so, they feel good.

Encouraging Referrals

Referrals are the lifeblood of a healthy practice. In fact, on average, 85% of the work you get will come through referrals. At first, these will come from inside the firm. But increasingly, they will come from outside the firm as you get better at connecting with others.

Referrals are powerful. They include an implied endorsement of you that makes getting the engagement easier. And yet, most of us find it difficult to ask for help. We hesitate to ask for an introduction or ask to be referred for work for any number of reasons - many of them wrong. Business professionals expect and even enjoy connecting and introducing others. Most business professionals and lawyers willingly give referrals when the person has a good reputation or a personal connection.

From Whose Plate Do You Eat?

It's important to know from where your work originates. Identify your best referral sources. Write down the names and practice areas or roles of the people who send you the most work. How often do they send you work?

Next, examine the relationship you have with each of those referral sources. What other ways have they helped you in your practice? What work have you sent them? How often do you send them work? Is there a trade surplus or deficit? How do their clients feel about the work you did for them? Are you adding to or subtracting from their reputation?

We expect referral relationships to be Quid Pro Quo relationships. But two professionals are rarely able to refer work back and forth in equal measure. If you are the recipient of work, explore ways in which you can reciprocate in other ways. Express your gratitude for the work and make them proud of your service to their connection or client.

If you are the one that refers a great deal of work to others, understand that the people you refer work to may not be in a position to return the favor. Don't be shy about ways that they can assist you. Suggest alternatives that would help you accomplish your goals. Most people are happy for the opportunity to help you out in return.

First Things First

You must earn referrals by being worthy of referrals. That means keep doing everything you do to be a good lawyer. Continue to be trustworthy and authentic in your dealings with others, and be an expert in an area of the law. Demonstrate your openness to building referral relationships by constantly looking for ways to help others. Your reputation, relationships, and knowledge all provide ways to help maintain the referral momentum. Cherish those relationships as you cherish your client relationships. They are equally important.

Use the Honeymoon

Most jobs and projects start positively. They are like the honeymoon phase of a marriage. That upbeat and optimistic time is a great time to plant the seed for referrals and testimonials. You can do this by saying, "I'm so pleased we're working together. I think I'll do my best work with you. If I ever fall short, though, I want you to tell me. Because I want you to feel comfortable referring your friends and business associates to me."

Plant the Seed

Mention in your conversations that referrals and introductions are important to your business - it's how you gain new clients. You can say something like this: "Most of my business comes through referrals from other professionals like you. I really appreciate the referrals I get from other professionals."

Unless you are comfortable making a direct ask, stop short of asking them to give you a referral. That's where it begins to feel uncomfortable for most people. And a direct ask is typically not needed. Most business people will get the hint.

Try a Social Referral

If you are uncomfortable suggesting referrals for work, try asking for referrals from people who have similar interests and hobbies. Mention that you are looking to meet more people who enjoy your hobby and ask that they refer anyone they know who enjoys the same activities. Surprisingly, this helps 'condition' the other person to think about you for referrals and can lead to referrals for work.

Help Others First

The best way to get referrals is by giving them. But like the people you ask to refer work to you, you may not know of someone with your particular legal needs at the moment. If you can't make a referral for work, you may be able to help them in other ways. The point is to 'always be giving'. Giving combined with a mention that referrals are the best way to get work, will often lead to new referral activity over time.

Fish Where the Fish Are

Identify people who could potentially send you work (or might know people who could) and make a list of them. Reach out to them regularly. Identify the types of people they would most like to meet, search your contacts and offer to introduce them.

Don't Expect an Immediate Referral

For a variety of reasons, referral activity takes time to develop. Most professionals won't refer simply for the sake of referring. They want to send good quality opportunities your way. Those don't come up every day. The challenge of referrals is to be the one they think of when they find a good referral opportunity. To increase your referral activity, mention the importance of referrals in every conversation, do good work, find ways to help others, and refer work to others whenever you can. Be sure to identify and talk to the people in a position to refer work. Do this consistently and you'll see your referral activity increase over time.

Don't Keep Score

The expectation of referral reciprocity is a dangerous, corrosive mindset. Keeping mental score of who refers work and who hasn't won't do you much good and will often be counterproductive. Focus on being the person who helps others and is a connector and influencer.

How to Say It

There are many ways to ask for a referral. It's important to find a way to phrase the request that works best for you and feels natural. A simple mention of the importance of getting referrals (a soft ask) can be an easy way to get comfortable with asking for referrals. Direct asks can be hard at first, usually because most of us underestimate the client's perception of our work or have lingering doubts about how the client feels about us. But the sooner you get comfortable asking for referrals, the more likely you are to get them.

Practice these 'asks' with someone else and get their feedback on how you come across to them.

- ✓ "Referrals are the biggest source of my work. As someone familiar with my work, I hope you'll think of me if you come across anyone needing help with [*service area*]."

- ✓ "Who do you know like yourself that would benefit from working with me?"

- ✓ "If you know of anyone needing help with [legal service], I hope you'll think of me."

- ✓ "It's hard for me to ask, but I need to make this request since I get most of my work this way. If you hear of anyone or any company with [legal problem], I would appreciate it if you introduced us."

✓ "I love meeting other professionals interested in [*topic of common interest*]. If you come across anyone, I hope you'll think to mention my name."

✓ "What groups are you involved in where you or your peers participate? Who do you know there that I can work with the way you and I work together?"

Difficult things become easier with practice. The more you make and ask for referrals, the easier it becomes and the more it becomes part of your regular business development strategy. Few things pay off as does the regular giving and asking for referrals.

Help Formulate the Pitch

When you refer work to another lawyer, it doesn't mean that they will get that work. But it does probably give them a leg up in getting the work since a referral is an endorsement of their capabilities. To help them get the work, ask a few more questions of the person asking for a recommendation. Try to find out as much as you can so you can help the person to whom you are giving the referral craft an approach that appeals to the company. I created the DRASTIC analysis as a guide to help identify the information needed to draft a compelling approach strategy. The additional information can help them position themselves better to get the work. And, by the way, it works equally well for the matters you are trying to get.

DRASTIC stands for **D**ecision makers and processes; **R**isks and rewards; **A**lternatives and competitors; **S**takeholders and influencers; **T**iming and time frames; **I**mpact and implications; and **C**riteria and unique needs. Each topic of the analysis will help you identify the information needed to develop a pitch strategy.

DRASTIC Factors Explained

The first is 'D', which stands for *decision*-makers and the *internal buying decision process*. Who makes the decision on how the issue is resolved and how does the decision process work inside the company?

R stands for the *risks and rewards* the company believes it will experience once the issue or problem is solved. What threatens the company, or how does the company stand to benefit if this issue is resolved? This drives at what is at stake for the company and its relative importance to the company.

Next, 'A' stands for the company's *alternatives* to solve the problem and the incumbent relationships available to it to deal with the issue. Who will they be competing against for this work?

S stands for the *stakeholders and influencers* inside the company who are interested in how the problem is solved. Who has a stake in the decision and who can influence it? Essentially, you want to know how much consensus there is inside the company for the best way to solve the problem.

T stands for the company's *timing and time frames* expected for the issue to be resolved. You want to understand the company's degree of urgency for solving the problem. That will also give you a sense of how quickly they plan to decide to hire outside counsel.

'I' stands for *implications and impact*. What unintended consequences or implications has the company considered might occur in resolving the issue? What implications are they suffering today? How will the company's operations be impacted by solving this problem? What changes are likely?

And lastly, 'C' stands for the *criteria* they will use to evaluate candidates and the company's unique needs that will need to be addressed in the solution or by the provider. What specific selection criteria will they use to evaluate solutions and providers? And are there any special or unique aspects they want included in the solution or provider?

Asking about the DRASTIC factors will help you better understand the issue and provide the insights needed to prepare a compelling pitch. Even if you can only get information on some factors, it will go a long way toward a clearer and more effective presentation, something both parties will benefit from.

Most referrals are simply the name and a brief description of the conversation. It is rare to get a referral that includes the additional information and thought about how to pitch their solutions to their issue. If you want to make a lasting impression, and create a deep sense of indebtedness, help the person you are referring with the information they need to hit the right chords in their discussions.

Is There Anyone Else?

You can also invite people to think of their own ways they can help you out. One effective way is to ask a version of the 'Is there anyone else' question. 'Is there anyone else' questions get people thinking about the people in their networks and the possible connections they can make. Even when they don't think of someone immediately, they often think of those connections in the days following your conversation.

Ask: Is there anyone else I should be talking to? Is there anyone else I can bring into our group? Is there anyone else who would benefit from this information? Is there anyone else who would value my input on this topic? Is there anyone else I could mentor? There are many ways to ask to bring others into your discussions and your network. Simply ask, is there anyone else?

Staying in Touch with Secondary Connections

Thus far, we have concentrated on outreach to your power network, which involves daily personal contact with your most influential connections. You likely have many more connections outside of your power grid. In this section, we'll talk about reaching out to the rest of your master list in order to stay on their radar.

Most, if not all, of the people who are on your master list but not in your power grid will be 'secondary' connections. To review, secondary connections are people you know, or once knew, and with whom you do not currently have a very close relationship. But, as we've previously discussed, secondary connections present tremendous opportunities because they give you access to networks of people you might not gain through your primary connections. They can also be a surprising and fertile source of leads for work.

In a 1973 landmark study titled *The Strength of Weak Ties*, Mark Granovetter, then of John Hopkins University, found that the best leads for job opportunities were more likely to come from distant acquaintances than close friends. Why? Cornell professors David Easley and Jon Kleinberg explained, "The closely-knit groups that you belong to, though they are filled with people eager to help, are also filled with people who know roughly the same things that you do." The point: distant acquaintances can expose you to opportunities that you and your friends just can't know about.

With so much potential from this group of connections, you obviously cannot afford to ignore them. Yet, with the time you are spending on regular and consistent outreach to your power grid— which includes perhaps up to 150 people—you probably don't have time for consistent one-to-one direct outreach to your secondary connections. That means you have to find a way to communicate with this group as efficiently as possible.

Develop a Marketing Communications Program

You can stay on the radar of your secondary connections by developing a marketing communications program. The objective of your marketing communications program is to keep your name in front of your secondary connections. You want to make sure that your extended network is aware of the type of work you do, your

271

recent successes, special areas of expertise, and that they know how to reach you should a need arise.

Your marketing communications program may include blogging, advertising, and publishing articles, in traditional media and on social media sites such as LinkedIn, Facebook, SlideShare, and JD Supra. But probably the most effective thing you can do to reach your secondary connections is to create a personal newsletter.

You should try to publish a personal newsletter every month or at least each quarter. Each issue should include information that showcases your knowledge and capabilities and that will, and this is important, be perceived as valuable by your audience. Avoid simply reporting on developments. Your writings should include your opinion, advice, or insights on how these developments will affect businesses or individuals. Be authentic and write so that your voice and personality come through each newsletter.

To keep the regular communications process manageable:

1. Plan to write and distribute at least one well-written and insightful article per month to your secondary connections.
2. Always include your contact information in case any of your readers have questions.
3. Add your monthly newsletter tasks to your calendar and prioritize producing your newsletter each month.

Keeping top of mind among your secondary connections will make them more likely to refer opportunities to you. And, of course, include the connections in your power grid on your mailing list. Your power grid contacts should also get any information you send to your secondary contacts.

While your newsletter can be published in print or electronically, electronic newsletters are especially easy because they can be automated and cost much less than a printed newsletter. If you don't have access to an email marketing program, considering subscribing to one like Mail Chimp, Constant Contact, Emma, or Infusionsoft. These programs make sending mass emails easy and usually have analytics you can review to improve your delivery performance over time.

They also allow you to create forms to collect contacts, conduct surveys, automate your emails with template designs, and schedule distribution of the newsletter in advance. Some of the email marketing programs are free for a certain number of email campaigns or under a specific volume of contact addresses. Many law firms already use email marketing software with professionals who support email marketing in the firm. If you have access to these professionals, by all means, use their services.

In addition to your personal newsletter, your law firm may publish a firm-wide client newsletter. Consider contributing to that as well. Ask the marketing professional for the editorial calendar for the newsletter, and note the due dates on your own calendar. Then give your draft to them well in advance of the deadline.

Another way to stay on the minds of your secondary connections is to set up card mailing. You probably already do holiday cards, but cards sent for special occasions such as birthdays, anniversaries, and notable achievements make a lasting impression, especially when they are handwritten and personalized. Consider a mail occasion that is out of the norm to create an even bigger impression. Be creative. Personalize the card and occasion to the individual if you can. If you both love music, send a note listing the upcoming music festivals. Send notes with interesting statistics if you're both into sports. Again, be creative, be thoughtful, and make it personal. Get help so you can do it consistently. Assign the system to someone who can do the hard part for you (so all you have to do is sign the card). Make it easy on you but an impact on your connections.

Reaching Out to Strangers

Most of the business outreach you do will be to people you know, some whom you know well, and others not so well. But sometimes the need arises to reach out to someone that you don't know at all.

For most people, reaching out to a stranger can be difficult and intimidating. In this section, I'll try to make that easier and alert you to some things to avoid when reaching out to people you don't know.

People who you do not know and with whom you do not share any mutual connection are referred to as "cold contacts." It is imperative you be selective about the cold contacts you approach. Avoid random acts of stranger outreach. Random outreach with no clear purpose is often ignored. That can be demoralizing and possibly tarnish your reputation if you do it too much. Social media sites like LinkedIn frown on gratuitous connecting, and too much of such activity can get your account privileges curtailed, and even get you banned from the site.

So, just as you would with a "warm contact" (that is, a person you already know), prepare for the outreach before you pick up the phone. Research the person and their business, think about the value you could offer, and make sure you can articulate a specific and legitimate purpose for asking for the person's time and attention. When you reach out to the person, explain how you know about them, what impresses you about the person, and why you want to connect. Make sure your research is reflected in these statements.

If you are leaving a voice mail, and most likely you will have to, speak slowly and clearly and give your name and phone number at the beginning and again at the end of your message. Keep the message short.

If you email them, don't include attachments that can get your email caught in their spam filters. If you have information you want to send them, ask for their permission to send it first. And keep the information short, concise, and easy to read. The more effort they must put in to understand your information, the less likely they will be to respond.

Avoid asking questions whose answers are obvious, can be easily researched, or are self-serving. If the person doesn't respond, don't pester them again and again. Send a second follow-up after one to two weeks. But, if they still don't respond, let it go and put your energies into someone else. You'll never know why someone doesn't return your calls or respond to your email so don't take it personally.

Getting an in-person meeting with someone you don't know is more difficult. But the same principles apply. Preparation is the key to a successful meeting. Try to set a meeting around mealtime, for coffee in the morning, or for drinks after work. Avoid dinners for a first meeting. Do not suggest an expensive meal or restaurant the first time meeting a person. Avoid lengthy, drawn-out meals for a first meeting.

For busier executives, an early morning meeting for breakfast or coffee is often preferable. Early meetings happen before the work day starts, making early meetings easier to attend, less of a distraction, and usually more productive.

Make it clear that you will pay for the meal. Find a time and location that is convenient for the other person. Show up early and choose a table out of the way of traffic. If possible, sit with your back against the wall, so the other person is facing you. This reduces the distraction the other person may have watching others in the restaurant and heps that person focus on your conversation.

Prepare for the meeting by researching the individual, the company, and planning what you would like to cover and accomplish in the conversation. Don't sell or promote yourself at this first meeting. Your objective should be to learn as much about the individual as possible. If you are talking more than 50% of the time, chances are the other person is not engaged and the meeting is not going well. Ask open-ended questions and probe gently for more information.

A mutual acquaintance who can make an introduction to a new person is always more beneficial than reaching out on your own. A mutual friend can turn a cold contact into a warm contact much more quickly. Don't forget to mine your master list to see who might be able to introduce you to new people you should know.

Soliciting Testimonials

Most people cringe at the idea of asking for a testimonial or review. Asking someone to praise you goes against everything we were taught. To many of us, it feels manipulative and sleazy. After all, most of us are introverts. Asking for a testimonial takes us way beyond our comfort zone. When I suggest to my coaching clients to request client testimonials, I usually get that stare into the middle distance that tells me they are frantically cataloging all the reasons they can't do it.

Testimonials are important social clues that help prospective clients determine whether providers are safe bets for their matters. You can find other ways to provide this proof (such as case studies, awards, and other third-party recommendations), but there are few tactics as powerful as the opinions of peers and clients.

But first, a note about using testimonials, endorsements, awards, and recommendations in your marketing materials. According to an article by Christina Vassiliou Harvey, Mac R. McCoy, and Brook Sneath entitled, 10 Tips for Avoiding Ethical Lapses When Using Social Media posted on the American Bar Association's website, lawyers should be cautious and make sure they understand the rules of their state when it comes to the use of testimonials and recommendations. These two paragraphs sum it up nicely.

"Many social media platforms like LinkedIn and Avvo heavily promote the use of testimonials, endorsements, and ratings (either by peers or consumers). These features are typically designed by social media companies with one-size-fits-all functionality and little or no attention given to variations in state ethics rules. Some jurisdictions prohibit or severely restrict lawyers' use of testimonials and endorsements. They may also require testimonials and endorsements to be accompanied by specific disclaimers.

South Carolina Ethics Opinion 09-10, for example, provides that "(1) lawyers cannot solicit or allow publication of testimonials on websites and (2) lawyers cannot solicit or allow publication of endorsements unless presented in a way that would not be misleading or likely to create unjustified expectations." The opinion also concluded that lawyers who claim their profiles on social media sites like LinkedIn and Avvo (which include functions for endorsements, testimonials, and ratings) are responsible for conforming all of the information on their profiles to the ethics rules.

Lawyers must, therefore, pay careful attention to whether their use of any endorsement, testimonial, or rating features of a social networking site is capable of complying with the ethics rules that apply in the state(s) where they are licensed. If not, then the lawyer may have no choice but to remove that content from their profile."

Despite this, I believe strongly that lawyers should use client testimonials in their marketing materials. There are enough easy ways to comply with state bar rules, and the benefits so compelling, it is worth the effort.

The Benefits of Testimonials

"What you say about yourself is promotion.
What others say about you is proof."

- Unknown

While you should proceed cautiously in using testimonials in your marketing, testimonials, and peer reviews are a powerful marketing tactics. A well-written and thoughtful testimonial is an *implied endorsement of your services* (which is why bar associations get so nervous about them). High client satisfaction from a respected company offers a form of *insurance* that you will perform equally well for them. And testimonials can suggest qualities that your prospective client hadn't considered in their analysis of your services. It is an excellent way to reveal the often hidden or personalized value you deliver in your work.

But not all testimonials must be written out and posted in your marketing materials. There are numerous other ways to benefit from the power of implied endorsements. Co-publishing and co-speaking is an excellent way to showcase your relationship and your work with a respected company, another lawyer, or a business person. Record the session and post it on your website or LinkedIn profile.

You can also request recommendations through your LinkedIn profile.
But if you want to get written testimonials, what's the best way to ask for a testimonial? It's simple. Ask directly and make it easy for them to do it.

How to Request Testimonials

There are two main reasons why people don't write testimonials. One, they lack the time. Or two, they lack the words.

When people can't think of what to write, they put it off for later. And that often leads to the testimonial not getting written. The formula for requesting testimonials addresses both of these issues. The more you can help people with what to write and do it quickly, the more likely you will get positive testimonials.

Avoid the Word 'Testimonial'

Avoid calling what you are asking for a testimonial. That word is fraught with danger and intrigue. Testimonial has a well-earned reputation for causing trouble and most lawyers avoid it like slow paying clients. Even business professionals find the work stressful and uncomfortable. It implies an officialness or permanence that seems more easily avoidable. Just refer to your request as feedback or input.

They are not committing themselves to recommending you. You are simply getting clarity on how you are being perceived, the ways you can improve your service levels and the impressions you leave on your clients. Keep it simple and uncomplicated. The value in asking is not just the information you get but it is also in the positive impression you make by asking. People are flattered to give you their input. So don't let them question that by calling it a testimonial.

Personalize Your Request

People respond better to requests for a personal favor when they are made in person. If you can't meet the person, schedule a video conference call. But try to make your request in person and personalize the request where you can.

Remind Them of Positive Events

If you recall a particular comment they made during your work together, include that in your request. Reminding them of positive moments makes it easier for them to transfer that experience into a compelling testimonial.

For instance, "I recall after we filed the registration that you commented how painless the process was. I was really flattered by that because it is not always a seamless and pain-free process. Of course, it helps to have organized and prepared clients."

You can also suggest your own impression of your work together. For instance, you may recall how busy they were when you were working together or specific situations where you helped them out.

You can write something like, "I remember you were buried with a big project that must have made it difficult for you to juggle getting our work done simultaneously. I hope working with me made it easier for you and that when we talked after work hours, it allowed you to concentrate better."

Remind Them that Their Comments Help Others

Legal services are complicated services to purchase. You only see the quality of the service after you've paid for it. You can't return the hours spent, rewind time, or unravel bad decisions. Testimonials and informal recommendations act as social proof of the quality of your lawyering and service skills. Prospective clients don't want to be the guinea pig on their important legal matters. People look for proof, recommendations from trusted friends and peers, awards, and other proof that their decision to use you won't turn into regret.

Remind clients that their comments will help others decide whether to hire you. It's not just a favor to you, but their review has a higher purpose- to help others consider you to determine whether your services are right for them. Well-written and thoughtful comments help prospective clients experience what it is like to work with you.

Make it Quick and Easy

Show that you are conscientious and care about the time it takes to draft a review. Estimate the amount of time you think it will take and let them know what you ask of them. Then structure your request to make it as easy for them as possible by including suggestions, links to websites, or by offering to write it yourself. The easier you make it for them, the more likely they will be to do it.

Ask Questions to Build a Powerful Testimony

Every purchase comes with some worry or concern going in to the purchase, especially in professional services. They could have been worried in the beginning about the cost, whether you have the experience, whether you possess the intimidation factor to the other side, or numerous other concerns. Asking about these concerns helps them think about specific examples of what it was like to work with you. Addressing the problems upfront leads clients to hone in on specific examples where they had concerns but were pleasantly surprised. That makes the testimonial more authentic and believable.

Encourage Authenticity

Lastly, ask them to write their comments just as they would if they were talking with a friend. Most people fall into their comfort zone of 'business or legal speak' when writing. This is a sanitized, bland, safe style of writing that works well for internal communications but sounds canned in a testimonial. You want them to write like a human being. By asking them to write the review as if they are writing to their best friend, you are permitting them to write more authentically.

Example

Seeing an example may help clarify why this formula is so much more powerful. Here's a typical recommendation:

"I attended Julie's session at HDI on Customer Experience Management. Julie was motivational and informative and made it very easy to engage throughout the session. She had great energy throughout and made great use of charts and statistics important to our industry. I would definitely recommend working with Julie or engaging her as a speaker."

Now, here's a recommendation in which an expression of the concern was solicited.

"I was initially concerned that Julie's Customer Experience Management session at the HDI conference was going to be another tired re-packaging of the same old, same old. Maybe I've been to too many of these IT conferences and seen too many sessions on Customer Experience Management. After all, techno-geeks are not known for their presentation skills or command of the audience's attention. But Julie was different. She blew my socks off! Her session presented new information and ideas. She was motivational and had a contagious energy level. If you get a chance to attend her session in the future, or better yet hire her to present it, I would definitely recommend her."

The expression of concern enables the reader to put themselves in the same place and relate better to the situation. It will produce more authentic testimonial language.

Other Testimonial Questions and Requests

Keep in mind that your clients think and speak more positively about you than you speak about yourself. For the most part, your clients are happy with your service and the quality of your work. If they weren't, I think they would let you know. If they didn't tell you directly, you would sense it intuitively.

The bridge we need to cross in our minds is to connect the specific instances, qualities and characteristics that your clients find helpful and transfer that to other clients and prospects. That takes courage. But knowing this is critical to building a reputation. And once you know it, that self-awareness will help you internalize those qualities and make it part of how you do business – how you deliver services.

Gathering this kind of 'practice-client service intelligence' enables you to build mini case studies to tell clients and prospects. When asked, you can share these comments or stories giving your claims more authority and credibility. You don't have to name your clients, the simple description of the situation will be enough.

This will also come in useful when you do the exercise to draft your unique value proposition. These comments will give you specifics you can point to and will help you write a more compelling value proposition.

To get these experiential case studies, ask your clients questions similar to the following.

- ✓ "How has my advice or my working style helped you do your job better?"
- ✓ "What have I done to make your job easier?"
- ✓ "What are some of the favorite things you like about working with me?"
- ✓ "How many other outside lawyers do you work with?"
- ✓ "If you had to rank me among the topics we're discussing, where would I rank compared to the others?"
- ✓ "What has kept you using me for so long?"
- ✓ "What specifically gets better when we work together over time?"
- ✓ "Does working with me save you time? How so?"
- ✓ "Does working with me save you money? How so? Can you ball park the amount you've saved?"

- ✓ "Do I help you make money? In what way?"

- ✓ "If you were describing my work to someone who doesn't know me, what would you say?"

- ✓ "If you were describing the experience of working with me, what would you say?"

- ✓ Are there any processes, checklists, or systems that we use together that you like? What are they and what do you like about them?

You may be thinking, 'Wow. I can't ask some of those questions.' Then don't. At least not yet. Pick the questions that you are comfortable asking and ask those. As you get deeper into conversation, those other questions will become easier to ask. Remember to write down as accurately as you can remember what was said. You'll be glad you have those comments later when you are in sales discussions, writing RFP responses, and educating your partners in how to sell you to their clients.

Using Testimonials in Casual Conversations

Obviously, you can use the comments you gather in your marketing materials, in RFP responses and your pitch deck. But most of the comments you gather are most effective when used in conversations. Here are some suggested comments you can use to work in the comments that clients make about you into your conversation.

- ✓ I recently had a conversation with a client of mine whose business is similar to yours. They commented on several ways that I had saved them money and time. Would you be interested in hearing their comments and seeing if it would apply to your business?

✓ My clients tell me that I save them about 20% more time on these matters. I'd like to bring savings like that to you. We can discuss how I do it and see how it might apply to you. Would next Tuesday at noon for lunch work for you?

✓ I recently completed client feedback interviews with my clients and received some insightful comments about my work product and service level. Can I share these with you?

Writing a Testimonial Request

The formula for constructing powerful testimonials asks clients to identify their concern in hiring you, to explain then what they experienced and finally, to write their review authentically. These three questions will lead them through the draft and result in a compelling review of your services.

1. What concerns did you initially have about the legal issue you were dealing with? Similarly, what concerns did you originally have about working with me?
2. What did you actually experience? What happened?
3. How would you describe working with me to a close peer or best friend?

With that said, here's my version of what I think you should say in this letter.

"Hi ___,
In today's connected and increasingly impersonal world, it is harder for people to know whether the services offered to them are truly as good as promised. The problem is especially acute for lawyers. Not only must we fight to get noticed in the online world, but we also want to attract the attention of prospective clients with whom we would enjoy working. I thoroughly enjoyed working with you and believe I did some of my best work under your guidance.

I'm writing to ask the favor of a testimonial. It should only take about 3-5 minutes of your time. And if you prefer, I would also be happy to draft one for you. Of course, it would be better to come from you, with your experience and perspective, in your voice, written informally.

Below, I've listed [number] websites where you can add your review of my services. Hopefully, you'll have the time to copy and paste your testimonial to all [number]. These help my website rank higher in search results. It also provides a sort of repository of all the reviews given of my firm. You can also find me on LinkedIn where you can record your recommendation by clicking here and scrolling down to the Recommendations section. (Hyperlink to your LinkedIn Profile page). I'd like to add the best testimonials to my website so if you are OK with that, please let me know so I can add your kind remarks. As a policy, I will only list your first name unless you specify that I can use your full name.

[If you have a specific situation you recall, you can add that here.]

To make it easier, I've included three questions that will, hopefully, help you draft your review.

1. What concerns did you initially have about the legal issue you were dealing with? Or, what concerns did you have about working with [me or the law firm]?

2. What did you actually experience? What happened? How were these concerns minimized or alleviated?

3. How would you describe working with us to a close professional peer or best friend? What results or benefit would you tell them about that occurred from working with us?

I can't thank you enough for taking the time to do this for me. I will, of course, reciprocate with referrals to your business or connect you with anyone you think would help in your success. We remain dedicated to providing the highest quality legal services and sincerely appreciate your past business."

10

Buying and Selling Legal Services

"People tend to look at their businesses from the inside out - that is, they get so focused on making and selling their services that they lose awareness of the needs and buying behaviors of their customers."

- Lawrence Bossidy

Throughout this book, I've talked about how to develop relationships, find work opportunities, and build a powerful network of connections. I have not discussed, at least not in much detail, how to handle inquiries from or sell to your connections.

Relax. I'm not a proponent of encouraging lawyers to use sales techniques. At least not the conventional sales techniques that use manipulative closing techniques or try to convince lawyers that they should 'always be closing.' I find that a lot of what is taught to lawyers about selling today can wedge you further from the close client relationships you've spent so much time developing.

If you have to use those conventional selling techniques, you've already lost the sale. Instead, I want to reframe how to think about the legal selling and buying process. I hope to explain how legal sales is different from the conventional sales training currently being taught throughout the legal industry. I hope to show you why each practice area needs its distinct sales process. And I hope to demonstrate how a facilitative or coaching approach will work better for most of the selling situations you will find yourself in.

In explaining all of that, I hope to sensitize you to what is going on with your prospect or in the discussions when you are trying to get an engagement. I hope to make you more observant and curious about where companies are in their internal buying decision process when they talk to you about their problems. And lastly, I hope to inspire more creativity in how you approach each selling situation, encourage you to adopt a positive frame of mind about selling, and help you begin and maintain your discussions as a business advisor and avoid selling.

How Did We Get Here?

Most of today's sales training, selling techniques, and sales processes evolved in the 1800s. John Patterson, the owner of the National Cash Register Company, was instrumental in developing the selling systems which continue to this day. There's a lot about John Patterson that is interesting to know. But for now, I'll try to get it short and on point.

John Patterson hired his brother-in-law, John Crane, to be one of his salespeople. And, unlike most 'I hired my brother-in-law to work for me' disaster stories, this one turned out pretty well. John Crane was an excellent salesperson. In fact, within a few short months of working at NCR, he was selling three times the number of cash registers than any other salesperson.

Patterson took notice and quizzed him about it. Crane explained that he had his talk that he used on every call and that his talk was obviously compelling. Patterson wanted to hear it and had John Crane sell him a cash register. That pitch put in motion most of what we know about selling today. Crane had devised a sales script that worked like a charm. Patterson was so impressed he had it transcribed and instructed every one of his salespeople to memorize and use the script. The sale of cash registers exploded as a result.

From there, Patterson and Crane broke the sales script down further and identified seven steps in the sales process. Little did they know, they had devised the very first sales process that continues today. As the company grew, it saw the need to formalize this training for its growing sales force. Eventually, they offered the training to other companies and created the very first sales training program – a sales training program that nearly one-third of all salespeople in the U.S. at that time learned. Patterson and Crane had a massive influence on modern sales training.

That original sales advice has remained relatively unchanged all these years, even though selling cash registers to mom-and-pop retailers is nothing like selling complex legal services to multinational conglomerates. Our conventional business development training programs follow a familiar path:

- Identify prospects.
- Qualify them.
- Gain their trust.
- Identify their needs.
- Present a solution.
- Overcome objections.
- Close the sale.

Our modern sales methods were further shaped in the mid-1930s by Dale Carnegie, who showed us how to win friends and influence people. He encouraged us to listen well; to use a person's name; not to criticize, condemn or complain; to be generous with praise; to be genuinely interested in the other person; and to be likable and charming. All of which is excellent advice.

Since his focus on building relationships was introduced, there have been roughly a dozen iterations to the basic sales methods that Dale Carnegie and John Patterson laid out. There is little substantive difference between them. Each of these sales program iterations has in common the basic tenet that selling is a repeatable process beginning with relationship-building strategies and, once a legal need is identified, a shift to persuasion skills to convince the buyer of the seller's qualification and fit.

Look closely at the sales processes and techniques of the most popular sales training programs such as Relationship Selling, Strategic Selling, Consultative Selling, SPIN Selling, Solutions Selling, Insight Selling, and the Challenger Sales program. The selling methods popularized over the past few decades share common methods and techniques and are based on assumptions that don't stand up to real-life legal selling experiences.

As popular as this sales process is, it cannot explain some of the fundamental challenges we often see in our sales pursuits. For instance, it can't explain:

- Why a prospect stalls or disengages from the selling process

- Why lawyers with strong company relationships and appropriate knowledge are not selected for engagements

- Why some engagements get signed quickly, and some take months, even years, to land, and

- Why some prospects recognize a need but don't resolve their issues or solve their problems.

These situations are a source of frustration for anyone actively selling legal services. Without an explanation for this seemingly erratic behavior, we assume that in-house counsel and business managers are sometimes 'irrational' - a characteristic of consumers, but not corporations. Businesses are anything but irrational. While their actions may appear erratic, companies are rational and calculated in almost everything they do.

It's hard to know whether a process is broken when we don't have a better process to which to compare it. It's all the more confounding when that process sometimes works, but we can't say why it worked. Unknowingly, we have adopted certain assumptions that obscure the fact that our process, and not our lawyers, is fundamentally flawed. The assumptions lead us away from a more effective approach. We assume that:

· When companies recognize a legal need, they are inclined to find a solution. As such, our approach has focused on helping companies identify their legal needs, even though most companies know their legal needs already.

· Buyers do business with people they know and like. As such, our approach has emphasized relationships as a required context for new engagements. But many engagements are signed before strong relationships develop.

· There is one person who decides to hire. As such, our approach has been to appeal to that decision-maker, when in fact many people inside the company have influence into the hiring of legal counsel.

· There is a single sales process and skill set that works for all selling situations. As a result, our approach has relied on training lawyers in a single sales process that emphasizes persuasion skills, even though persuasion tactics rarely tip the balance in our favor and the sales process doesn't track the actual selling experience.

Conventional business development methods ignore a critical aspect of the legal services selling process- one that turns out to be a key to understanding the uniqueness of our selling processes and getting better at it. This aspect is the legal services buying process.

To sell, we must understand how and, more importantly, why buyers buy. But we can't fully understand how and why buyers buy until we have insights into how buyers *decide to buy*. We think carefully about what we should do to persuade a prospect, differentiate our services, and negotiate the best terms for each engagement. And yet we spend almost no time thinking about what the buyer must do inside the company to prepare the company to hire a solutions provider and the changes inside the company that that solution may provoke.

Sales Strategy Changes Based on the Buyer's Readiness to Buy

The techniques required to advance an engagement change depending upon where the buyer is in their buying process. When a buyer is ready to buy and has decided on the provider and solution, your task as the chosen provider is to negotiate the terms of the engagement. In this sense, negotiation skills are most valuable. I call this a *contractor role* at this stage of the buying process. It is primarily focused on negotiating the engagement.

If the buyer is ready to buy but not sure about the specific contours of the solution strategy or the selection criteria for potential providers, consultative selling skills and competitive positioning techniques can help you to stand out as the best choice with the best solution. I call this a *consultant role* for this stage in the buyer's process. This role is primarily focused on consulting and advising the buyer in formulating the right solution.

But if the buyer is not ready to buy, no amount of persuasion, competitive positioning, or negotiation skills will convince them to engage outside counsel. At this stage, the company is primarily evaluating whether or not to solve for the issue. If they have not made a buy decision, the company is evaluating the problem or issue. Keep in mind that the buyers of legal services have reasons to choose not to buy legal services, delay the purchase, or reconfigure solutions that don't include outside counsel.

To get better at selling, we need first to understand where the company is in this evaluation process and why it decides when (or even whether) to solve their legal issues and problems. I call this a *coaching role* at this stage of the buying process because the company needs objective feedback and guidance in whether or not to solve the problem or issue. They need education and objective questioning and guidance, guidance that has only a focus on making the best decision for the company regardless of the coach's continued involvement. This is the stage in which authentic trusted advisor relationships a develop with company representatives.

This last part is what is wrong with legal selling today. The gurus teach sellers how to sell but very little about how buyers buy. The focus is on how to sell regardless of where the buyer is in their buying decision process. It assumes that skilled selling can overcome any internal resistance to change. If you haven't made the sale, it is because you are not selling effectively enough. Hog wash.

Understanding what is going on inside the company in the earliest stages of the internal buying decision process explains why companies stall, disengage, or take so long to make a decision. I believe that understanding the internal buying decision process is the key to a more effective business development process for a number of the legal services being sold. But I don't believe it works for all legal services. It depends upon where you enter the buying process (problem resolution consideration process) and the type of legal services you sell.

To illustrate this point further, consider when a company is hit with a hefty lawsuit that has strategic importance or risk for the company. In that situation, the company needs to fix their problem, and they are ready to buy the services of the lawyer they feel can help them do that. In this case, the lawyer with the best reputation for winning these types of cases is the one that gets the call. Maybe that lawyer will have an existing relationship with the company, but maybe not. Watch those interactions, and you'll see almost no selling taking place. The lawyer needs to understand the case and negotiate the terms of the engagement. And, the buyer tends not to have as much price resistance since the impending matter promises severe business disruption, and they want the best lawyer on their side.

In other situations, the company recognizes that they need legal services but haven't yet determined the exact solution or the best provider. For example, think about a company that has undergone strategic planning and decided that it needs to find a company with whom to merge. The company has aligned behind the need to merge or acquire another business but not the particular solution (which business) or which provider will help them. The lawyer in this situation can use consultative selling skills and competitive positioning techniques to influence the selection.

For the last situation, let's use the example that you are pitching a banking technology company on the need to redraft contract language for potential changes brought about by new regulations. While the company recognizes the need, to be ready to 'buy' the redrafting of its contracts, the company will first need to answer a host of questions to determine the implications and impact of these changes on its current operations. They'll need to talk to the stakeholders to understand the impact on various departments of the company such as IT, training, marketing, and customer or supplier relations. And they need to go through a cost-benefit analysis to understand the impact of the changes and how they could affect how the company operates. All of this needs to happen before the company can be ready to begin the provider selection process.

In reaching out to these companies (who we know has a problem we can solve), we are starting sales discussion when the company is still in its early buying decision stages. They have not made a 'go or not go decision on whether to or how to make the change. As such, we are trying to sell a solution before they are ready to buy.

The company must first work out how to address the changes before it can hire a lawyer to make the changes. Rather than selling, at this point, we should be educating and facilitating understanding of the risks and implications based on our knowledge of similar companies and situations. Selling and persuasion at this point fall on deaf ears because the selling process is not aligned with the buyer's internal buying decision process.

It's not hard to understand why addressing the internal buying decision process has been overlooked in contemporary sales training. You are on the outside of the company. You are not privy to the internal politics, the relationship dynamics, the internal back and forth about problems and solutions, the cultural norms and values, the history and hard-fought lessons that determine how the company operates, how it makes decisions, and how it selects providers. You are not part of the buying decision process.

But you can help facilitate the decision process from outside by helping your connection ask better questions, get better information, and more clearly understand the resistance to the changes some legal solutions will cause inside the company.

Expanding our definition of the selling process to include the buyer's internal buying decision process helps shed light on why buyers buy from providers who have no preexisting relationship with the company. They are looking for someone to solve their unique business problem and seek providers with that unique expertise. It helps to explain why a company with a problem you can solve doesn't always solve those problems (it's not a big enough 'pain point' or it can be fixed in the next budget cycle). And, it helps to explain why some sales cycles happen quickly and others take months if they happen at all (they are having trouble inside the company getting alignment behind a solution strategy).

Our ability to manage a sales conversation through phases of the sales process is overrated. When an experienced lawyer approaches a company to sell their services, they are successful only about 10 percent of the time. Even when companies approach us (which we can infer means that the company has recognized a legal need and also that we have the capabilities to solve their problem), we are only successful in getting the engagement about 30 to 40 percent of the time. Why is that? The truth is, selling doesn't cause buying. Aligning with the company's internal buying decision process enables selection.

When John Patterson developed his seven-step sales process, he did it to give his salespeople a road map. The process was intended to help his salespeople understand where they were in their sales script and what to do next in order to keep moving toward a sale. Sales methods since have based their sales process on that fundamental assumption- that the sales process drives the buying process. I think that's backward- at least for many legal services.

Patterson's customers were all small retailers with the same problem of inventory control and employee theft. His cash registers were the only product that produced a printed receipt. That receipt solved both of their problems. His sales process simply had to confirm the need, explain the difference his registers offered, show how they paid for themselves, and overcome any objections (there weren't many). It all seems pretty straightforward.

Applying a single sales script and process to guide us through a complex sale to a highly matrixed organization doesn't make sense and, as the 10 percent statistic suggests, doesn't work. Buyers don't follow our sales process. They follow their own buying process. We would be well-advised to change our approach and our seller mindset.

Every Practice Area Has a Unique Buying-Selling Process.

As I've argued, one sales process does not work for every legal practice area. For some practice areas, decisions to hire can be made quickly. For other types, companies must carefully consider the ramifications on the company's operations before determining the solution. The latter requires a much different sales approach than a practice area with little impact on the company's operations. With complex problems, issues, and opportunities, the impact and implications must be understood before the best solution can be envisioned. That happens differently in different companies and at different speeds, and it makes sense that it would also happen differently for different areas of the law. For legal services, where you enter the company's buying process also makes a difference.

No two business situations are the same. No two practice areas are the same. Traditional selling relies on persuasion skills, while selling to corporations is more complicated and nuanced. It seems common sensical that one must first understand the context of the selling situation to sell effectively. Understanding how prospects determine which problems to solve, how they decide to solve them, what motivation they have to solve their various issues, and what value they perceive in your consultations is a better way to understand the context of the selling situation. And this will lead to better sales strategies and better results.

You should understand the selling situation you often encounter in your practice. Ask yourself, does this prospect recognize a need for the legal solution I'm proposing? Do they understand the implications to their business of solving or not solving the issue? Do I have a good enough understanding of how the business operates that I can be sure I know what ramifications my solutions may cause?

If they understand the need and the implications to the business, is there an incumbent provider currently doing the work or easily accessible? And if they recognize the problem and there is no incumbent provider, why haven't they resolved the issue? These questions will help you get closer to the appropriate approach to how you can help that company.

Rather than focusing on how to sell the prospect, we need to shift our focus to understanding the dynamic challenges inherent in every company's buying process. Understanding the buying process and the internal dynamics that slow, obstruct or fuel purchasing decisions can give you insights into how to meet each business's unique challenges.

That may sound like simply the rephrasing of 'understanding the prospect's legal needs.' But it's not. It's much deeper than that. It is the more profound understanding of a company's business and industry that in-house counsel wants in their legal partners. When they find that in you, you will be an irreplaceable resource.

Think Change Management, Not Sales Management

Buying legal services is a dynamic process full of politics, operational considerations, shifting priorities, and analysis. It is fraught with risks and unintended consequences - the kryptonite of business managers. Managing the sales process with companies should look more like change management than sales management. This is because the changes brought about by legal solutions can affect many different parts of the company in many different ways.

In working with large corporations, it's better to keep in mind the change formula and ignore the sales formula. The change formula is this:

Change = (D+V+S) > (C+R) (Dissatisfaction with current situation + Vision for a better situation + Solution available) > (Cost + Resistance)

The change formula is considerably different than a sales formula. There are two essential elements of change (in brackets). The readiness to change (D+V+S) and the resistance to that change (C+R). And the readiness to change must be greater than (>) the resistance to change for change to occur.

Change occurs in both companies and individuals in the same way. It occurs when *Dissatisfaction* with the current state is acknowledged and shared among stakeholders. This is combined with a *vision* for what the future state could look like and a clear path to a *solution* is understood. Evaluating the reason for Dissatisfaction helps define a Vision for a better Situation and the criteria for the best solution.

This combination, however, must exceed the *Cost* of that change and any internal *Resistance* to the change. In other words, the company (or person) has to see the need to change, understand how to make the change, and see a clear benefit to the change. And it has to overcome resistance to the change and improve the situation without causing too much disruption.

Helping companies make positive changes is at the heart of good lawyering. To do that, you must build your business acumen. To understand how these changes affect the company, you must learn to be a good business person as well as an exceptional lawyer. Without a clear-eyed, keen understanding of the business, there are limits to the degree to which your lawyering will stand out.

The Four Selling Situations

Every practice area has a different sales cycle, different criteria for selecting outside counsel, and varying degrees of risk and importance associated with the problem, opportunity, or issue under consideration. As you've already read in Chapter 8, understanding the urgency, strategic importance, and priority that the company has placed on the legal issue, problem or opportunity is the starting point for understanding the best sales process for your practice area. Understanding this from the client's perspective – meaning the 'business need' perspective – is the first step in positioning yourself as the provider of choice.

The second step is to understand their basic selling situation and how your approach must change to address each situation.

You can evaluate the company's selling situation using two factors: 1. The recognition by the company of a legal need, and 2. The presence of an incumbent provider. With these two criteria, you can evaluate what type of selling situation you face. When companies consider buying legal services, they fall into one of four basic types of selling situations.

> 1. The company has a recognized legal need and is looking for a provider.

> 2. The company has a recognized legal need, but there is an incumbent provider already in place providing those services.

3. The company does not recognize the legal need, and therefore no incumbent provider exists. And,

4. The company recognizes the legal need but has chosen not to address the issue (either they have chosen not to address it at all, they have developed a workaround solution, or they have chosen to delay resolving the issue).

This may seem overly simplified to you. But you'll be surprised at how helpful this orientation exercise will be. Each selling situation requires different marketing and business development strategies.

The first selling situation requires a competitive positioning strategy. The second selling situation requires a displacement selling strategy. The third selling situation requires an education selling strategy, and the fourth selling situation requires a discovery sales strategy.

Competitive Positioning Selling Strategies

The first situation, *recognized need, no current provider*, should seem familiar to you. The company knows they have the problem and need outside counsel to help them solve it. Your job is simply to identify those companies and pitch your services.

To pitch them, you'll need to position your services as *the* competitive choice. In other words, your selling strategy will be to identify companies that may need your assistance and then focus on differentiating your service delivery. You should emphasize the results you've achieved, explain how you align your solutions to the unique needs of their business and provide objective evidence of the quality, prestige, and value of hiring you as their lawyer. It is how you probably sell your services today.

Too often, lawyers assume there is a legal need and that there is no incumbent form. That is, the competitive selling strategy is used in most situations. I believe that is because most lawyers are taught this conventional selling strategy and not taught how to determine whether it is applicable, resulting in the low success rates we see in proactive selling efforts.

As a side note, brand new or emerging issues often fall in this selling situation type. With new or emerging legal issues, there can be a gold rush mentality of lawyers flocking to the new issues to be the first to market expertise and pick up the easy engagements. Unfortunately, those don't come along every day for most practice areas. Instead, in most legal selling situations, there is an existing incumbent provider.

Displacement Selling Strategies

The second selling situation, *recognized need, incumbent provider present*, is the most difficult. It requires you to not only convince the prospect of your capabilities but make a compelling case that they would gain more value from working with you than they get from their current provider. That's a very tough selling situation. But not impossible.

The key to this strategy requires the company to reassess the quality and value they get from their incumbent provider. As I tell my clients, companies don't consider changing providers until they first question the quality and value of their existing providers. It's not easy to ask directly about the company's experience with its current providers. It puts them on the spot and can be perceived as overly assertive, especially in a budding relationship. However, you can't develop an effective sales strategy unless and until you know the vulnerabilities of the incumbent provider.

In my experience, the best approach is to ask a question that indirectly encourages the prospect to think wholistically about their current relationship with the incumbent provider and follow up that question to explore all aspects of their service levels and work product quality. Asking directly (What do you like or not like about such and so) can make people retrench or defend their current choice of provider. Behavioral psychologists call it the status quo bias. And it has the unfortunate effect of making people more resistant to change when they feel confronted with their prior decisions. In contrast, indirect questions keep them open to evaluating the provider and the possibility of change.

To ask indirectly, use a form of this question:

"How would you know if it were time to reconsider how these matters are currently handled?"

This is a classic coaching question that coaches use to get their coachee to think more objectively about their situation. It's a question that encourages them to articulate how they would know it was a time to change what they were doing.

For a prospective client, this type of question encourages the prospect to recognize the possibility that a change could be in order. It forces their mind to inventory the sometimes unrecognized or ignored issues they may need to address. But it does so in a way that maintains the individual's control of the analysis.

Follow-up questions can help the prospect go sequentially through each aspect of the provider's services, their results, and the process they follow, all in a more critical frame of mind. It can lead them to the answers to what they need to do to improve that part of their system. It forces them to evaluate their 'status quo.' And by taking part in this conversation with them, it can provide you with deep insights into the business and a view into the sales strategy that would work best.

To be effective, you must take on the role of a coach rather than a salesperson. Coaches facilitate introspection and understanding without regard to a specific outcome. Whereas the 'sales mindset' wants to direct, advise and guide. The conversation will fail if you attempt to steer the conversation toward a self-serving result. You may even be perceived as manipulative. So, stay objective, helpful, and curious.

By the way, curiosity is a powerful rapport-building quality. People are naturally flattered by another person's curiosity about them or their challenges. You must genuinely be curious in a way that helps your prospect evaluate, as objectively as possible, their current situation. But done well, the coaching role can position you as a trusted advisor who now, through effective questioning, has the inside knowledge to help formulate the best solution.

Keep in mind that this strategy may take some time. It is developed and reinforced over time. But with persistence and skill, the conversations that evolve from the 'how would you know' question can provide you with the insights and inside track to oust the incumbent provider.

Provider Switching Strategies

The displacement strategy encourages a prospect to consider alternatives to the incumbent provider. But companies try to avoid disruption at all costs. Once successful in evaluating options, your next job is to lower the barriers companies face in switching providers. Give them the situations when they should call on you and make it easy for the company to try out your services. When prospects are open to considering other providers, these strategies can help you get your foot in the door.

1. Position for trial when the incumbent is conflicted

2. Position for inclusion on outside counsel panels

3. Position to be an outsource when in-house counsel are overworked

4. Position using a trial or loss leader appeal, or

5. Position for the wholesale acquisition of all of the work.

The first two strategies are relatively easy. It amounts to asking to be considered when the current provider has a conflict. The key here is not to forget to ask. Simply say, 'I would appreciate the opportunity to work with you if your current firm is ever conflicted out of a project.' Keep it short and straightforward.

The second is a request to be included on their panel of approved outside counsel for those matters. That may be a little more involved as it may require you to provide panel counsel information so that they can evaluate your capabilities against the current panel counsel.

The third strategy is appropriate when the company has in-house counsel or incumbent handling most of the matters. If they are overloaded, you can suggest that you offer to work on the overflow, or some portion of the work, in heavy workflow periods.

The fourth, a trial or loss leader appeal, involves an offer to do a test matter. This is where you agree to do a matter so that they can try out your services. Put another way, you agree to do the work at a reduced fee as an incentive to them to let you demonstrate the quality of your work. This strategy can help you get in the door for those matters.

In your displacement conversations, you should be able to explain how you handle matters more efficiently, how you integrate technology, the processes you use to keep the client informed of progress and issues, and how you make your clients' jobs easier. Ideally, you have good relationships with company insiders and a good understanding of the company's business and industry. Lastly, all of this should be packaged with evidence of your capabilities vis-a-vis client lists and testimonials, value-added services that you provide, examples of your work, and examples of your process improvement and project management capabilities.

The displacement strategy is a long-haul strategy. You must meet with the prospect and ask about their business, legal service expectations, and their recent experiences with outside counsel. The questioning strategy is where you go through an interview-like process to review all the points of comparison of legal counsel subtly. The objective is to make them question the current provider's quality of service. I said earlier that this is a difficult and more advanced strategy. You should prepare carefully and thoroughly and, if necessary, get training in how to use this type of questioning strategy to unseat the competition.

Education Selling Strategies

In the third selling situation, *the unrecognized need, no incumbent selling situation*, the company doesn't know they have the issue or problem and, of course, has no one helping them with that problem. Here again, marketing can help you find potential companies with the problem. An education strategy can help raise awareness and identify the risks of not addressing the issue. Education selling strategies often use thought leadership and content distribution mediums to create awareness of the issues. This can include publishing articles about the issue, speaking at conferences and client seminars, and posting on social media to educate and raise the awareness that you handle these problems. This strategy is also one that should be familiar to you.

Discovery Selling Strategies

In the fourth situation, in which the company *recognizes that it has a legal need but has not addressed it*, there is also an opportunity to win the engagement. It requires a change away from the conventional sales approach. Companies decide not to address problems for a variety of reasons. They may not know the best way to address the problem or may not understand the risks associated with the issue. Or, the problem simply may not be a priority for the company.

There are selling opportunities when the company is uncertain about what changes in the company's operations will be affected by addressing the issue. The company may have developed a workaround solution that works well enough to keep the problem at bay but might consider a more permanent solution. Or, they may not address the legal need due to internal political, cultural, technical, or operational conflicts inside the company. There are many reasons why a company postpones or decides not to solve legal problems that they recognize they have. And in understanding their internal deliberations, selling opportunities abound.

As you might have guessed, it is essential to understand the company's decisions about the issues, problems, or opportunities. If they have decided to postpone or ignore the problem, your job is to understand why. Understanding the factors considered in making that decision is critical to finding an approach that might allow them to revisit their decision. I refer to this as the company's *decision strategy*. The decisions the company has made covers a range of considerations including decisions about the available resources that will be needed to solve the problem, decisions regarding the priority that problem's solution will have in the company, and decisions as to who will be involved in making sure the solution works within the context of the company's operations and business model.

The decision strategy affects how you approach the company. Your sales approach when a company doesn't know it has a problem is different than the approach you would take with a company that knows it has the problem but has not made fixing it a priority. You can develop a better approach if you understand how the company arrived at its decision.

The key to discovery sales strategies is in your ability to facilitate the decision on whether or not and how to solve the issue, problem, or opportunity. I call this *decision coaching*. But before I explain the decision-making process, you should know a few things about how companies operate.

Corporate Buying and Decision-Making

Corporations and small businesses share common qualities that influence their buying processes. These are not facts. Instead, they are common traits that I have observed over many pitches and presentations. Knowing companies have these qualities helps you understand what happens throughout the buying-selling process. These observations help explain a number of the moves a company makes that can confound us. They look irrational from the outside but, viewed through these principles, begin to make sense. See if you don't notice them when you are talking to a prospect about representing them. Pay attention to the cues of whether or not they have made a decision to proceed or whether they are still in the evaluation stage.

The following are a set of principles about companies and their buying processes that I think are helpful for you to know.

Companies Have a Bias for the Status Quo

The decision strategy (whether and how to solve the issue) takes into consideration the impact a solution would have on the company. Company representatives study the implications, look for unintended consequences, review options, and assess the costs and resources required. They devise a 'business case' for implementing the solution so that those with interest in the decision can share in the understanding of what the company expects or will try to achieve by making the change. What may look like a simple change in the clause of a contract may have far-reaching implications and may be beyond the understanding of company outsiders.

Companies have an inherent bias in favor of the status quo. Smooth running operations assure consistency in profits, workflow, operations, and customer experiences. The anticipated changes that solutions to legal problems could bring about are closely evaluated. And they are sometimes resisted. Suppose the solution means a shift in how the company operates, and that solution does not promise a compelling reward, reduce risk or alleviate a threat. In that case, there is a likelihood that the company will not pursue the solution.

Every Company Has a Unique Internal Buying Decision Process

Every company is unique. Their internal decision processes are like a secret sauce made from the mix of internal politics, culture, available resources, organizational practices, and historical experience. Your ability to gain access to and understand these dynamics is the key to navigating many types of selling situations and winning the engagement. You can gain access to this understanding by developing relationships with company insiders and asking thoughtful questions about how they make decisions, allocate resources, and prioritize projects.

Organizational Decision Complexity and the Strategic Importance of Solutions Drives the Decision Process.

Solutions that affect key strategic activities of the company require more careful consideration. The problem, issue, or opportunity complexity drives the decision process's pace and information requirements. Solutions that do not affect strategic areas of the company's operations do not require the same level of consideration. When issues are complex, have implications that affect many areas of the company's operations, or have the potential to affect customers or the company's business model, the potential solutions to these issues require study and careful evaluation.

When the strategic importance of an issue is high, and the implications for the company are narrow and well known, the company's decisions can be made more quickly. When the strategic importance is high, and the implications for the company are broad or unclear, the company will act more cautiously. When the strategic importance is low, but the issue presents a broad range of implications to the company, companies typically break down the issues into more manageable parts and deal with the issues selectively. And finally, when the strategic importance is low, and the implications are known and narrowly defined, companies may opt to ignore the issue. The chart exemplifies the decision strategy graph. Look at your practice area and the issue you deal with and try to determine where those issues fall in a company's decision strategy. It should be instructive to you in how you approach clients.

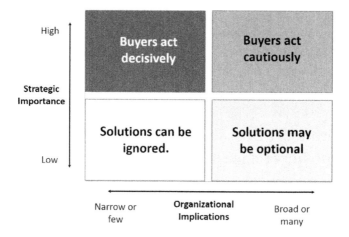

Stakeholders and Influencers Must Weigh In

Companies determine the requirements of legal solutions by involving the business line managers, department heads, and various disciplines within the company to understand what effect the issue has on the company, its operations, its suppliers, or its customers. They ask for input into how the company should solve those issues. These are the stakeholders and influencers, and they play an essential role in how companies arrive at the solutions they decide to undertake. They are also the people who often must implement the solution within their areas of responsibility.

The company must build consensus among all of the stakeholders who may be affected by the solution to ensure they agree on how to solve the problem. Stakeholders have unique insights into their areas of responsibility or expertise. They know how the company operates and are the best people in the company to project or anticipate how issues will affect their area of responsibility. Company decision-makers want the input from stakeholders and influencers.

Companies Must Understand the Implications of Solutions

Stakeholders report back on their assessment of the suspected implications, being careful to understand the risks, unintended consequences, and costs of proposed solutions. That can take time. Some legal issues have far-reaching effects on the company with implications that cross multiple departments and processes or extend into the company's supply chain. Stakeholders must try to anticipate how the issue will impact the company, but stakeholders are also the people who must implement any change brought about by the legal solution. Their involvement is critical in some legal solutions. The *implications scanning phase* is crucial in outlining the criteria for a solution as well as the requirements needed in their prospective providers.

In this implication scanning phase, sales discussions often arise. This is because company representatives usually research the topics to get the information needed to understand their issues as well as possible. They may come across your blog, attend one of your seminars, or read an article on the internet that you wrote. Inquiries are sometime made during this phase. However, those inquiries do not mean they are ready to solve the issue, let alone engage your services. They may simply be researching the issues to make sure they have scanned their operations for all of the potential implications of solving the legal problem, issue, or opportunity.

Understanding the Decision Stage is Critical

As I hope you can see, understanding where the company is in its decision process is important, especially so for some practice areas. In many cases, you can help the company decide to solve by equipping it with the knowledge and expertise from your experience working with other companies on similar issues. When companies are in the phase in which they are researching the implications of their issues, they will be more likely to partner with you so that you can help them through this implications scanning process.

In essence, your role is to advise them on what to think about when scanning for implications, talking to stakeholders, and determining the provider selection criteria. This role is a coach's role. You act as a 'coach' to help guide them through their internal decision process. Acting as a coach rather than as a salesperson puts you in the advantageous position of being a resource that helps them navigate the complex challenges of determining the best solution. That's precisely the position you need to be in to get the information for a compelling proposal.

The Buying Decision Process

Companies each have their unique process for determining how the company will allocate and invest resources. This process considers the company's business strategy, its business model, current project priorities, and numerous other factors. Generally, the company moves through the buying decision stages below. A decision to hire (or not to hire) is typically not made until the company has identified a solution strategy and the provider selection criteria, that is, they get to step five below.

IPO = Issues, Problems or Opportunities

Some issues are ongoing problems for companies with the decision process largely delegated to the procurement department. Many companies have approved panels of counsel to which they can turn when these problems crop up. But one-off issues, or issues that arise from changes in the operations of the company or new products, services or strategies, or anything that is not an expected development in the company often requires an internal review before a decision is made. It is in those situations that this process most applies.

Determining the Decision Stage

To determine the best approach, it is essential to determine what stage the company is in in its buying decision process. Essentially, you want to know whether the company has a firm grasp of the implications an issue may have on the company's operations, whether there is consensus inside the company in how to proceed and whether a decision has been made to hire outside counsel. In some cases, they may not know about the issue, in which case, they are starting at square one in the graphic above.

There are several questions you can ask to determine the decision stage. Work back in the decision diagram above (from the right-hand side) by asking the questions for each stage. Keep working back until you determine the decision stage and the scope of their evaluation of their options. Use your own version of these questions.

First, find out if they have a solution in mind by asking:

How would the company describe its ideal solution to this issue, problem or opportunity? How would the company describe the most likely solution it will try to implement? What compromises might the company agree to in order to fit a solution into its current operating model?

Next, find out whether the company has a grasp on the impact a solution would have on the company by asking:

What would happen in the company if the problem is not solved or the issue goes unresolved? What gains, losses, risks, or rewards can the company expect? In what time frame would the company see that impact play out?

Next, find out whether the company has assessed the implications on the organization of the problem by asking:

What possible implications could result if the company does not change what it is doing? What unintended consequences could arise?

Next, find out if the company has identified the team of people (stakeholders) who should be involved in determining the solution criteria by asking:

What are all the areas of the company affected by this problem or issue? Who are the stakeholders or people responsible for those areas? Who influences how resources are used in the company that might want input into the solution (or could obstruct the decision process or even say no to the solution)?

This questioning process is loosely defined. The questions are meant to give you an idea of how you can go about learning the key information that drives the decision process inside companies. Your prospect may not have all of the answers to your questions. It may take several conversations to get the information. And you may need to probe continuously to get more and better information.

Regardless, by holding this type of discussion, you and your prospect will learn a great deal about where the company is in its decision-making process. And it will give you the information you need to craft a business-specific, prospect-focused proposal.

Selling legal services, I think, is a misnomer. Our conventional idea of what selling is doesn't portray the role or the activities that lawyers actually engage in to win engagements. The most successful lawyers-sellers that I've observed don't follow the seven-step sales process, they don't use closing techniques, and they don't try to persuade, or worse, manipulate a prospect into engaging them. Instead, they act as advisors and freely share their experiences and knowledge of similar situations. They explore causes, desired outcomes, and unintended consequences to help prospects better understand the contours of their challenges. It doesn't look like selling. It looks like serving.

The idea of selling is anathema to many lawyers and for good reason. The concept of selling or being a "sales" person (as it's commonly thought of) runs afoul of the gravitas and trusted advisor standards that most business lawyers hold themselves to. Lawyers don't like to sell and, more importantly, business managers don't like to be sold. Thankfully, serving is what encourages buying. I hope the takeaway you glean from this book is to build a power grid that will fuel your success and that you focus on serving your way to new engagements.

11

Final Thoughts

Congratulations. You've made it to the end of this book. That, in and of itself, is an accomplishment. More importantly, it shows me that you are serious about building a power grid and becoming more successful in your professional life.

But being serious about something and doing it are two different things. In reading this book, I think you have recognized the need to do more to build your book of business. What I've laid out is a step-by-step process along with some concepts to better understand your practice and what it takes to win engagements. You've already done the hard part- you learned the steps and taken note of the advice. Now it's time to get into action.

The single biggest killer of dreams is the lack of action. Lots of people dream big. Most of us can imagine what it would be like to accomplish our vision of success. But only a few actually do it. Do you want to know why?

Because doing it means doing it every day. That is incredibly hard. Doing what you know you need to do in some small way every day takes commitment and discipline. It's tough because progress only shows up in hindsight, sometimes hindsight that sits far down the road. Staying focused and doing what you need to do consistently, that grit, is the key to success. Doing it in the face of all those important things pulling on your time is the magic you create for yourself.

Don't let yourself fall prey to the dark knight of excuses. Do one little thing every day. Make one call. Send one e-mail. Work for five minutes getting your contacts organized. Spend 10 minutes learning about your client's business. Then tomorrow, do two little things. Do a little more each day. Work it in to your schedule. Keep building momentum. There is a virtuous cycle created when you do something every day consistently.

As a kid we had an above-ground, circular-shaped pool in our backyard. We used to create whirlpools in the pool. Each time you walked around the inside perimeter of the pool, you pushed against the volume of water. It was hard at first. The volume of the water far outweighed our tiny bodies. But each time around created momentum and you could walk through the water easier and easier. After a few times around, the water began to form a whirlpool. Our continuous circling made the pool whirl faster and faster. It gave in to our continuous circling. It became easier. The whirlpool grew stronger each time you circled the pool. Until finally, the whirlpool carried you. You could lean back, pick your feet up, and the water moved you around the pool.

That's how power grids work. You talk to your contacts consistently every day, and in time the power grid fuels your practice. Eventually, you won't have to try so hard. It's only in the beginning that the effort is the hardest. But that's like everything you do, isn't it?

Disciplined practice, or as we called it in college 'your time in the woodshed,' will produce results that multiply your first efforts. Don't focus on whether you have the water circling fast enough. Focus on walking. The water will eventually carry you. Don't worry if you sound like John Bonham. Just keep drumming. Show up every day. You'll hear Bonham in your paradiddles eventually. Persevere. Keep going. Work on the little things every day. It is the single thing you can do to be successful. And it is the one thing you can totally control. You can make at least one call happen every day. Each of us have it in us to persevere.

We can all make a call.

About the Author

Eric Dewey is an expert in driving growth and efficiency in professional service firms through innovative and practical marketing and client development strategies. With over 25 years of marketing and business development experience in five service industries, Dewey has counseled hundreds of attorneys in prospecting, client development, marketing effectiveness and presentation skills.

Eric owns eLegal Training, LLC, an online eLearning website for lawyers with hundreds of video training courses covering business development, business writing, getting and giving feedback, delegation, negotiations, time management, and more. He is also a leading U.S. authority on lateral partner hiring performance. He is the co-author of *Surmounting the Lateral Partner Hiring Challenge: Lessons Learned, Best Practices and Tools for Success*, a research publication of ALM Intellgence and Group Dewey Consulting. He provides lateral coaching, interview training, lateral hiring program analysis, client book due diligence, and other services related to lateral recruiting, hiring and integration.

Eric regularly contributes to, and has been quoted in, numerous top legal and business publications and blogs including The American Lawyer, Law Practice Management, Legal Marketing Strategies, Marketing the Law Firm, The Recorder, The Wall Street Journal, Professor Stephen Harper's The Lawyer Bubble, numerous business journals and related publications. He is one of the top authors on the topic of legal marketing and business development on JD Supra. A frequent speaker, Eric's innovative concepts in practice development, lateral recruiting, competitive and client research, business development, and cross selling have been featured at national and regional conferences and seminars of The Association of Legal Administrators, The Legal Marketing Association, The American Association of Law Librarians, The American Bar Association, The Managing Partner Forum, and many others.

Eric holds an MBA from Ohio University, a Certified Financial Marketing Professional (CFMP) designation through the American Bankers Association and the University of Colorado and a Certified Marketing Director (CMD) designation from The International Council of Shopping Centers and the University of Michigan. Dewey has held the senior-most marketing professional positions in two AmLaw 200 law firms, the largest securities class action firm in the U.S., a regional bank holding company and several commercial real estate developers.

Special Thanks

Several people have provided valuable insights in their early reviews of this book. I deeply appreciate the feedback provided by them. In random order, they include Bruce Heintz, Steve Shapiro, Barb Shepard, Patrick Fuller, Patrick McKenna, and Linda Hazelton. Thank you all from the bottom of my heart.

I'm here to help. Please feel free to call me with any questions or to share your stories and thoughts. Call me if you want to brainstorm ideas for how to pitch important clients, for how to build your power grid, or displace an entrenched competitor. I want to help you take your practice to the next level.

Write me at eric@eLegalTraining.com or call / text me at 502.693.4731

Printed in Great Britain
by Amazon